WORK
AND
INTEGRITY

ALSO BY WILLIAM M. SULLIVAN

Reconstructing Public Philosophy

Habits of the Heart

The Good Society

WORK

AND

INTEGRITY

*The Crisis and Promise of
Professionalism in America*

WILLIAM M. SULLIVAN

HarperBusiness
A Division of HarperCollins*Publishers*

HarperCollins books may be purchased for educational, business, or sales promotional use. For information, please write: Special Markets Department, HarperCollins Publishers, Inc., 10 East 53rd Street, New York, NY 10022.

FIRST EDITION

Designed by George J. McKeon

Library of Congress Cataloging-in-Publication Data

Sullivan, William M.
    Work and integrity : the crisis and promise of professionalism in America /
William M. Sullivan.
        p.   cm.
    ISBN 0-88730-727-2
    1. Professional ethics—United States. 2. Professions—United States.
    3. Professional socialization—United States. 4. Integrity. I. Title.
    BJ1725.S85   1995
    174—dc20   94-37870

95 96 97 98 99 ❖/HC 10 9 8 7 6 5 4 3 2 1

To Robert N. Bellah and Robert C. Neville
Teachers Mentors Friends

CONTENTS

ACKNOWLEDGMENTS

The idea for this book originated in a project on The Public Role of the Professions organized by the Hastings Center, and I am indebted to the project's codirectors, Daniel Callahan and Bruce Jennings, for the invitation to participate. While the participants in that project provided many leading ideas about the situation of the professions in contemporary society, they are of course innocent of any of the egregious twistings I may have subsequently given their views.

I owe considerable intellectual debts to friends and colleagues who provided many insights in pursuit of the themes of this book. By provoking new questions they inadvertently extended both the reach of the investigation and its duration. I am especially grateful for the continuing good fortune of association with Robert Bellah, Richard Madsen, Ann Swidler, and Steven Tipton, who gave stimulation, support, and friendly criticism. Dennis McGrath, Wallace Katz, and Richard Wenner provided invaluable critical perspective by reading parts of the manuscript, while David Smith of the Poyn-

ix

ter Center at Indiana provided a forum in which to test some of these ideas in public. I am especially indebted to my agent, Doe Coover, for her enthusiasm, and to Janet Goldstein of Harper-Collins, for just the right mix of editorial patience and stimulus. I also wish to thank Betsy Thorpe for timely help in the final phases of preparing the manuscript.

INTRODUCTION:

The Importance of Being Professional

Americans find themselves increasingly drawn into the currents of a new global economy. This emerging economic system is both the cause and effect of only dimly comprehensible social changes. It is less and less deterred by national boundaries. Driven by dizzying mutations in technology, new flows of information, money, goods, and people are already disrupting and reshaping the social fabric of every nation. American society, which has prided itself on leading the advance into successful modernity, is today more like all others and has become enmeshed in networks of interaction which while proliferating across the planet, nevertheless spread the effects of the new economy very unevenly.

The disruptive dynamism of these currents makes some people and places, even within the same society, winners while others lose in a competitive contest with few clear rules which has so far defied efforts to control it. The dynamism of this new order does not distribute its benefits everywhere. It favors certain places, privileged city-regions spread primarily through the most developed and prosperous nations of the Northern Hemisphere, and certain people, primarily those with education, skills, and the capacity to organize themselves for enterprise. In this uncertain environment, Americans can no longer look to the future with their old confidence.

One of the most striking features of the new order is the rapid shifts it has occasioned in how economic value is generated and who benefits from it. In shorthand: the age of mass manufacturing is giving way to an economy in which value increasingly clusters around products, services, and distribution systems which are tuned to meet rapid and subtle differences in demand. This tendency has given a substantial competitive advantage to those who can generate expert knowledge and organize expertise, opening new opportunities for individual and collective enterprise. Expertise and professional knowledge have become more central to life than ever before. New industries, new fields of knowledge, new professions keep appearing, but older ways of doing business, less skilled workers, whole communities, find themselves rapidly driven to the wall. Avoiding social catastrophe will require that, along with others, Americans learn to respond not only to opportunities but to the demands of interdependence.

To its celebrators, such as Francis Fukuyama, this form of civilization represents the "end of history," the culmination of a universal human struggle for "recognition and self-worth" which can finally satisfy both the material desire for comfort and the spiritual aspiration for moral significance.[1] Critics of this triumphalism see the emerging pattern with less elation. Daniel Cohn-Bendit, once a leader of student activists in France during the turbulent 1960s, now argues that "We live in a global society that is highly unequal with respect to chances in life yet is geared, in the post–Cold War era especially, to common consumer expectations."[2] In the same journal in which Fukuyama announced his "end of history" thesis, Samuel P. Huntington has suggested an even more ominous possibility. For Huntington, the most likely consequence of tighter global relations will be to rally increasingly disoriented peoples around the cultural legacies of the historic civilizations presently eclipsed by the West. The result is likely to be intensified cultural conflict across historical, religious, and linguistic frontiers.[3] These divergent assessments reflect more than personal whim. They reflect the ambiguous, even contradictory processes with which people everywhere must struggle.

This dynamic instability is likely to be the source of vast moral and political struggle over how the new order will be organized, within societies as well as among nations. On the one hand, increased economic interaction and cultural contact have vastly expanded individual opportunity, especially for the most advantaged groups. This is expressed in the moral value accorded to the freedom, in theory, for all persons to make as much of their talents as circumstances permit. Across the world's prosperous regions, a moral consensus is evolving according to which each person, regardless of background, should be able to hope for financial reward and respected status by contributing to meeting social needs. On the other hand, fewer grasp that these opportunities could only have grown up as part of an ever-denser network of interdependence. This network is actually a nexus of relationships in which many anonymous parties feel the often unintended consequences of the pursuit of individual and collective opportunity. It is a circumstance in which inherited inequalities in wealth, power, and skill ensure that some are in dramatically worse positions to pursue their goals than others.

The celebrators focus on the positive sides of this dynamic. These interactions have developed the skills and capacities of a vastly greater proportion of the human species than has any previous form of society. In its most successful instantiations, it has probably succeeded in providing more individual well-being and social mobility than ever before in history. In these ways the triumphalists are right. However, it is also producing great cleavages, even within the successful countries, between the fortunate minority able to ride the waves of its planetary dynamics and those who are being inundated by them. The destructive aspects of these same processes, though catastrophic for the unlucky, are often dismissed as mere inconveniences by the successful. In reality, however, they cannot be ignored, not only for moral but for hard-headedly practical reasons.

The moral recognition of the good of opportunity has produced the idea of individual rights, which now enjoys wide acceptance in the industrial nations. However, growing interdependence also makes moral claims and demands a parallel recognition. Interdependence means not only that individuals are dependent on the actions of many unknown others for their opportunities, but that they also either support or undercut these others by their own activities. The spreading networks of interaction which make possible the openness of modern life for individuals are at the same time in a real, if often only vaguely understood, way under the care of the persons they support. The needed moral recognition is responsibility, a disposition to act with regard to the good of self and others within the larger whole, a disposition stemming from an understanding of mutual dependency. Without widespread recognition of the importance of responsibility, and without its effective institutional embodiment, the web of interdependence being woven by the global society will prove terrifying and destructive. As the environmentalists already know, a good life for anyone now depends upon conduct that is collectively as well as individually responsible.

In the United States, the market forces of "creative destruction" have complicated the problem by producing a growing disconnection between the most educated and economically advantaged portion of the population and the rest. While the long-term welfare of the successful is demonstrably intertwined with the fate of their less fortunate neighbors, the more immediate awareness of interdependence which developed in the more localized conditions of the early twentieth century has faded. This secession of the successful is certainly one of the most ominous signs for the future. Educated, middle-class Americans, the bulk of the twenty percent of the workforce classified professional and managerial, seem to be losing concern about their fellow citizens even as they scramble to keep up with occupational changes which offer them advantageous positions in the emerging global order. This group, like their peers in other societies, embodies enormous human capital in the form of knowledge, skill, and organizational abilities. These are key resources, not only for the growth of the world economy, but for any conceivable solutions to the problems of global population growth, social conflict, and environmental degradation. The nature of this new civilization will be determined by many factors, but one of the most important will surely be whether or not those who wield professional skill do so with a large sense of their responsibility for enhancing the quality of life for all.

These tendencies toward secession pose a growing peril to the emerging global civilization. The problem is that the operations of the world market do not by themselves engage sufficient human effort toward the enhancement of the positive potentials of the new civilization and the containment of its negative effects. Nor can expert steering by national states or global corporations be looked to as the solution. Because of the interdependence of the contemporary world, often tightening between national societies even while it is loosened within them, attention to the needs of sustained cooperation is increasingly necessary for human survival.

Integrity is at once an aspect of individual responsibility and a source of human dignity. Its roots, however, extend beyond the individual into the social subsoil of personality, to the implicit judgment that others can prove trustworthy, that one can engage with them in common undertakings because, in the main, cooperation enhances rather than undercuts the possibilities of living. At the other end, integrity and responsibility need knowledge and orientation. These depend upon institutions which are organized to recognize and promote the application of expertise toward those socially and environmentally conserving functions which are needed to rescue competitive striving from its self-induced narrowness of sympathy.

These contemporary demands give a new currency to the ideal of professionalism as it was put forward by reformers in Great Britain and the United States early in this century. Then, the reckless pace of industrialization also threatened social solidarity by flouting claims to social justice in the name of economic competition. The advocates of professionalism countered with a conception of highly skilled workers who could bring to a variety of occupations a broader, more socially responsible sense of calling, combining something of religious dedication with the civic ideals of traditional humanism and the scientific virtues. They wished to transform the cultures of business, government, education, and the trades with a professional understanding that could transcend divisions of interest by infusing into these spheres a public spirit. They sought to embody this spirit in a politics of civil argument which respected diverse viewpoints, while aiming at a consensus about common purposes.[4]

The enormous growth of professionalization since that time has severely disappointed those hopes. Public alarm at professional dereliction of duty is today often of a piece with worries about the secession of the successful, so that professionalism has for some come to mean little more than a cover for self-aggrandizement. Others note technological developments out of control, posing military, social, and environmental threats, tracing the problems to irresponsible specialists unaware or unconcerned about the wider effects of their particular expertise. Yet, to resort to external regulation to control expert functions, from physicians to teachers to scientific researchers, is not by itself an adequate response. Neither economic incentives, nor technology, nor administrative control has proved an effective surrogate for the commitment to integrity evoked in the ideal of professionalism.

This book is an exploration of the fortunes and prospects of professionalism. As shown in the varied development of professional occupations, professionalism can mean a number of things and produce profoundly divergent outcomes. At its worst, professionalism can lock individuals in a narrow focus upon technical competence, and sometimes individual success, to the exclusion of all other considerations. At its best, however, professionalism has been far more than that. By taking responsibility through one's work for ends of social importance, an individual's skills and aspirations acquire a value for all. Professionalism thereby forms a crucial

link between the modern individual's struggle for a fulfilling existence and the needs of the larger society, so that individual opportunity can serve the demands of interdependence.[5]

The divergence between the narrowness of the purely technical
versions of professionalism and the breadth represented by its civic
development has two causes. The institutional organization of different spheres of professional life strongly shapes from without the
form professionalism takes. However, the way in which professional education and practice are themselves articulated and understood by professionals, whether professional life is in practice narrowly technical or broadly civic in intent and reference, also makes
a difference, one all the more crucial because it comes from within
professional practice itself.

Professionalism has sometimes been treated as a mere reflex of
the economic division of labor. It has been minimized as a largely
defensive ideology employed by privileged strata of the modern
workforce. Against these determinisms of technology or class, this
book emphasizes the ways in which professional development has
been both effect and cause of changes in the patterns of work. It
will examine professionalism as a sometimes successful and creative, sometimes failed and calcified, response to changing condi-
ions. Reformers as well as hacks, prophets as well as apologists
e shaped the professional enterprise into an important part of
iern civil society.[6]

In no modern society has professionalism loomed larger as a
social ethos than in the United States. Of all nations it has been
most hospitable to the generation of forms of professional enterprise. The United States can therefore stand as a sort of test case of
the significance of professionalism as a distinctively modern form
of vocational ethos. The strategy of the following chapters will be
to first survey the contemporary complaint about the professions
and professionalism, then to describe how the professions have
developed historically from a limited kind of genteel occupation
into one of the most widely emulated and sought-after models of
work. This change includes the rise of the complex institutions of

industrial society, especially the university, the common school of the professions, as well as the bureaucratic structures of business, government, health care, and education, the major homes of professional work.

Throughout this story, the focus of attention will be on the differing ways in which professionalism has been understood and articulated in American culture amid changing forms of professional organization. The tale is in some ways a great success story, as professionalized forms of work have advanced the welfare of American society, greatly expanded the educated middle class, and provided important vehicles of upward mobility for once-marginalized immigrants, minorities, and women. However, it is also a story of dashed hopes and of public trust betrayed, a project somehow gone awry or fallen sadly short of its human potential.

The explanation that is offered for this ambiguous outcome is that professionalism's loss of direction has been due to its disconnection from the culture of civic democracy. In American public culture, a long tradition stretching from Alexis de Tocqueville to John Dewey has warned of the dangerous consequences of reducing social energies to the pursuit of single goals, economic or technical, acting in the naive belief that public happiness would somehow result automatically from private preoccupations. Today, it ha become almost a truism that in the global economy, an educa engaged, and well-organized workforce is the basis for the lo term success of any economic entity. It is still less widely unde stood that these factors, which are cultural, even moral in nature rather than economic or technical, are themselves only sustainable within a certain kind of social and political climate.

Some societies, and certain regions within those societies, are proving far more able to navigate the currents of the world economy with a greater sense of direction and socioeconomic success than others. Recent research argues strongly that a key determinant of such success is the presence of a vital civic culture, in which accepted practice demands being alive to the concerns of others, tolerant of difference, supportive of others' dignity, and willing to talk and work together across a wide spectrum of vital associations.[7] As we will see, these findings confirm the thesis of the theorists of the American civic tradition, that in the modern world, humanly successful societies are those in which the path to individual fulfillment lies through that enlargement of perspective and heightening of responsibility which come from participation in the life of civic democracy.

The tradition of civic democracy has old links to the idea of professionalism. Reformers of the Progressive Era promoted professionalism precisely as a project for keeping the imperatives of democracy and public service alive within an ever more complex occupational world. Today, increased concern about the nature and role of the professions has begun to create conditions in which the idea of a civic professionalism may again become a practical force in public awareness. Within the practice of professional fields, as in the workings of the advanced economy, civic norms of reciprocity, tolerance, and common deliberation seem needed by the evident failures of the inherited system of myopic specialization.

This book makes a case that professional life can and needs to be restructured in ways that suffuse technical competence with civic awareness and purpose. Thanks in part to the challenges unrelentingly posed by the new global society and its host of attendant problems, specialists find themselves increasingly having to learn the principles of each others' specialities. They must also learn to relate their expertise to publics concerned and affected by change. In response to these challenges, new understandings of professionalism and forms of professional practice are emerging. These emerging forms of practice recognize that there is finally no successful separation between the skills of problem solving and those of deliberation and judgment, no viable pursuit of technical excellence without participation in those civic enterprises through which expertise discovers its human meaning. In these developments we can glimpse the possibility of transforming existing models of professional thinking and practice, along with the benefits such changes can bring.

1

PROFESSIONALISM:

Part of the Problem or Part of the Solution?

SYMBOLS OF SUCCESS

They are not everywhere. The briefcase has become one of the most recognizable emblems of status in modern society. Every weekday ranks of these status symbols, gripped like the leather shields of an invading army, inundate every metropolitan center. In the same metropolises, and a host of suburban office parks, those human waves are almost always smartly dressed. Even if they tread softly in running shoes, the shoes are uniformly in good taste. The briefcases and their bearers may not turn many heads, but they still emanate an alluring scent of success.

In modern life briefcases are more than substitutes for rucksacks or paper bags. They are signs of a certain status. A briefcase announces that its bearer holds an occupation sufficiently responsible that work is not confined to a production shift or opening hours. Carrying a briefcase advertises that its bearer commands ample amounts of the rarest form of credit: autonomy in work. The briefcase asserts that this person can be counted upon to do the job without direct supervision, out of the shop, and off-hours. If asked

1

to name this kind of highly valued, highly trusted kind of work, most of us would be likely to say, "professional work." Those who do such work seem to occupy an important and enviable place in the world.

Professional is a very loosely defined term. Originally, of course, it referred to the classic honorific occupations of medicine, the bar, and the clergy. These occupations certainly enjoy high status. When asked to rank the most desirable jobs, Americans have consistently placed medical doctors just below Supreme Court justices, the top-ranked job. Lawyers, clergy, dentists, college professors, and architects always appear among the top twenty ranks.[1] Professions are typically described as occupations characterized by three features: specialized training in a field of codified knowledge usually acquired by formal education and apprenticeship, public recognition of a certain autonomy on the part of the community of practitioners to regulate their own standards of practice, and a commitment to provide service to the public which goes beyond the economic welfare of the practitioners.

Observers of modern society have repeatedly pointed out great changes in the world of work. As farming, then manufacturing has absorbed less of the American workforce, those occupations involving services and information have expanded enormously. In particular, the jobs classified as "professional and managerial" have become increasingly numerous and important. The reasons are not hard to see. As American society has shifted from a rural, local base to an urban and technological pattern of life, expertise and coordination have become increasingly essential. The complicated organization of the modern economy has made us all far more interdependent than in the past. Our livelihoods, our health, our knowledge of the world, the whole quality of contemporary life, depend upon the integrated meshing of a vast number of skills and capacities. It is this complex interdependence which has set the great waves of briefcases in motion across America.

Skilled professionals have become indispensable to modern society. They provide the specific skills that are basic to the operation of complex modern institutions in the spheres of industry, government, education, health care, and the law. Professionals such as therapists and social service providers help negotiate that complexity as they aid many in seeking direction and assistance amid the often harsh accidents of life. Historian Harold Perkin has characterized British history during the last century as dominated by the professional organization and outlook.[2] Similar views have been put forward about modern societies generally, and the United States in particular.[3] Because of their knowledge and the strategic importance of their functions, professionals are frequently beneficiaries of trust and high expectations on the part of the larger society. The professions depend upon a kind of social compact of reciprocal trust and good faith between the practitioners and the publics they serve. In some cases, where professional fields are licensed, this compact may be quite explicit, but it is always presumed. This is one reason why malfeasance on the part of professionals can excite moral outrage.

Popular moral vocabulary has come to give special prominence to professionalism. It has emerged as a widely esteemed and sought-after virtue. To act "professionally" is high praise in any situation, while the most damning epithet hurled at politicians, financiers, and athletes by their enemies is the charge of being "unprofessional." So seriously is it taken that even in the contemporary climate of moral relativism, when the substance of formerly solid terms such as "indecent" and "disrespectful" have been opened to question, few speak of professional behavior as existing only in the eye of the beholder. Examples of the importance of the public concern about the moral health of the professions appear daily. When an underfunded New York hospital whose patients are poor in disproportionate numbers found its supply of medical interns was to be cut off because fewer interns chose to train among the poor, an anguished staff member remonstrated: "If everything was perfect, we wouldn't need them the way we do. . . . I thought they [physicians] took an oath."[4]

In the case of the traditional professions of the clergy, the bar, and medicine, clear standards affirm professional status. That is the effect of official licensing, specialized university education, and the

3

codification of formalized expertise combined with jurisdiction over vital public activities. There is more ambiguity in the public mind about which other occupations are really professional. The picture is complicated by the increasing tendency of managers to seek professional status: witness the explosion of the Masters of Business Administration degree.

There is a difference in status between the MBA-credentialed executive of a firm and the manager of a local McDonald's. But it is noteworthy that the latter is also likely to speak of managing as an important and specific sort of art—and to carry work home in a briefcase. In other words, modern management clearly aspires toward a recognizably professional identity. Becoming professional is a key dimension of success for occupational groups as well as for individuals. The very disputes over just which occupations deserve to be called professions indicate the symbolic power of the designation "professional." However, the aspiration to being professional connotes more than a claim to higher social status. Professional work also requires the practitioner to adhere to demanding standards of competence and public service. When professional groups fail, as they often do, to hold their own members accountable to these standards, charges of malpractice can, in some fields, be taken to court.

Far more than the symbolic briefcase, then, professional work is freighted with moral weight. But this moral aspect of professionalism is also a source of ambiguity. A young beginning professional, Susan Evans, recently made this discovery. Susan takes pride in being both the first woman in her family to have graduated from college, and the first member of her family to have gone on to professional school. Following a time-honored ritual passed on through generations of students, her graduation from law school meant trading her worn, familiar student's book bag for a genuine leather briefcase. Again, following hoary tradition, Susan Evans went to a professionally recommended, and it should be noted, discount leather and luggage store downtown to select a proper case. Everything proceeded smoothly, including getting the proper monogram imprinted on the case.

As the sales clerk handed it over, he smiled, patted the case, and boomed good-naturedly, "Hope you make lots of money with it!" Susan was stunned, looked around embarrassed, imagining, she later recalled, that "this is how it would feel to be caught buying pornography in public view." She made a rapid exit. Once outside, however, she began laughing nervously. "It was a moment of truth," she recalled. She was, after all, beginning work with a prominent law firm. And yet, somehow, the whole incident did not seem right. "Isn't there," she remonstrated with herself, "more to it than that?"

That remonstrance might have been an echo of the conscience of the profession. The "more than that" is the special dedication and clear accountability which, to common sense, distinguishes a profession from trades and businesses. A profession is "in business" for the common good as well as for the good of its members, or it is not a profession. To demand of any occupation that its members act professionally is to appeal implicitly to the kind of social covenant which explicitly governs professional fields.[5] As Evans realized, however, there is considerable tension between a profession as an ideal, a vocation capable of giving life meaning, and the way in which that occupation is situated—and is perceived—in contemporary society. In Evans's case, the most distressing phenomenon is what she perceives as a steady erosion in the sense of the law firm as a collegial enterprise. She notes that as the competitive pressure on the firm mounts, the partners seem to have few qualms about trying to squeeze more and more out of associates, even as they squabble among themselves over payment formulas to reflect the relative business potential of individual lawyers. What is being lost in the scramble for clients and fees, she believes, is the sense of common purpose, the satisfaction of contributing to a worthwhile public enterprise.

CALLING OR CAREER: THE TENSION WITHIN PROFESSIONALISM

Susan Evans had worked hard through professional school to become good at the craft of law, and her education would continue as she began practice. The goal of these efforts, as she saw them, was to be able to respond self-confidently to someone who had been counseled to "get a good lawyer." By defending and counseling those in need of justice, such a lawyer certainly performs a vital, and difficult, public office. At the same time, we can also imagine that she chose her profession in the hope that it would prove a means toward a dignified style of life. In part that means being successful in the economic sense. In America achieving economic well-being has long been a significant and honorable aspect of professional identity. But it has always meant more than that as well. A profession is understood to provide a career, an opportunity for social and economic advancement, while professionalism demands the kind of dedication to purpose characteristic of a vocation or calling. Not infrequently, these two elements of career and calling pull against each other.

An authentic profession can provide a strong sense of identity because, beyond providing a livelihood, it is a way of life with public value. It is the kind of thing one can build a life around. For the person possessing the requisite capacities and sufficient commitment, a profession can provide not only a career but a calling to useful work as well. Providing counsel and care, curing illness, bringing justice, teaching: these are activities which provide more than jobs and satisfactions for individuals. By their nature they create goods which at some time are essential for everyone, and important for society as a whole.

These functions are carried on in a commercial society in which professional skills, like others, are marketed. The labor market puts pressure on professionals to behave competitively toward their peers, and to accede to the demands of profit when these conflict with professional standards of excellence. Indeed, it is in part to combat these market pressures that professional organizations exist. The situation of professional life is further complicated by the fact that today most professionals are no longer the solo practitioners of popular image, but parts of large bureaucratic organizations. The purposes of these organizations, like the profit motive of the market, do not always support service according to high professional standards.

The advances of modern technology have also accented the tension between intrinsic professional purposes and the imperatives of organizations which employ and train professionals. Especially in the health professions, the aura of technological wizardry has redefined the healer. Less the caregiver of old and more the technician able to engineer health, the physician has become increasingly tied to the high-technology medical center, exchanging the old humble function of care for a less personal, if more effective, role as technician. At its extreme, the redefined physician in the medical center can manage a career almost entirely in terms of technical and economic success, giving little attention to the human meaning and moral ties which give healing its purpose and value. This narrow conception of professionalism has been strengthened by the economic imperatives of the health care marketplace, but it is also fed by the belief that modern technology has banished the vulnerability and mortality of the human condition, and with them the need for the physician as bearer of solace and giver of care.

Nothing in recent memory has so challenged the comforting belief that technology has secured modern individuals against the ravages of disease and death than the AIDS epidemic. Yet this very epidemic, while it threatens the dream of invulnerability through technological "modernization," has also called out responses within the medical world which proceed from a very different model of the physician's calling.

John Turner, M.D., is an endocrinologist in his forties with a successful private practice. He is also treating nearly eight hundred people infected with the AIDS virus. He receives about seventy-five telephone calls a day from patients and their caretakers and works excruciatingly long hours. John Turner's practice no longer fits within the scheme of technological modernization. "If anyone would have told me then [in medical school] that I'd be taking care of people my own age or younger—many of them dreadfully sick, many of them dying—it would have seemed preposterous." After seven years treating the prematurely, mortally ill, he reflected that such experience "forces you to confront mortality square on and to

7

redefine what is important to you to get done in your life."[6] Clearly, for Turner, what is important is extending care to those who find it very hard to get.

Despite the burden of caring for so many in such dire straits, John Turner's complaints are not about the caseload. They are directed at the paucity of response to AIDS patients among physicians and hospitals in the Philadelphia area where he practices. Turner explains the reluctance of doctors, hospitals, and medical schools to become identified with the AIDS epidemic because "they're afraid it will be bad for business." Some of Turner's colleagues avoid AIDS patients, he says, because "a lot of care for people with AIDS is free. People lose their jobs, they lose their insurance. You don't discharge them as patients." Institutions have often been reluctant to take the lead in treating a disease identified with such socially stigmatized groups as homosexual men and IV drug users. Yet, Turner does not see the situation as entirely bleak, despite the undeniable battle fatigue of his rather lonely struggle against the disease.

In John Turner's experience, the epidemic has also called out humanly positive responses from both individuals and institutions. Among the AIDS victims themselves, Turner notes that he has seen "amazing strengths of character float to the surface in people who had no idea they were going to be called upon to consider final events." He reports seeing friends and "sometimes anonymous buddies" stand up and "dedicate their lives to helping," particularly when those one would expect, "clergy, and hospitals and families," withdrew. And Turner, with his companion, Bernardo, in fact seems to have done something like this himself. At last, Turner and other Philadelphia physicians involved with AIDS patients have succeeded in galvanizing major institutional support for an AIDS Education and Training Center. Turner described this development laconically as "very important . . . those of us who do see AIDS patients are all getting, well, a little tired."

For physicians like John Turner, the tragedy of AIDS has brought home all the vulnerability of what used to be called "the human condition." The epidemic has enabled Turner and those like him to rediscover the truth of human interdependence, people's need for each other. More particularly, the response of professionals like John Turner has helped otherwise less-responsive institutions and professional associations to realize that to be professional means to carry an obligation to promote the general good. But Turner's example of leadership also shows that an ethical professionalism is only viable within an institutional context attuned to human needs and part of a larger civic life. This kind of civic awareness was missing in the defensive turf-protecting and narrow self-interest which Turner at first encountered among some parts of the health care world. Ultimately, the potential power latent in his kind of civic professionalism is that it works to wake up professional groups to their larger obligations. It makes them more attentive to the larger purposes for which they exist and which give their work meaning and, at moments, moral splendor.

In Susan Evans's field of the law, recent discontent with the narrow defensiveness on the part of the bar has hastened a similar awareness and another potential opening outward of professional concern. An American Bar Association commission of the late 1980s conceded that there was no real basis for the claim that "lawyers have the exclusive possession of the esoteric knowledge required and are therefore the only ones able to advise clients on any matter concerning the law."[7] The ABA commission concluded from this that it would be desirable to license paralegal practitioners to handle some legal work. At the same time, more radical critics from both ends of the political spectrum have pushed for an end to all governmental regulation of entry into legal services, thereby challenging the jurisdiction of state and federal bar associations over the practice of law.

The professional organizations themselves have become concerned about these perceptions of their own narrowness and complacency, at least to the extent of worrying about their public image. At the end of 1987 the prestigious journals of the American Medical Association and the American Bar Association carried a unique joint editorial, signed by the editors of both periodicals. Entitled "50 Hours for the Poor," the editorial began with the reminder that doctors and lawyers, along with the clergy, belong to "the classic learned professions." It went on to distinguish these from businesses on the basis of a "true profession's . . . special relationship with the poor."

The editorial stressed the duty to serve the poor without pay as the concomitant of "the privilege to practice law or medicine," duties spelled out in law and medicine's official codes of professional conduct.[8] The editors then asked rhetorically how many members of the two professions "deliberately care for the poor in a voluntary and uncompensated way?" Their answer was, "many but not enough,"—only fifteen percent of lawyers, for example, take part in organized pro bono programs for the poor. Each doctor and lawyer, according to the editors, should donate a minimum of fifty hours of professional time annually, or about one week of service to the poor "without expectation of financial remuneration."

The editors concluded by invoking the "great tradition" behind the "giving of this gift." In the church, they wrote, "it is called stewardship. In law, it is called *pro bono publico* (for the public good). In medicine, it is called charity. In everyday society, it is called fairness." The editors were invoking something fundamental to professionalism. This is the ethical spirit of civic life manifested and given specific direction in professional life: the spirit of profession as a calling. Within this civic understanding of the professional vocation, each specific professional responsibility gets its point and value from the contribution it makes, through shared commitment, to the good society and the good life.

For a viable democratic society, a sense of collective purpose needs to operate in the public sphere, especially in politics, the law, and civic deliberation. But it must also be made effective in the everyday realms of work and living. The professions are important because they stand for, and in part actualize, the spirit of vocation. Professionalism promises to link the performance of specific tasks with this larger civic spirit. By enabling workers to connect their activities and careers to the service of public ends, professionalism suggests how to organize the complex modern division of labor to ensure that specific functions are performed well and with a sense of responsibility for the good of the whole.

For physicians like John Turner, attorneys like Susan Evans, and surely many other professionals in all fields, their work is more than "just a job," their lives more than just a career. Professionalism remains a powerful source of moral meaning. But professional life and its institutions are far from being in the best of health. The pressures of market competition and organizational demands threaten to distort the defining purposes of professional work. Within as well as without the professions, there is unmistakable skepticism and cynicism about the whole notion of professionalism. In the face of these forces, a clear understanding of the positive meaning of professional work, and the institutional conditions needed to sustain it, are needed if the professions are to take their place as responsible occupational communities. Without such understanding, and the will to make it effective in institutional reform, the potentials of professionalism, no matter how well exemplified in individual practice, will remain largely a frustrated wish, a romantic, if noble, intention.

The Call to Serve

As long as we equate the "learned professions" with knowledge in the specialized, technical sense, John Turner's dedicated public service can only appear as an admirable but accidental feature of his career. At best, it will seem a personal moral heroism only tangentially related to the practice of medicine as such. But this would be a mistaken view. There has historically been a close relationship between the learned professions and the ethic of public responsibility. Though embattled, the learned professions' sense of special responsibility persists.

The professions have long espoused an ethic of responsibility for the whole of society. The classic learned professions have traditionally served many functions for Americans, and have accordingly played public roles. The ministry, in particular, has been centrally involved with the ethic of public service. The ministry, not law or medicine, is the oldest of the learned professions in America, and the ministry has long had close connections with education. The churches were the first promoters of schools in English North America. The earliest institutions of higher learning, the colleges of Harvard and Yale, were founded expressly to train ministers. From the seventeenth century on, Americans continued to found liberal arts colleges across the continent, principally to train men and women as ministers, teachers, and missionaries.

The ranks of the clergy provided the earliest American intellectuals. Clerical intellectuals have continued to play major public roles in the twentieth century, as names such as Reinhold Niebuhr, Paul Tillich, or Martin Luther King, Jr., clearly indicate. In several ways, the idea of the ministerial profession, with its dedication to the public welfare, in both the material and the moral sense, has exercised a profound effect on the culture of professionalism. That influence has been perhaps the more profound for having been so much taken for granted. The reverence Americans show for knowledge, even mixed with a demand for practical results, suggests the lingering aura of the sacred which once attached to the pursuit of learning. Most important, the ministry has shaped the ethic of service as a distinctive part of professional identity.

The term profession is itself religious in origin. It derives from the act of commitment, the declaration to enter on a distinct way of life, as in the profession of monastic vows. It was, at least in theory, a response to the belief that one had received a "call," not an action imposed by economic or other necessity. Profession entailed a commitment to embody the virtues needed to realize the community's highest purposes. Religious institutions have perennially attended to considerably more than the individual's conscience. They have also addressed key social needs, not only in education, but by the provision of health care and social services of many kinds. The vitality of this spirit of dedication to the commonweal is exemplified in the career of David Gracie.

12

For nearly three decades, the Reverend David Gracie has served as a priest in the Episcopal Church. Until recently, he served as campus chaplain in Philadelphia. But, like his fellow Philadelphian, John Turner, David Gracie's activities are not circumscribed by any job description. "The word I'd use to describe David Gracie most of all is 'involved,'" said a fellow minister. "But he's thoughtfully involved. Dave has always had a well worked-out rationale for what he does. I've urged him to publish some of these reflections; they would make very valuable reading. They would shake up a lot of complacency."

For years, David Gracie worked out of an office in an unimproved row house which also provided housing for several university students and university organizations. Gracie thinks that the ministry "always has a potentially important role" not only within a religious organization but also in society at large. "The church," he believes, "should be a training ground for leaders, enabling them to go into the world, hopefully, with a deeper faith." The inspiration for Gracie's conception of ministry and the role of the church may well lie in the example of his father, a Scottish immigrant worker in the auto plants of Detroit. "My father became a member of the board of deacons in the Baptist church we attended when I was a boy," explained Gracie. "The church really allowed him to develop capacities which his lack of formal education made it hard for him to exercise elsewhere in society." Gracie generalizes this point to say that the church's mission is ultimately persuasive: to transform human society globally so that all can take part in life with dignity.

For David Gracie the ministry, when it is at its best, is a "public work." His exemplars are figures such as Charles Andrews, an Anglican cleric who became one of Gandhi's closest friends and collaborators in the nonviolent campaigns of civil disobedience which Gandhi led for justice and participation in South Africa and India. Gracie has written on Andrews, and finds his example important for defining his own sense of mission. In the days of the Civil Rights struggles of the '60s the newly ordained David Gracie became an urban missionary in Detroit. There he opened his church to the high school students who, under the banner of "quality education" declared a strike against the city's public schools.

"The participation of the church was important to that movement," Gracie recalls. It provided a sense of "sanctuary, a feeling that this is a safe place," and an institution which belonged to the students, their families, and neighbors. The "freedom school" organized with Father Gracie's support in the church provided an alternative and a goad to reforming the public high school. For Gracie, the story is exemplary of the kind of empowering, transforming function he believes religious communities are called upon to fulfill for the sake of the society as a whole.

"As a Christian," he explained, "I am committed to see things in the perspective of 'the Light which enlightens everyone who comes into the world.'" As an heir to the Anglican tradition, Gracie is inclined to "take the order of the world seriously," though not in the sense of accepting the social order as it is, but by "demanding that it live up to its truth." As contemporary examples of this view of things, he cites the leadership of Anglican Archbishop Tutu in South Africa, and the recent acceptance of women into the priesthood of the Episcopal Church.

Over time, however, the effective concern of much of the clergy narrowed more and more, turning away from public matters to specialize in the world of personal morality and intimate concerns. The result has been to redefine the minister, priest, and rabbi in ways quite unlike David Gracie's conception of ministry as public work. In an increasingly competitive cultural environment, religious professionals are often hard to distinguish from therapists, guidance counselors, and other human services personnel.

"In days of yore," comments an article on the changing nature of the rabbinate, "rabbis served as sometimes absolute arbiters in their communities, sitting in legal judgment, attending to adherents' spiritual needs and even assessing taxation." Today, however, the scope of the typical rabbi's activities, like the that of the minister or priest, has narrowed to administration, "officiating at life-cycle events," and providing comfort and counsel. But while the scope has decreased, the new situation places a host of new demands on the rabbi. "Because synagogues must compete for a congregant's time, rabbis are expected to be attractive, with winning personalities." One consequence, according to Rabbi Gilbert Epstein of *Conservative Judaism in America*, is that "some younger men and women have second thoughts about going into a pulpit rabbinate because of these tremendous demands."[9]

Despite these perplexities, those twentieth-century professions with a mission to maintain and develop human resources are in spirit, and often in fact, outgrowths of the ministry. One effect on American culture of the extended sense which the Reformation gave the term vocation has been the continuing insistence that the professional be a person of moral as well as intellectual culture. Something like this diffusion of purpose from the sacred to the secular sphere has been a large part of the story behind the development of a social conscience within the American middle class. For that conscience, social life gains significance from ethical and civic purposes. That view, however, has long been at odds with another orientation toward life which takes as its purpose the efficient deployment of techniques for enhancing individual satisfaction. Professionalism has long been divided between this utilitarian tendency and the understanding of society as constituted by ethical ends. The problem for professionalism today centers on how strong the force exerted upon professional life by the one or the other orientation.

THE PROFESSIONS UNDER SCRUTINY

The continuing appeal of professionalism shows that it articulates a hunger for something which is often missing or suppressed in work. That something is a sense of engagement, through one's work, with shared purposes which give point and value to individual effort. These purposes—dignity, justice, fellowship—make possible a civil and meaningful public realm. They are the promise of professionalism. They are also the goods which engaged professionals such as those we have met in this chapter have in abundance. But these are not goods which individuals can possess or enjoy alone, or even achieve entirely by their own efforts. We can see these as the goods of self-discovery and purpose, even a satisfying kind of self-fulfillment, though this self-fulfillment is not what often goes by that name. It comes, almost paradoxically, through a kind of transcendence and change of self, gaining a wider sense of identity through engagement with technical excellence while taking responsibility for shared ends.

John Turner has found in medicine this enlargement of identity and purpose by assuming the responsibilities of leadership in the face of the crisis of AIDS. David Gracie has found significant engagement through making his own the traditional commitment of his church to responsibility for the world's betterment. With Susan Evans this sense of significant engagement in her field of calling remains elusive, though an object of passionate concern. As Evans's incomplete quest indicates, however, the achievements of all committed professionals remain precarious in the absence of strong institutions committed to the same ends, institutions whose working secures the integrity of individual dedication. The fragility and relative scarcity of such institutional arrangements is part of what has prompted a significant series of attacks on not only particular professional abuses, but the notion of professionalism itself.

This is a time of scrutiny for all the institutions of American society. It is also a time of widespread disaffection, alienation, and resentment at virtually all established organizations which are perceived, often rightly, as having failed to address effectively the challenges of the present. But this tone of scrutiny and skepticism also makes it difficult for those who wish to conserve and expand the moral resources of professionalism. In what follows, we will examine three recent critiques of professional life, the first by James Fallows, the second by Barbara Ehrenreich, and the third by Christopher Lasch. We will take them up as participants in a public argument, structured by a profound clash between two rival conceptions of what is most important in modern society. The clash is between the view that society ought to be seen as a system for maximizing individual utilities or satisfactions, versus the notion that a viable society must pursue civic as well as utilitarian ends. It will turn out that these commitments about the nature of social life also produce opposing assessments of the value of professionalism and professional work which powerfully affect contemporary conduct.

James Fallows's book, *More Like Us*, bears the clarifying subtitle, *Making America Great Again*. It is significant that a central theme of his argument is that America has been deflected from her natural path of development by the imposition of "Confucianism," the ascendancy of a kind of mandarinate of credentialed professionals. Fallows sees the United States as a dynamic society of "constant, unstructured change," in which individuals could advance, and gain that often crucial "second chance," thanks to a remarkable open occupational structure, fed by a market economy driven by the winds of "creative destruction."[10]

Fallows contrasts this picture of the United States with his experience of the more institutionally static societies of East Asia, particularly Japan. Since World War II, however, Fallows sees America as having drifted in something like an Asian direction, toward becoming a more Confucian society characterized by deference to credentials earned through long formal schooling, and a sense that individuals should have an assigned place in life.

"With the rise of educational requirements and licenses," Fallows writes, "the formula for success and mobility changed. How someone prepared for a job became at least as important as how well he actually did it."[11] This development has had baleful effects. It has hurt the sense of possibility, especially the possibility of the second chance in life, which Fallows believes has been key to American energy. Professionalism has also created an American version of the British "gentlemen's work," implanting a sense of snobbery about what kinds of work are suitable for the talented, thereby steering talent away from potentially creative and useful jobs toward fields considered safe and dignified, such as the law.

Fallows makes clear in this discussion that his concerns are ultimately for the civic health of the United States, especially whether it will live up to its promise of open access for all, especially for those previously held down. Given this moral purpose, his critique of the constricting and often unjust effects of much of the organization of "meritocratic" schooling and professional work seems on point. Fallows urges that we would do better to emphasize proven competence as the test for access to occupations over the alleged capacity of testing and schooling to predict "ability." However, in mounting his critique, Fallows slides, perhaps unknowingly, into a conception of society quite different from, and largely indifferent to, the moral and political appeal his book is making.

The attack on professional Confucianism is posed in an economic idiom made popular by the current vogue of free market theories. Fallows adopts a conception of society as the playing field of self-interested individuals who seek their particular satisfactions by striking the most advantageous possible deals with each other. The happy paradox, according to this view, is that individual satisfactions, in the aggregate, will be best achieved if everyone seeks individual well-being while playing according to general rules of cooperation. These rules, however, do not require altruism or consideration of some general good; their real force comes from their theoretical ability to promote the greatest efficiency in the allocation of scarce resources and, thus, in the long run, the greatest satisfaction for all the parties.[12]

This is a familiar picture. It is derived from the utilitarian theory which has long been a strong component within philosophical liberalism, a theory which, dismissing talk about moral and political ends, places its hopes for progress on understanding and mastering the forces of nature, such as the alleged "laws" of market activity.[13] Imagining society as a simplified and idealized version of the marketplace writ large, the best society is the one in which there are few impediments to the rapid exchange of goods, one that least inhibits individuals in their search for the best deal, in work as in consumption.

Professional licenses or schooling requirements, then, are to be deplored like government regulations and for the same reason. Professional requirements block the process of "constant, unstructured change" which is, by assumption, believed to be the source of both economic efficiency and individual satisfaction. In other words, the great obstacle on the way to a better world is the tendency of individuals and groups to seek, for their own particular advantage, to slow or impede the winds of "creative destruction" by building dikes and dams. This process generates inefficiencies of which monopolies are the worst example. Professions represent similar efforts to restrict free trade in services and, as a consequence, rigidify social relations. Thus, professionalism is a source of social friction and, if unchecked, of Confucian stagnation.

There are several major problems with Fallows's argument. First, it is not clear that the laissez-faire model of economics which he espouses is really a very good guide to economic success in the actual world. As Lester Thurow, another contemporary diagnostician of the American political economy has pointed out, the more successful capitalisms of Germany and Japan cannot be said to have "less government nor more motivated individuals," the two objectives Fallows hopes to achieve by opening up markets. On the contrary, what distinguishes those economies from the American is their far greater emphasis upon institution-building and the "careful organization of teams": their programs of "communitarian" as opposed to "individualistic" capitalism.[14] Through their educational systems these nations combine academic learning with practical training in institutionalized patterns that link government, business, and schooling.[15]

Second, and more seriously, Fallows's embrace of the utilitarian theory contradicts the core argument of his book. Fallows is searching for social conditions which would foster more significant engagement in work. He wants to find these for the good of America as a national community for which trust and justice, not merely utility and efficiency, are the measures of well-being. Even the problems Fallows singles out as the evils undercutting American "greatness" are really moral and social rather than economic or technical in nature. Without a belief that they are getting a fair chance, Fallows believes, Americans will not do their best. His attack on the usefulness of professional credentials and his prescriptions for opening up the occupational order on the basis of tests of competence are premised upon the efficacy of moral incentives and priority of a shared, civic sense of trust in the fairness of their nation's system of opportunities and rewards.

When Fallows assails professionalism as a force which undercuts trust among citizens, he is implicitly admitting that even national economic success depends upon the maintenance of civic values such as mutual trust, cooperation, and concern about the interests of one's fellow citizens. The utilitarian picture of society cannot account for the very moral concerns which give Fallows's argument its poignancy. Indeed, Fallows himself, on another occasion, has well described the fatal limitation of the theory he here espouses by noting that "People don't live in markets, they live in societies."[16] Yet, Fallows's civic ends themselves tend to be one-sidedly private and individualistic. He writes at length about individual freedom and success but says little about that fuller sense of dignity and amenity which makes societies worth living in. Fallows is repeating the old tendency of the utilitarian theory to take seriously only individuals, while reducing relationships to so many instruments toward subjective satisfaction, ignoring the institutions necessary to sustain the public goods of mutual trust, justice, and the sense of place and purpose without which no individuals, and no society, can live well.

Barbara Ehrenreich's critical analysis of the "professional middle class," *Fear of Falling*, appreciates, as Fallows does not, the significant engagement manifested in professional work. As she hyperbolically puts it, the professional middle class has found a "secret pleasure principle" in the form of work which is a source of satisfaction sufficiently deep to provide an "alternative to the less satisfying, and hence more addictive, hedonism of the consumer culture."[17] This is a social analysis at odds with the reduction of social life to economic utilities. For Ehrenreich, the key problem of professional life is precisely the tendency toward loss of the intrinsic rewards attendant upon significant engagement in worthwhile work and their replacement by the anxieties and fevers of a utilitarian culture dominated by instrumental values.

The story Ehrenreich tells spans the years since World War II, and it too is highly critical of the direction American life has taken, especially since the 1970s. Since that time, Ehrenreich stresses, American society, which had during the postwar decades made modest strides toward greater socioeconomic and racial equality, began to slide toward an increasingly polarized situation, a nation divided into an increasingly affluent minority—including the professional class—and a large majority whose living standards continue to fall. The story's collective protagonist, the professional middle class, has forsaken its most promising possibilities as a force for significant reform and greater equality, and instead come to behave more like a defensive and beleaguered oligarchy.

As Ehrenreich sees it, the blame for this unhappy outcome rests in part upon the character of the professional class itself. Ehrenreich ascribes, in the traditional manner of the political left, primary causal force to the workings of the capitalist economic order, but she seems determined to provoke the conscience of the professional class itself. In the end, this division of responsibility allows her to suggest a positive role for a reformed professional middle class: consciously working to compensate for the market's tendency to produce an ever more unequally divided America by striving to make their secret "pleasure principle" of dignified, meaningful work available to all.

The professional middle class, as Ehrenreich describes it, is defined by a guild-like period of training, centered in higher education, which instills social cohesion and a self-directed work discipline. The class is also defined by occupations which are generally salaried, rather than remunerated by fees or hourly wages, organizational in structure, and self-directing. Professionals' incomes range considerably, from schoolteachers to doctors to some corporate CEOs who have joined the "corporate rich," but it is generally adequate to secure a lifestyle which eschews the mass-produced in favor of "the authentic, the natural and frequently imported."[18]

The great problem for professional workers in contemporary capitalist society, writes Ehrenreich, is that their very autonomy in work requires "self-discipline and self-directed labor." But these ascetical values conflict with the dreams of affluent ease which the consumer culture imagines to be the only reason for working. Thus, the pursuit of affluence, while seductive, comes to be experienced as a threat, identified as it is with "hedonism and self-indulgence." This contradiction between the lures of affluence and the demands of work discipline generates a pervasive "fear of falling" through "inner weakness . . . losing discipline and will."[19] Here lies the larger significance of the story of the professional middle class: it is the site of the "most acute conflict over hedonism . . . between modernity and tradition, consumerism and self-discipline."[20]

The saving grace for professionals, of course, has always been that sense of significant engagement with publicly meaningful work which makes up vocation. Although Ehrenreich is not clear as to who and what is responsible, she argues that the vocational sense has weakened, not only in the face of a more immediate pleasure principle, but from the fact that successful careers have increasingly come to entail the sacrifice of intrinsically meaningful involvement for the sake of compensation and status. This, anyway, is how Ehrenreich explains what was called the "Yuppie syndrome" during the 1980s. These tendencies weaken the viability among the middle class of appeals to conscience and responsibility just at the moment when social polarization and the weakening of the public sphere of common life most need vocal and committed reformers. Ehrenreich characterizes the professional class as an uncertain elite, strategically positioned, both economically and culturally, now largely part of the problem, but potentially a potent force for moving the nation toward a more egalitarian and inclusive society.

Ehrenreich is in many ways persuasive in her analysis. From it we can see how the public ends of civil society which have been embodied in professional work are being subverted by the pressures of market competition and consumer culture. The challenge which Ehrenreich presents is to discover ways to strengthen society's common purposes against the anarchic tendencies of the market. The hedonism of consumer culture has rendered this process much more difficult than it once was. Thus, professionalism has been stripped of much of its power to challenge the conscience of either the professional class or society at large.

The implication of this analysis is that professionalism cannot be separated from the larger economic, political, and cultural currents which have shaped contemporary society. In different ways, both Ehrenreich and Fallows illustrate the social importance of professionalism, not merely in an external, instrumental way, but as a cultural source through which modern people shape their identities. However, Fallows and Ehrenreich fall out in making almost symmetrically opposite judgments of the value of professionalism as a source of identity and meaning: the former condemning it as an impediment to the openness of American society, while the latter praises it as a potential alternative to the seductions of consumer society. What neither notes is that professionalism itself embodies the contradiction we have seen between the enhancement of individual satisfaction and the demands of social well-being.

By contrast, a third contemporary critic of professional life, Christopher Lasch, challenges professionalism squarely as a powerful—but corrupting—source of identity and meaning. In *The True and Only Heaven* Lasch acknowledges the important function of professional knowledge in defining reality for modern societies. He is critical, however, of the tendency of educated professionals to define themselves through belief in progress, which he sees as a continuation of the Enlightenment's faith in the emancipating powers of reason. As Lasch stingingly puts it, "we can readily agree with [the description] . . . of the professional class as the 'most progressive force in modern society': the question is whether that can still be regarded as a virtue."[21]

23

Lasch raises several severe objections to the value of "progress" as a guiding belief, and these objections are bound up with what Lasch takes to be the distinctive culture of professionals. Progress, according to Lasch, has been driven by two factors above all: the "intoxicating prospect of man's conquest of the material world" which derived from seventeenth-century natural science and, secondly, the capitalist appetite for acquisition. Along with the modern nation state, Lasch believes that capitalism has drawn its energies from the scientific attitude toward the world. Together, these two forces have created a self-generating spiral in which "the definition of human needs and wants was thought to expand as those needs and wants were progressively satisfied."

The long-term consequences, however, have turned increasingly sour: the psychic dislocation and social breakdown attendant upon the ruthless mobilization of human resources mirror the ecological destruction which is the effect of these "growth processes" on the natural habitat. As an inner attitude, progress has meant the hope for "the eventual triumph of critical intelligence over superstition, cosmopolitanism over provincialism, man over nature, abundance over scarcity."[22] These attitudes are widespread in all modern societies, but, according to Lasch, it is among the professional class that they are found most virulently and less diluted by residual premodern loyalties.

Lasch argues that the professional faith in progress is of a piece with what sociologist Alvin Gouldner identified as the "culture of critical discourse." Lasch accepts Gouldner's contention that this "culture of critical discourse" is the source of a common ethos shared by members of the professional middle class. For those initiated into this culture, "nothing is sacred . . . nothing is exempt from reexamination." As Lasch sees it, this critical temper is predisposed to degenerate into cynicism and opportunism, as well as "snobbish disdain for people who lack formal education and work with their hands, an unfounded confidence in the moral wisdom of experts."[23] The habit of criticism, transmitted by the university and often glorified as the greatest spiritual achievement of modernity, Lasch brands as the chief cause of the utilitarian "disposition (the natural out-growth of irreverence and distrust) to see the world as something that exists only to gratify human desires," a spirit which "unleavened by a sense of its own limits, soon reduces the world to ashes."[24]

The central thrust of Lasch's critique is that the culture of critical discourse *is* the defining feature of professionalism and that this culture is nihilistic at its core. Lasch contrasts this Promethean culture for which "nothing is sacred" and which knows no limits with another, still extant version of modern culture. This is contained in what appears in modern American political discourse as "populism," though its moral sources antedate the Enlightenment. This other current of modernity has always been skeptical of the notion of unlimited progress. Its civic home has typically been communities of artisans and agriculturalists, and it has found its political expression in movements such as labor syndicalism and agrarian populism, which were among the chief victims of the consolidation of the industrial order. Today, it is embodied in the culture of the working people of the lower middle class often despised, Lasch believes, by members of the professional middle class.

Populists, in Lasch's reconstruction of their tradition, rejected the allure of unlimited abundance, the very heart of the dream of progress. Instead of abundance and luxury for all, populists extolled "a competence . . . a piece of earth, a small shop, a useful calling." Competence, so understood, referred to "the livelihood conferred by property but also to the skills required to maintain it. The ideal of universal proprietorship embodied a humbler set of expectations than the ideal of universal consumption . . . it embodied a more strenuous and morally demanding definition of the good life." Against the ideal of a society of "supremely cultivated consumers" this artisanal moral source imagined "a whole world of heroes."[25]

For Lasch, populism is a tradition which grew up in the shadow of a morally strenuous Calvinist Christianity. At its center lay an essentially religious affirmation of the inescapability of natural limits on human freedom and the necessity of work as both a submission to the sovereign power of God and that through which

25

humans can transcend the limits of necessity. Lasch notes no such religious ethic in connection with professionalism, which he sees as lacking any sense of either reverence or the limits of its own powers.

While for Fallows the organization of the professions is a deplorable impediment to the benefits attendant upon utilitarian progress, Lasch identifies professionalism as a chief carrier of the pathology of progressive ideology. Fallows denounces professionals as would-be monopolists; Lasch attacks them as technocrats without conscience. He would reject Ehrenreich's attempt to strengthen professionalism as a source of meaning alternative to consumer culture, insisting that the consequences of the one are as destructive of humane values as the effects of the other. Neither professionalism nor consumerism possesses that reverence for being which can provide a critical distance on the social and ecological depredations of the modern state and economy.[26] Thus, more than the other two critics, Lasch poses a profound question about the soundness of the modern project as we have been living it out in the late twentieth century. Finally, however, his portrait of professionalism is sweeping caricature, penned with the righteousness of a prophetic outsider who sees no hope for reform.

MAKING SENSE OF THE PROBLEM OF THE PROFESSIONS

To judge from these critics, the professions have become flash points at which conflicting tendencies in American economic, social, and cultural life meet and assume shape. As we have seen, the critics differ widely in the stance they take toward professionals. They focus upon different issues, beginning with issues of economic and social opportunity and proceeding to link the rise of the professions to the fate of cultural meaning and moral purpose in the contemporary United States. When Fallows suggests dismantling much of the edifice of professional education and work in the interests of economic efficiency and civic equity, he is focusing mostly on the economic and social aspects of the professional phenomenon. By contrast, Ehrenreich's muted hopes for spreading and democratizing the professional ethos emphasize the dimension of moral meaning intrinsic to professional work. Lasch extends the focus on culture and morals through his historical narrative. As Lasch tells it, the morally rootless ways of cosmopolitan professionals have impoverished rather than enriched modern life by their ascendancy over the culture of work, family, and local community which he identifies with populism.

Each of these different criticisms, however, fails to see the organizational, cultural, and historical dimensions of the professions in clear relationship to each other. To understand how and why the professions have reached their present important but uncertain state, the changing structures of professional life have to be acknowledged as participants in the larger evolution of American society. For this purpose, a historical approach is essential because the professions, like all enduring social groups, cannot be understood apart from the process of their development.

Even in today's society, dominated by large-scale, bureaucratic organizations, professions such as engineering and management, which arose with twentieth-century industry, are intertwined with forms of professional life which derive from earlier phases of the national past. The continued coexistence of these newer fields, in the company with an expanding number of emerging professions, with the older learned professions such as law, medicine, and the ministry becomes intelligible when viewed as the continuing presence of historically distinct lines of professional development. An archaeological approach which views social forms as superimposed, often conflicting, layers of social evolution illuminates present anomalies by laying bare, as it were, the different institutional purposes and habits which operate in today's professional society. This approach will also make it easier to grasp both the limitations and potentials of the several types of professions for responding to the challenges of the present.

This approach also sheds light on the crucial cultural dimension of the professional enterprise. Reconstructing the socioeconomic and political contexts which gave rise to the particular professional types will make it clear how and why the meaning of professional life remains a contested issue. So, the qualities of autonomy, personal probity, and social leadership associated with professionalism derive from the early learned or liberal professions which formed around themselves the aura of social responsibility and leadership. In a parallel way, the ascendancy of confidence in learned expertise, specialization, and the applicability of science and technology to human problems, indicate the continuing currency of values which launched the later technologically oriented professions.

Tracing the conflicts and innovations through which the several types of profession arose will also indicate their close association with characteristic institutions and influential currents in American culture. The most constant tension, as we have seen, has been between a technical emphasis which stresses specialization—broadly linked to a utilitarian conception of society as a project for enhancing efficiency and individual satisfaction—and a sense of professional mission which has insisted upon the prominence of the ethical and civic dimensions of the enterprise. This conflict within professionalism has at times mirrored a wider conflict within American society, while at other times the direction taken by the culture of professionalism has held a leading part in the larger drama of cultural change.

This framework of analysis makes no pretense to neutrality in the ongoing contest over the identity and destiny of the professional enterprise. It seeks to reclaim and continue a tradition of civic professionalism. This is a tradition which, while acknowledging the genuine importance of technical proficiency in every field, views the professional enterprise as humanly engaged practices which generate values of great significance for modern societies. The burden of the several chapters which follow is to show how the civic orientation in professionalism has been eclipsed by a more narrowly technical understanding, often to the detriment of professional life and the social compact which links professions to the larger society. The latter part of the book attempts to make constructive use of this analysis in order to discern and explore the possibilities which a renewed civic professionalism hold out for American democracy.

2

---◆---

THE EVOLUTION OF
THE PROFESSIONS:

From Professions of Office to the Organizational Professions

Today the professions appear a natural and established feature of American society, as of all developed nations. In fact, however, the professions' achievement of social importance was hardly an expected nor necessary feature of the development of the United States. Since its founding, American society has been especially agitated by conflicts which pit a belief in egalitarianism against an ideal of individual achievement. This conflict has led to dramatic swings, at one moment toward public recognition of the competence of certain specialized groups to regulate a whole occupational sphere, such as health care, while at other moments public opinion has stripped occupational groups of any special prerogatives or privileges.

Since the professional career has always been a route to individual success, professions have been focal points in the struggle to

29

balance democratic openness to individual achievement with the need for the professions to be trusted to work for the benefit of others, in pursuit of agreed-upon, common ends. Professionals take part in commercial society as the owners of a special type of wealth-producing property or "capital" of a peculiarly intellectual sort: the skills and knowledge acquired through their specialized training and experience. This is sometimes referred to as "human," as opposed to physical, capital. Like physical capital, human capital can be traded in the market and, like physical capital, it can be possessed by individuals. Also like physical capital, its security and negotiability depends upon a structure of legal definitions and procedures.

The human capital of professionals, however, is peculiarly dependent upon the public, legal acceptance of the value of services offered by the professional. The professional's services are often beyond the lay buyer's ability to understand or fully judge. There is thus an inescapable, reciprocal fiduciary relationship between the professional and client. That is, the professional, including the group of professionals providing a certain service, must persuade clients to accept the professionals' definition and valuation of that service, even as the clients must acknowledge and trust the competence of the providers. In this way, professionalization is always the result of a two-way process of political accommodation. More than many other kinds of property, the human capital of professionals is visibly a social and political artifact. Hence, it can only be secured so long as, in the main, the terms of reciprocity seem fair to the public or the profession can wield political power to uphold its privileged position.

In this sense, the professions live a precarious existence in a democratic society. Ideally, they operate within a social compact, one which has required that in exchange for their elevated status and a regulated market for their services that ensures a good livelihood, professionals demonstrate civic responsibility and even community leadership. These capacities have rarely been in abundant supply in any group, and their appearance, nurture, and uncertain functioning among professionals is a major part of the story of the rise of professionalism in the United States, a story which unfolds within a larger struggle over the moral legitimacy of professional standing itself.

From the beginning of European settlement, the colonists of British North America seemed to prefer the risks of individual opportunity to the relatively secure but limited prospects of the European craft guilds and estates. For much of American history, an egalitarian "can do" spirit of self-help and spontaneous mutual aid seemed sufficient to most needs. This has been a nation which has embraced the all-around individual who could learn whatever special skills might be needed to grasp an opportunity. At the same time, however, Americans also embraced the promise of the European Enlightenment that everyday life could be significantly improved through the application of trained reason to all areas of human affairs, including the realm of the arts and crafts as well as medical, legal, and academic scholarship. Thus, while the traditional professions had always been distinguished by confidence in learning, in modern society the professions have been supported by public confidence that the application of rational reflection is a main engine of progress. In the American experience, however, it has rarely proved easy to reconcile this confidence in the value of trained expertise with the moral claims of a strong egalitarian populism.

By contrast, in Continental Europe the professions grew up under the tutelage of the established institutions of church and state. Like the United States, the modern European nations developed on the basis of an expanding commercial system and new or violently recast national states. There, too, scientific scholarship and expertise were embraced by the leading groups in the population. Only in Europe the state and its institutions, often encompassing both the academy and the church, were felt to carry the collective purposes and values of the national spirit. The European nations, including Britain, gradually created a central core of national institutions to handle the complexity and conflicts set in motion by the industrial and democratic revolutions.

From the late eighteenth century onward, European states founded new institutions of learning or renovated old ones to train a new class of prestigious professionals: the pastor, the lawyer, the judge, the military officer, the professor, the civil servant. All were professionals of office. They drew their authority from the institutions they served and to which most of the educated ranks of society were connected, at least through education if not direct employment. Today, as civil servants in those societies, contemporary European professionals continue to identify themselves closely with the institutions which they serve and the state-related university system which educates them. By contrast, in the United States, "professional" designates an independent status, different from business or wage labor, but less tied to authoritative public institutions than its Continental relatives.[1] For most of its history, the United States has lacked the central core institutions of the European national state. Consequently, and momentously, the American professions have been far more diversified, competitive, and ambitious than their European (or Japanese) counterparts, less identified with the prestige and larger purposes of public institutions and more focused upon the rewards of commercial success.

The significant exception to the typical American pattern was, in this as in many ways, New England. In the colonies settled by English Calvinist dissenters, deliberate and major efforts by the colonists saw to it that the authority of church and state was strong. Calvinism was in part a movement for communal renewal and when, as in New England, it had a fairly free hand to fashion society in its terms, the result was a corporate polity with established ecclesiastical, educational, and judicial institutions supported by taxation. There two of the early modern professions of office found a central place, as the minister and the magistrate, the theologian and the jurist, became the chief figures shaping the direction of the new society. [2]

The Calvinist emphasis upon law, both religious and civil, ensured that learning, rational debate, and persuasion would play major roles in ordering public life. Intellectuals could outrank men of wealth in such a polity, and New England institutions encouraged the identification of both men of intellect and men of property with the order represented in church and state. From this development has come the notion that professions ought to have "missions," sacred trusts to promote and act for the sake of declared common purposes, in terms of which practitioners are to be held accountable before the public as a whole.

The paradigm case of this understanding of the profession of office in America was the New England Congregational minister. Trained at publicly sponsored schools and a similarly sponsored college such as Harvard or Yale, the minister was an elected and publicly funded official of the town. As historian Donald Scott has put it, "The minister conducted what was referred to as 'public worship,' performing the rituals and delivering the Word that ordered the community as an organic whole. In this sense the minister belonged to the town."[3]

With the coming of the Revolution, the chartered royal governments collapsed, while religious establishment fell into bad odor in most of the new states (though not in Massachusetts). Tolerant, multiethnic Pennsylvania, rather than hierarchical and established Massachusetts, became the more typical pattern for the new republic. The great waves of egalitarian spirit and republican hopes which the Revolution sent abroad eroded the earlier tendencies toward a society controlled by local gentlemen. The vertical ties of personal economic and political patronage which had held colonial society together loosened in new and unexpected ways with the spread of the horizontal bonds of commerce. Accelerated commerce weakened older dependencies and intensified the division of labor, giving rise to new groups of economically independent, politically enfranchised citizens.

Under the new conditions, the inherited conception of the common good, as a balanced and just ordering of a whole made up of unequal parts, gave way to the dynamic image of networks of exchange binding yet propelling independent individuals forward in time and space. For many of the founding generation of American leaders, such as Thomas Jefferson and John Adams, the experience of revolution and nation-building proved a sobering one. Directly opposite to the unifying and centralizing tendencies then explosively at work in European nation-states, the United States after independence expanded rapidly but with little central coordination, despite the efforts of the Federalists. This pattern fostered dispersed loyalties and narrow perspectives but also a leveling spirit, especially along the ever-expanding frontier in the West, along with great commercial vitality.[4] At first, the expectation had been widespread that the new freedom and equality would spontaneously generate "civic virtue," an ideal of public spiritedness once confined to a ruling class. But in fact, individual liberty tended more often to the assertion of self-interest, now released to compete in a free market of both property and votes, than of republican virtue.

In this emerging civil society of unfettered commercial exchange, many looked to the state to underwrite faster development. But concerned republicans such as Jefferson began looking for ways to ensure that leadership would reside in the hands of what he called a natural aristocracy: those of all stations who demonstrated both capacity and virtue in assuming public responsibility. This was his more egalitarian alternative to the strategy of John Adams and Alexander Hamilton to solidify a powerful, and hopefully responsible, aristocracy of birth and wealth. It was to identify and train his natural aristocrats that Jefferson urged the establishment of education, including a state-supported university. Education would introduce those with promise of high achievement to the ideals of civic humanism and the techniques of science in order to counterbalance the blandishments of irresponsible wealth.[5] Something of the public spirit of the professions of office continued to cling to these proposals. Jefferson and the Federalists agreed at least on this: that the well-being of the republic required the promotion of learning and intellect, infused with a spirit of public service, in order to develop an expanding class of responsible social leaders.

THE FREE PROFESSIONS: RISE, DEFEAT, AND METAMORPHOSIS

In fact, the nascent civil society of nineteenth-century America was to prove far more fluid, and more allergic to the institutionalization of either intellect or leadership, than even Jefferson imagined. During that time, the learned professions of law, medicine, and the ministry (largely including education) were forced to seek a new institutional form. This form was what has been called the commercial or free professions. In the early period, the free professions linked themselves with the wealthy gentlemen farmers and merchants of the eastern cities and towns. By means of gentry influence, professional licensing was established in many states, and the formation of professional bodies as separate, privileged occupational groups was under way. Through attendance at the colleges which served the sons of the socially established, aspiring members of the bar, the clergy, and medicine joined the circle of this eastern gentry. They shared with much of this gentry a humanist education, a cosmopolitan culture and outlook linked to Europe, and they often married into prominent families.

The United States in the first decades of the nineteenth century, despite the tolerance of slavery and the slow engulfment of the Native American nations, was by world standards a comparatively open and egalitarian society. The atomizing effects of rapid economic and geographic mobility were to some degree offset by shared legal norms and an internalized morality which defined clear identities for both men and women and subjected them to close scrutiny by their neighbors. Individuals were tightly bound into local communities and graded as "respectable" or not as they approximated notions of "character," encompassing the virtues of hard work, honesty, loyalty, and fair play. This fluid, loosely articulated society sustained a boisterous public realm in which diverse interests could clash and struggle openly.

Centered on the mercantile towns and cities, a broadly democratic civic culture was supported by voluntary societies, educational organizations for working people as well as merchants, newspapers, and political clubs. In this locally based society, professionally trained men were often conspicuous leaders.[6] Alexis de Tocqueville, visiting the nation during the 1830s and 1840s, no doubt noticing the public sway of figures like Daniel Webster, Henry Clay, and John Calhoun, identified the lawyers as playing the role of an American aristocracy, balancing the egalitarian passions of democracy with a conservative feeling for continuity and precedent.[7] However, in the struggle to control public opinion, the nascent free professions suffered the enormous setback signaled by the election of Andrew Jackson.

Jackson combined the egalitarian enthusiasm for economic independence with resentments against the gilded privilege of the eastern elites to fuel a powerful political movement hostile to professional privilege in any form. Led by the vigorous President Jackson, a wave of populist sentiment overwhelmed the bastions of gentry strength and professional privilege, ending licensing of doctors and religious establishment, even in the New England states.

Andrew Jackson's first inaugural address proclaimed the theme. "Let us go on elevating our people," Jackson cried, "perfecting our institutions, until democracy shall reach such a point of perfection that we can acclaim with the truth that the voice of the people is the voice of God."[8]

Those events of the 1830s continue in powerful ways to affect the American present. When late twentieth-century politicians intone the phrase "traditional values," it is usually an idealized version of the Jacksonian persuasion which they are invoking. Jacksonians opposed "the people" to "the interests" of privilege. Andrew Jackson himself defined his constituency as "the real people, the bone and sinew of the country ... whose success depends upon their own industry and economy."[9] Denouncing privilege and celebrating the virtues of hard work created a bond of moral agreement among a very diverse constituency. The "people" so described actually included southern, slave-owning planters along with western farmers and eastern mechanics and laborers. The people's enemy was not wealth as such; everyone aspired to that. It was rather those interests which required grants of special legal privilege which were the objects of anger and attack. This class included those with an interest in professional licensing and the credentials of learning.

Democrats, as Jackson interpreted the term, wanted to clear the land of all obstacles to economic opportunity. This is what linked together the otherwise disparate features of Jackson's presidency. The attack on the federally chartered Bank of the United States, forcible removal by the great "Indian Fighter" of all Native Americans living east of the Mississippi, and the delicensing of professions and institutions of learning: all these were successful efforts to clear the ground for the people's entrepreneurial energy. Would-be professionals frequently adapted by acting as free economic agents themselves, hanging out a "shingle" and plying the trade of their fancy. So successful were the Jacksonians in identifying individual economic opportunity with democracy that when institutionalized credentials and professions began their comeback at the end of the century, their advocates would justify them by reason of their usefulness, especially their potential contribution to national economic progress. This was arguing the case for professions on terms Jacksonians would understand, if not always accept.

Jacksonian America relied upon a simple, replicable, uniform culture to stabilize and guide the disorientations attendant upon the policy of laissez nous faire. This common culture was based upon the (Protestant) Bible, the family, enterprise, and the presumed equality of all native-born white males, according to the same rules of fair play. Modern populist passion has continued to draw strength from latter-day versions of this moral system, somewhat broadened over the intervening time. American populism has generally been in favor of rural life and small, homogeneous communities, but it has also strongly endorsed economic advance through market competition. It has been hostile to inherited privilege and urban life, skeptical of cosmopolitan culture, irreligion, intellectuals, artists, and moral experimentation. This combination of themes reveals its origins in a social environment where the household was the economic unit and enterprise was small, unspecialized, and local in scope.

The center of the Jacksonian moral world was the figure of the independent citizen, in which the lore of Ben Franklin, if not the full reality, lived on. This figure has continued to reappear at the center of American aspirations as the successful breadwinner, husband, and father who "knows best."[10]

Contemporaries could be quite blunt, and revealing, when assessing the political significance of the independent citizen ideal. Near midcentury, Martin Van Buren, Jackson's successor as president and leader of the Democratic party, wryly summed up the reasons for the continued success of the party of Jackson. Van Buren found the key in a prevalent social cleavage. Very simply, Van Buren said, Jacksonians spoke for the mass of "sweats" as against the few educated "wits" of the nation. As long as there are more "sweats, especially farmers and mechanics," any political party, such as the opposition Whigs, perceived as the preserve of the "wits," was bound to fail.[11] All this seemed confirmed when the Whig party, led by gentlemen opponents of the Jacksonian Democrats (and soon to be reborn as the Republicans), finally found in Abraham Lincoln a "wit" leader acceptable to many "sweats."

"Honest Abe" Lincoln, the rail-splitter from Illinois, seemed the perfect image of the self-made man from the West, a Ben Franklin for the times. Lincoln articulated the party's platform stands against the expansion of slavery and in favor of expanded property ownership. But Republican party propagandists were also proud to assure voters that Mr. Lincoln had risen to fortune as a legal professional, not only a defender of the people's rights but once the general counsel to that pioneering high-tech corporation called the Illinois Central Railroad. And in fact Lincoln, Janus-like, could assume both faces. Part of Lincoln did look to the homesteads and Main Streets of sweat equity, local entrepreneurship, and democratic fairness. The other Lincoln understood and functioned within the emerging industrial society of hierarchical, highly technical organizations which often worked closely with government, of which the Illinois Central was a harbinger. Lincoln himself had anticipated the national trend in moving from "sweat" to "wit" while, like every successful politician after him, nurturing ties to both constituencies.

In his fateful role as president, however, Lincoln became the free professional in heroic proportions, the counselor to a bitterly divided nation who tried to shape American dispersion into a coherent national society. As the self-declared admirer of that earlier advocate of national unification, Henry Clay, Lincoln brought to the presidency a vision of national unity and greatness unseen since the era of the revolutionary gentry's ascendancy. Even during the height of the conflict over slavery and the Union, Lincoln worked methodically to develop and expand the nation into the West under federal aegis, chartering the transcontinental railroad, promoting the Homestead Act, and using the power of the national state to foster higher education through land grant colleges. Significantly, during the early years of the Civil War which brought Lincoln to tragic greatness, his son was among the "wits," studying at Harvard. Yet, Lincoln's goals of a more just yet unified national society were to be realized only in part. In nineteenth-century America, the claims of enterprise, equality, and institutional authority seemed unable to find a stable point of balance.

THE FREE PROFESSIONS AND THE SEARCH FOR PROFESSIONAL INTEGRITY

In *Democracy in America*, Alexis de Tocqueville interpreted the new democratic country he had visited during the Jacksonian era as a glimpse of the likely future of all modern nations. He saw America's historically unprecedented commitment to individual liberty and equality as embodying at once a great moral gain and a fundamental human dilemma. To Tocqueville, the United States was the advance guard of a new kind of society, which he called "democratic," where individuals had gained a novel degree of dignity and freedom to define themselves in ways of their own choosing. Previously, in Europe and other civilizations, people had lived according to inherited codes, distinct from each other in hereditary groupings, bound into a stratified order. Tocqueville termed this type of society "aristocratic." Since he was writing for the political enlightenment of public opinion in less-egalitarian Europe, Tocqueville sought to warn his readers of what he saw as the difficulties inherent in the democratic type of society.[12]

Individual freedom was not a natural condition, as Tocqueville saw it, but a collective achievement. It could only be maintained by persons who understood that their individual well-being, because it was interdependent with the well-being of many others, required taking responsibility for maintaining the patterns of life which ensured their security and freedom. Tocqueville gave famous expression to this notion by arguing that Americans combated the atomizing effects of individualism through a variety of civic institutions operating according to the principle of "self-interest rightly understood."[13] He also pointed out that freedom in a democratic society required stabilizing practices: vigorous religious morality; civic participation; and what he termed "the severity of the *mores* surrounding marriage" which he thought gave American women greater standing and freedom than their European counterparts while it helped domesticate their husbands.

There was a further, more troubling dimension to the paradox of democratic equality. Tocqueville believed that in a commercial society, individuals, now free from dependency upon social superiors, would define their liberty in mostly material terms, taking security and comfort as their defining life-goals. But this "virtuous materialism," because it focused narrowly on the individual and a small circle of family and associates, undermined the very moral capacities which gave meaning to the idea of freedom. Unless the democratic individual came to understand that real fulfillment came not in comfort alone but through engagement with things of intrinsic significance and high value, democracy would slump into a dull materialism without spirit. As it was, the utilitarian cast of democratic life tended to undermine institutions of authority, allowing few bases for distinction other than raw power and ostentatious wealth. Such a society would become easy prey to would-be despots only too ready to allow the many their pleasures. In a word, the great promise of democracy, human dignity, and excellence for all, would be lost.

The key problem, Tocqueville thought, was that in an egalitarian society it was harder, not easier, to distinguish true freedom from its counterfeit. In Tocqueville's time the powerful surge of romantic culture gave a new importance to realm of the arts. For romantics, the idea of beauty, the "purposeless purposiveness" of things of recognizable intrinsic excellence, seemed the perfect refutation of the utilitarian tendency to see all values as mere instruments to satisfaction. In the aesthetic realm, the disinterested concern for quality and the integrity of objects and actions seemed to point out truths which the world of commerce had forgotten. Beauty, for the romantic sensibility, served as an aesthetic analogue for moral and religious truths. Tocqueville, too, found in the practice of the arts an important analogy for understanding the peculiar features of democratic society. His description of the paradox of artistic freedom in America would prove prescient regarding the key social problem facing the free professions of those days, the problem of the integrity of professional work and standards.

"Democratic peoples," wrote Tocqueville, "habitually put use before beauty, and they want beauty itself to be useful."[14] The situation was quite different in those societies which had been formed by a long tradition of aristocracy, such as Tocqueville's France. In aristocratic societies, "the practice of almost all the arts becomes a privilege, and every profession a world apart into which all and sundry cannot enter." Within these "professional" worlds, a "corporate public opinion" and a "corporate pride" soon develop. Hence, no craftsman can pursue his fortune except by submitting to the standards of the guild. "Corporate interests count for more with him than either his own self-interest or even the purchaser's needs." The consequence, argued Tocqueville, is that such a social context places the craftsman's emphasis on "doing things as well as possible, not as quickly or as cheaply as one can."[15]

The contrast with the typical arrangement in democratic society is dramatic. There every art and craft is open to all, since it is believed that all should be able to try—and quit—any field of endeavor. There is consequently little stability in any craft community, "the social link between them is broken, and each, left to himself, only tries to make as much money as easily as possible." Thus, the only restraint and guidance which the artist feels come from the market, in the form of the customer's wishes. Furthermore, Tocqueville continued, the market for the arts is itself very differently organized in the two types of society.

In aristocratic conditions, because the patrons occupy secure positions, or aspire to a way of life defined by long-established institutions and practices, customers "naturally like things very well made and lasting." This taste in turn "affects the way a people looks at the arts." That is, the practices and tastes of the larger society support and encourage the smaller community of artists in their identification of their interests with the standards and reputation of their guild.

In democratic countries, as Tocqueville saw things, the art-buying and appreciating public have few such inherited standards to guide their interaction with the often equally isolated artists. Lacking secure social standing based on considerations other than purchasing power, the customer in the democratic society typically wants not high quality but "a look of brilliance." Since democratic competition always provides a "crowd of citizens whose desires outstrip their means," the common interest of craftsman and customer is to make and sell as many products as cheaply as possible. There are few institutional supports for standards of excellence which could counter or qualify the activities of either producer and customer. The whole artistic enterprise tends to become *only* a market, directed not by aesthetic values as such but by the pursuit of maximum financial gain. Thus, Tocqueville concluded, in both the fine and useful arts, "quantity increases; quality goes down."[16]

What makes this analysis particularly striking is that Tocqueville could have been describing the problems faced by responsible free professionals in nineteenth-century America. The root of the professional problem, like that of the arts, stemmed from the anomalous status of the professions in a utilitarian commercial society, a situation they shared with the arts, education, and religion. In the first place, a profession is "in business" for more than itself. In the case of the professions of office this had been inherent in becoming a public official. For the free professions, however, the situation was more ambiguous. Professionals competed, after all, in the labor market and typically offered their services in exchange for fees. Yet, they explicitly served public, even transcendent ends. Public values are necessary in order to secure the goods of civilized life, but they can only be secured for each citizen when all, or nearly all, citizens, contribute to their support. This is plain in such simple cases of public goods such as security. If there is too little general contribution in the form of law-abiding mutual trust, then individuals find themselves put on a defensive posture, forced to restrict contact with strangers and dependent upon private defenses, in an escalating spiral of defense and withdrawal until the once-sought public good is lost altogether.

For the nineteenth-century free professions, the problem was to convince not only the public at large, but also the mercenary and the eccentrics calling themselves doctors, lawyers, and preachers to act toward their clients with fiduciary responsibility. The laissez-faire environment of American life made it difficult to establish the idea that to be a professional means acting in the interests of one's client. The client often depends on the wisdom and integrity of the professional's judgment. The professional, on the other hand, cannot be simply the client's tool or instrument. The professional is accountable *to* the client as to whether the professional is serving the client's best interests, but the professional is also accountable *for* the public purpose for which the profession exists. Thus, the lawyer is rightly called a "counselor" and attorney, since the lawyer's task is to apply trained judgment in acting for the client in seeking his or her best interests in regard to justice. The same is true in the case of the physician with regard to health, and similar responsibilities apply to the other professions.

The common problem for the free professions was—and is—to

nizations to provide themselves with "market shelters," areas of activity protected by law or contractual agreement from encroachment by competitors from other sectors of the economy. The result was an upsurge of agricultural cooperatives, trade unions, and new or revived professional organizations.[18]

This was a social environment considerably more receptive to aspects of the professional enterprise than antebellum America had been. If Jacksonian Americans had thought about opportunity largely in the horizontal terms of an expanding frontier for self-reliant household enterprise, increasing numbers of Americans would come to understand opportunity in vertical terms. The image fit with the realities of a career in the large and impersonal organizations, operating as part of a national system, which were taking over area after area of economic life.

The new era was to be the age of the career. The stability of a career in a prestigious occupation lifted those who could attain the educational credentials toward the possibility of dignified and well-paid work within the expanding national networks of commerce. The new universities, themselves often founded or funded by the wealthy creators of the corporation economy, were critical to this development.[19] Professionalism, often defined less as a civic art and more as the capacity to solve technical problems, would over time enable the middle class to make peace with the plutocrats. The unsettled social conditions of the time also provided the opportunity for enterprising profession-builders to persuade influential publics of their value to the nation.

For this was also the age of experts. The organizational professions of the late nineteenth and early twentieth century, such as engineering and management, introduced into the professional enterprise a new emphasis upon science, efficiency, and technical expertise. Experts, in the sense which Americans of the nineteenth century might have recognized the term, were typically the learned judge, the theologian, the scientific scholar, the ingenious inventor who benefited the community. Such expertise derived from learning, and often from demonstrated practical wisdom as well. It carried overtones of the fiduciary qualities characteristic of the professions of office and the free professions. In its new sense, however, expertise connoted someone who "knows how to get things done," the person able to wield sophisticated techniques as means to produce desired ends. At its most expansive, the new notion of expertise meant the capacity to solve problems, the kind of skill which expanding industrial America greatly needed and very much admired.

"Little noticed in the heat of the nineties," wrote Robert Wiebe, "a new middle class was rapidly gathering strength." That "class . . . covering too wide a range to form a tightly knit group," included significant groups of those "with strong professional aspirations in such fields as medicine, law, economics, administration, social work, and architecture." Notice that this list includes not only two of the three traditional professions, but such newcomers as academic social science and professionalized administration. Wiebe also noted that "consciousness of unique skills and functions, an awareness that came to mold much of their lives, characterized all members of the class."[20] This was to be professionalism's heroic age, when it came forward as a new American moral ideal. It was also a time of major conflict over the meaning of professionalism. That conflict would result, by the early decades of the twentieth century, in the identification of professionalism in many fields with technical expertise, to the detriment of the civic orientation characteristic of earlier professional ideals. That development continues to produce negative effects today for the larger society as well as within the professions.

What made possible the appearance of the organizational professions, far more tied to large formal organizations than the free professions, was a revolution in both social organization and attitudes toward specialization. That change, however, was not accomplished easily nor without painful conflict. It is hardly an exaggeration to say that the organizational professions were born out of profound social crisis. By the late nineteenth century many Americans could no longer make sense of their social world in the inherited terms of their local civic creed or through the idiom of open opportunity. As farmers and townsfolk became drawn into the geographic and cultural orbit of the industrial metropolis, the familiar idea that some benign natural harmony underlay the apparent randomness of market society was in retreat. Those who could make sense of things were suddenly in demand. Social analysts and prophets abounded.

It seemed clear to all that the optimistic republican dream of a harmonious and classless civic community was being torn to pieces in conflicts between opposed economic interests. Members of the middle class felt themselves caught in a squeeze. On all sides they saw powerful forces which were essentially outside their familiar cultural and political world.[21] The middle class was horrified by class struggle, sensing that it marked the end of the old American ideal of civic community. The United States was changing dramatically in ways that created new kinds of differences and antagonisms among groups. The age of specialization and differentiation was at hand. The question was whether and on what terms a new social integration was possible.

"The fate of classes," wrote the economic historian Karl Polanyi, "is much more often determined by the needs of society than the fate of society is determined by the needs of classes." In terms which illuminate the rise of the professions, Polanyi argued that at moments of major social change, the success of classes and groups "will depend upon their ability to win support from outside their own membership, which will depend upon their fulfillment of tasks set by interests wider than their own."[22] All the segments emerging out of the industrial maelstrom faced the problem of securing public legitimacy. Populist farmers appealed to the Jeffersonian heritage, while Samuel Gompers's trade union movement sought approval on grounds of the fairness of labor's demands. Socialists like Eugene Debs invoked the republican heritage to condemn the new system of industrial oligarchy. The leading financiers and industrialists invoked the social Darwinist vision of progress through competitive struggle to justify their rise to dominance.

In similar vein, the new professional middle class strove to cast its new occupational specialties as the bearers of a better future. The new professionals sought to establish themselves by bringing new techniques for coping with the challenges presented by urban, industrial disorder. They also linked themselves to the wonders of technology, appearing as ministers of the better life promised by scientific enlightenment. In early twentieth-century America, the professions thus waged a two-front battle for legitimacy. The developing professional fields strove to attract members by providing obvious benefits such as rising salaries and improved conditions of practice. Their other challenge was to convince the public of their value to the society and their worthiness for legal protection and philanthropic largesse.

Professionals were often at the forefront of efforts to find solutions to the new problems of the industrial era. In time-honored American fashion, these efforts typically went forward through a maze of voluntary associations led by local notables, often one organization for each issue, such as public health and sanitation, immigrant resettlement, charitable work, and the rest. Now, however, the emerging middle class professionals received unexpected assistance from some of the very plutocrats they feared and distrusted. Great captains of industry such as Andrew Carnegie and John D. Rockefeller were by the turn of the century also attempting to win the hearts and minds of the public they had so often outraged just years before. Such industrialists sought to soften their public image, and genuinely to adopt positive civic roles by establishing vast new philanthropic foundations. Scientific medicine, for example, received a major boost by attracting the attention of the Rockefeller philanthropic interests.[23]

The philanthropic foundations established by the corporate empire builders invested in a host of new or expanded institutions designed to ameliorate the conditions of economic and social turmoil which their founders had done so much to cause in the first place. So, what was typically done in other societies by institutions of general competence, chiefly church and state, was done in the

United States by the most powerful private persons to emerge from the competition of the civil society. Whether the new philanthropy did a great deal to change public attitudes toward the donors remains debatable, though it certainly moved some of the plutocracy toward a larger sense of social responsibility, linking their aspirations—and sometimes their lineages—to those of the nineteenth-century gentry.[24]

These same developments aided the organizational professions' search for legitimacy and importance. The philanthropies of the plutocrats, the universities, specialized institutes for research and training, and settlement houses and other organizations aimed at easing the horrors of mass urban poverty each became, in turn, crucial sites of training and employment for the developing professions. Through their association with these causes and these new institutions, professionals gained greater public acceptability as a key resource for expertise in meeting the threatening challenges of an urban, technological society.

EXPERTISE MAKES ITSELF INDISPENSABLE: FREDERICK W. TAYLOR

Of the many heralds of the new scientific and technological virtues of the professions, none was more successful, nor ultimately more important, than the engineer, Frederick W. Taylor. He was to the organizational professions roughly what Morgan, Rockefeller, and the others were to corporate capitalism itself. The corporate economy promised vast increases of productivity, national wealth, and individual opportunity. Taylor, who began his career as a mechanical engineer and went on to fame with his time-and-motion studies of worker efficiency, intended to be far more than a mere servant of corporate wealth. His purpose was to spread the benefits of efficiency and productivity into all sectors of American life.[25] Taylor set out to show that by applying rational principles of "scientific management," not only industrial productivity but the whole of modern life could be made far more dependable and efficient, opening a vista of unlimited satisfaction for all. Not coincidentally,

Taylor's vision also included the prospects of new and exciting careers for the effectively educated.

Though he thought in terms of the public interest, Taylor's chief means toward that end was emulation of the organizational patterns of business, a conception which, not surprisingly, found widespread approval among influential businessmen. The impulse toward bureaucratic organization, for Taylor, was a historically significant innovation which would stabilize the dangerously antagonistic social relationships threatening the cohesion of the United States. Nonpolitical, neutral experts could work to reshape these conflicts by acting as mediators between big capital and labor, and by staffing new institutions of government which would put social "efficiency" ahead of partisan advantage. As Taylor saw it, the key to scientific management was the replacement of personal authority and judgment with rules developed scientifically, by experiment.

"Questions which are under other systems subject to arbitrary judgment," Taylor wrote, "are therefore open to disagreement." By contrast, "under scientific management" these same questions "become the subject of the most minute and careful study in which both the workman and the management have taken part."[26] These rules could then be codified and applied impartially, to govern both worker and manager. On an expanded scale, the same approach might be applied to the operations of whole industries, cities, even the national government. The vagaries of discretion were to be traded for the predictability of formula and algorithm.

One of the direct effects of the growth of professional management along Taylor's lines was to sanctify with professional certification the complete subordination of employees to their employers. The Taylor principles insisted on the need strictly to divide and define tasks for maximum efficiency. The minutely specialized operations could then be coordinated from above by the manager. This was to be done in the interests of economic, and ultimately social efficiency. Rising productivity in mass production would ultimately lower the cost of goods and so benefit everyone: workers, managers, and the owners of capital alike. But scientific management also removed from workers all discretion in organizing and controlling their work.

While the spread of scientific management through industry and into government and all large organizations created demands for new kinds and levels of knowledge skills, it also worked to "de-skill" many of the artisans whose capacities had previously been essential to industrial life. The rise of scientific management thereby marked the irreparable decline of traditional skilled labor of the artisan type, and with it the loss of one version of American republicanism.[27] Organizational professionalism on the technical, managerial model thus complemented the dominant organizational form of the new order. The notion of administration or management as an ethically neutral, technical body of knowledge has long outlived Taylor's direct influence. It has been the dominant approach to administration in American organizational life, in the public as well as the private sector, ever since. Likewise the organizational career usurped the older aspiration toward private practice as the typical pattern for many professional careers, at least until the onset of large-scale restructuring in American organizations at the end of the twentieth century.

Success in a professional field is very often now a story quite similar to success in a business organization. It means a climb toward higher degrees of competence in narrower areas of responsibility combined with expanded supervision of more similarly specialized subordinates. This structure is predicated, in ways Frederick Taylor would have applauded, on the supposition that the skilled specialist, properly organized and deployed, is the key to solving the problems of living as well as those of producing. Along with the establishment of the research university as the model for the educational enterprise, the development of that notion of expert problem solving through organization set the context within which the organizational professions of the twentieth century would come of age.

FROM ALMA MATER TO INCUBATOR: MODERNIZING THE UNIVERSITY

The new organizational professions, by making their own the prestige of expert knowledge, solved the previously daunting problem of professional authority. The institutional basis which made this possible was the new research university. Possession of higher educational credentials gave the aspiring professional a kind of movable capital upon which to trade in the increasingly specialized marketplace. Through the new model of education it established, the university became the one institution shared by all professional fields, aspiring and established.

Harold Perkin has called the university the "axial institution of the modern world." While its roots and some of its forms date from the premodern era, Perkin notes that the university was essentially reinvented in Europe during the nineteenth century. The key innovation was to link the traditional function of preparing students for careers that required special training, usually professions of office, with a new one: the advance of knowledge itself. Worldwide, the foundation of universities has been one of the crucial marks of modernization. It is typically in universities that members of national elites have been identified and trained, and, since the revolutions of nineteenth-century Europe, university students have often been the vanguard of political change. Yet, increasingly, it has been the increase of knowledge through specialized research which has come to seem the core purpose of the university.[28]

Until the time of the consolidation of the corporation economy, the United States had a diverse array of academies and colleges for preparing future leaders and free professionals, but no universities of the modern type. The American university appeared on the scene quite suddenly after the Civil War. Sometimes new starts, such as Johns Hopkins, Cornell, or Chicago, and sometimes a renovation of old colleges as with Yale and Harvard, these institutions set out to both advance knowledge and produce skilled graduates. Just as at this time the founders and key personnel of the leading economic enterprises began to coalesce into a national, as opposed to merely local or regional, elite, the research universities were spurred by their own interest as well as by patronage from the same sources to become the sites where ambitious Americans could obtain the credentials and connections to make their way in this new national society. The period of the foundation and early growth of these new national educational institutions, like that of the modern professions and indeed the whole industrial system, coincides with the two decades on either side of 1900.[29]

The new American universities were eclectic in drawing upon British, French, and especially, German university patterns. In Germany, the universities had been developed principally to train expert personnel and advance scientific research. They were directly tied to the state which provided support and access to a host of careers, from teaching and the ministry to much of engineering and medicine. In the United States, by contrast, private trustees and businesses came to share the role of patron with state governments. It would not be until after the World War II that the American university would assume a role of comparable social centrality, but the basic pattern for that development was set in those formative years around the turn of the century. This was the time when the pattern of the university teacher and researcher crystallized, displacing the clergyman and sometime scholar as the archetypal figure in higher education.

While more diverse and competitive than British or European systems, the American universities also came to standardize the requirements for degrees, particularly in the growing professional schools. These were sometimes, as in the case of medicine, law, and divinity, postgraduate in character, and sometimes, as with engineering, both undergraduate and graduate schools. The once common conflation of professional status with anyone who could claim higher educational experience was becoming differentiated into a clearer system of credentials: the bachelor's, master's, and doctoral degrees which connoted a pyramid of increasingly prestigious learning, in which scientific research held pride of place, with "clinical" practice always a second.

The new basis of professional authority in specialized expertise, like the research university itself, represented a departure from the earlier pattern of the free professions. For the free professions, the question of authority and of standards was tied to social acceptance of the professional's claims to public value. In the earlier pattern, technical competence was visibly linked to civic involvement, since the professional's livelihood depended upon his reputation with the public for good practice judgment and benevolence. Parallel to Tocqueville's observations concerning the arts, American professionals struggled throughout the nineteenth century to establish their claims to status independent of their links to elites of property. In these efforts, they were largely unsuccessful, indicating the limited authority of expertise or even scientific knowledge per se at the time.[30] When all this changed around the turn of the century, it is not surprising that not only the new, aspiring fields such as management or engineering would turn eagerly to appropriate the prestige of expertise for legitimacy, but that the old free professions would attempt the same.

Nowhere was this effort to reinvent the free professions so successful as in medicine. There a gathering improvement of scientific knowledge of disease, European in origin, found spectacular success in public health improvements. A new medicine, rooted in techniques of diagnosis, promised a new age of control over disease. The hospital, a venerable charitable institution presided over jointly by free professionals and local men of property, now became the site for the practice of this new medicine, attracting even the wealthy and middle classes out of their homes for treatment. The hospital taught physicians and the paying public the benefits of research, cooperation, and high standards of competence. At the same time, beginning at the Johns Hopkins University, medical training was standardized and brought into line with the new advances.

Spurred by philanthropic support, and legitimated by the widely praised Flexner report carried out for the youthful American Medical Association under the aegis of the also young but already prestigious Carnegie Foundation for the Advancement of Teaching, the medical profession began a new phase of consolidation. In ways that resembled the theological seminary, medical students now entered only with collegiate degrees in hand, took a controlled course of basic science, followed by years of closely supervised clinical study as interns, then specialized residents, all the while being socialized into the professional norms of the hospital.[31] By raising the cost of medical education and practice while reducing the number of schools and entrants to the field, the reforms boosted practitioners' income and enhanced their competence and social prestige.

Here was the classic case of a profession capitalizing on the growing prestige of science that served to bolster and consolidate its authority. By the 1920s these developments gave medicine prestige as a collective body through the American Medical Association, and set the field on the road to becoming the recognized model of the successful professional enterprise.

Through these developments, the new universities came to resemble in organization and ambition the great corporations, as their critics liked to observe. The ties between the professions and the universities would involve the professions in much of the criticism the universities began to receive. "The men who stand for education and scholarship have the ideals of business men," complained John Jay Chapman of early twentieth-century Harvard, continuing that the university's administrators "are very little else than business men, running a large department store which dispenses education to the millions."[32] Of course, Chapman was exaggerating. Only a small percentage of the nation's youth was actually attending college or university, and those who did were overwhelmingly white, male, and from comfortable backgrounds.

There were exceptions to this generalization. Beginning with the founding of Vassar in 1865, women's colleges began to provide a way of successfully challenging the assumption of separate male and female spheres of competence and concern. African Americans, too, would often make their way more effectively in their own liberal arts colleges and theological seminaries than in the national universities. Black intellectuals such as W. E. B. Du Bois invoked the ideal of the civic professional in a new context when he argued that educated and professional Blacks had a responsibility to take on the task of community leadership, with an ultimate aim of leavening the materialism of American culture.[33] Still, John Jay Chapman could have added in his critique of Harvard that the ultimate purpose of higher education was indeed the kind of social standing conferred by a career in a professional field.

Within the universities a battle was going on among faculty, trustees, and presidents over how this "education for the millions" was to be organized and at what it should aim. Led by Harvard's charismatic and innovative president, Charles W. Eliot, many advocated specialization to foster social usefulness. Elsewhere, especially among representatives of the old colleges, the notion of a generalist education in which a "man of learning" would have "an uplifting and unifying influence on society" continued to have force. However, the premise of that older vision had been that "higher learning constituted a single unified culture."[34] More and more, however, curricular integration would seem more an act of political will than a natural complement to the contours of modern learning.

At Johns Hopkins, for example, the emphasis from the start was on graduate training for specialized scientific research. Unlike the traditional American college, Johns Hopkins, at first an all-graduate institution, operated on the assumption that the old unity of culture had been surpassed by the progress of the sciences. Standards for degrees and the basic organizational structure became general fairly quickly. In this sense, the structure of the American university became fixed by the first decades of the century, but no single model of curriculum and organization appeared which fully and successfully resolved the differences in educational philosophy.[35] In one important sense, however, critics like John Jay Chapman and Thorstein Veblen were on to something. Like major philanthropy, the universities seemed to receive the largesse of the barons of business in large part because they appeared to exemplify the idea that social progress was primarily an affair of an ever more effective application of expertise.

From such a perspective the civic ideals of the old liberal arts college appeared as outmoded as its classical curriculum. The literary and rhetorical culture of the gentry elites was shouldered aside in the curricular battles of the time in favor of more useful knowledge. The model for this notion of useful knowledge was the scientific-technical culture exemplified in fields such as engineering. The contest was, as the contemporary German thinker Max Weber described it, between the traditional ideal of the "cultivated man" which had provided the basis of social esteem nearly everywhere, including among the British and American gentry, with the new "specialist type of man." The trained specialist, argued Weber, was increasingly in demand—and in charge—due to "the irresistibly expanding bureaucratization of all public and private functions of authority." This fight, wrote Weber, "intrudes into all intimate cultural questions."[36]

THE PROFESSIONS AND THE NATIONAL SOCIETY

The professions thus began to win their battle to gain social support for expertise. The tentative new middle class of educated "knowledge workers" of the 1890s was on the road to becoming a growing, confident, and successful sector of the society. A career in a profession had become a mainstay of educational ambition as state after state had moved to license professionals in a variety of fields, and money poured from corporations and philanthropies to universities and hospitals. Meanwhile professional organizations such as the American Bar and Medical Associations had emerged as the voices of socially significant groups, and aspiring fields such as nursing, social work, accounting, and architecture struggled to find their niches. The professions were taking up positions within the new national economic order according to that order's own organizing principles. Within this national system, the professional's role was typically specialized and technical, so that collaboration among differentiated fields increasingly depended upon the skills of yet other specialists, the managers and financial technicians, all as Taylor had theorized it should be. The old, personalized ways of doctoring or pastoring or the life of the bar seemed simplistic by contrast and decidedly out of date.

By contrast, the nineteenth-century free professions had lived and taken their direction not from a small and distant federal government, but within the civic order of the American town. Compared to the smoothly managed processes of the new national order, the civic context was a contentious one, far more interactive, and far more demanding of the individual's loyalty and active engagement. As we have seen, that cultural world, while regionally diverse, was at one in its attention to an ideal of a unified, morally responsible character, the independent citizen, who embraced the disciplines and limitations of local civic life for the sake of the dignity and purpose which it provided. American civic culture also supported a genuine public space, open at least to all male citizens, a forum of often raucous contest over the terms of the civic compact. Free professionals frequently sought to enhance their prestige and public leadership through painstaking demonstrations of impartiality and benevolence in community affairs.

That civic culture had played a key supporting role as a civilizing and stabilizing influence upon the main protagonist in the American drama, the heroic push beyond all boundaries in the quest for expanded individual opportunity. By the turn of the twentieth century, however, the national drama's principal theme was being orchestrated by an industrial economy that transcended and despised the constricting boundaries of those local civic cultures. Wherever possible and convenient, the huge national corporations simply colonized local communities. Yet, those eclipsed civic cultures had "multiplied local winners" while protecting "the self-respect of many citizens with small incomes but good reputations."

Instead, the expanding national system "funneled a few winners to the top, dramatically extended the distance from there to the bottom, and stripped an anonymous poor of their residual sources of respect."[37]

This new order was truly national in reach and advanced by the great, hierarchically integrated corporations. Here the comparative weakness of the country's national core again proved decisive in setting the United States on a course of social development different from that typical of Europe and Japan. Private considerations of profit and competitive victory would determine the pattern and pace of economic development, with little admixture of public concerns with national welfare or social justice. Centered upon the raw industrial cities, these corporate giants married technological advance to financial and administrative technique, thereby setting a new model for the efficient and businesslike organization of social functions. As we have seen, the new organizational professions excelled at the very functions which the new order needed: specialized expertise, scientific research, planning, managerial coordination.

Professionals thus came to the forefront among the growing segment of the population which was oriented more to this national system than to local society. Compared to the citizens of the towns and rural communities, these metropolitan Americans were more narrowly specialized in work but less bound by convention in the rest of life, opening up the possibility of a uniquely private realm in which the individual could aspire to sovereignty. A sharp division developed between these two groups, the one looking outward to nationwide, even international networks, the other focused inward on the local civic community. The ensuing clash of perspectives, values, and ways of life would become an increasingly significant and conflictual cleavage in American life. Professionals would be central actors in this twentieth-century story, functioning both as bridges between the two groups and as the chief agents by which metropolitan values and practices would penetrate popular life.

While this new industrial order was growing over the heads of most Americans, its captains defeated the efforts of populist farmers and urban workers to bring political controls to bear upon it. By the turn of the century, however, the vast hopes and angry energies generated by these changes gave rise to new efforts to reassert the values of American civic culture within the emerging metropolitan society. These currents took form in a series of reform movements collectively known as Progressivism. The old American civic order had relied heavily upon voluntary association and involvement. The effort to develop a contemporary and national version of that civic creed would likewise rely heavily on voluntary participation in social movements to win the minds and hearts of Americans. Just as the lack of a powerful centralized state enabled powerful groups to push their interests until they overreached themselves or encountered strong opposition, so the lack of a center also meant that reformers had to struggle in the public forum to win the minds and hearts of Americans to a new vision of a more civic national society.

Professionals and their aspirations would be central to Progressivism. In the ensuing debates and struggles, some influential members of the new professional class would develop a conception of professionalism opposed to the narrowing implicit in its technical form, a professionalism designed to complement and strengthen a new civic politics. We will call this development civic professionalism.

3

A METROPOLITAN MATURITY:

The Progressives' Struggle for a Civic Professionalism

PROGRESSIVISM AND THE PROFESSIONS

The professional enterprise of the twentieth century has been at its core a metropolitan phenomenon. All the critical sites of professional development, from the university to the teaching hospital, the corporation, and government, expanded and proliferated in the industrial cities. It was also against the stormy backdrop of America's twentieth-century urban expansion that professionalism found convincing formulation. Or, rather, formulations, for the meaning of professionalism was a disputed matter throughout the crucial formative period of the organizational professions, those two decades on either side of 1900 which also witnessed the nation's epochal transformation into an industrial, metropolitan society. That was a time of extraordinary social and political volatility as the nation struggled toward a new institutional order appropriate to the changed circumstances. The institutional order which resulted has provided the basic pattern for American life throughout the twentieth century, and professionals were very much a part of this ferment, especially in the social movement known as Progressivism.

The major aims and themes of the Progressive movement fit well with the need of the growing professional middle class to find a place within the emerging industrial order. In broad outline Progressivism represented an effort, particularly congenial to the middle classes, to bring the giant financial powers of the corporation economy within the American civic order. Like the populism of the farmers and the socialism and labor activism of industrial workers, the Progressivism of the professional middle class sought both social justice and a place for themselves in the emerging metropolitan society. It was a crusade to re-enfranchise citizens dispossessed or overawed by brutal new powers.

Progressives generally sought neither a return to the unregulated market economy of the nineteenth century which had given rise to the financial giants, nor the extirpation of private property by the state. Rather, as a middle class whose capital lay in occupational skill, as opposed to the dividends or rents of the upper classes, adherents of Progressivism espoused the adoption of common civic values and standards, enforced by new governmental initiatives, to bring equity and balance into the economic order. Progressives championed gradual social reform to extend democracy to the social and economic spheres through governmental planning, subvention, and regulation of the economy for the sake of social justice. Intellectually, American Progressives shared with certain contemporary European currents of reform a new confidence that knowledge and judgment could be founded in experience rather than abstract reason or ideology.[1] This confidence found its most influential form in the philosophy of pragmatism, as exemplified in the influence of William James and John Dewey.

As a social movement, Progressivism contained diverse currents. It could be both cosmopolitan and hostile to immigrants, confident of the eventual triumph of universal moral principles over parochial attachments and shrill about the corruption of political bosses. Progressives embraced the expansion of the division of labor; they thought of scientific knowledge and the new technologies of transport and communication as potentially civilizing forces. They opposed social Darwinist ideas of progress through competition to the death, as they sought ways to institutionalize social purposes as counterbalances to the relentlessly utilitarian tendencies of the market economy. They exalted education and, in a way new to the United States, many Progressives saw urbanization as a potentially positive transformation away from the rapacious mores of the frontier rather than as a corruption of rural virtue.

The mutual influence between the Progressive movement and professionalism was ongoing, and long after its eclipse following World War I, Progressivism's impact on professionalism remained considerable. Professionalism became one of the pillars of the Progressive movement by providing, in the professional career, a design for living that promised to give individual occupational achievement moral meaning through responsible participation in a civic life. In practice, however, the Progressives' efforts to articulate a new social whole revealed fissures in their projected edifice which ensured that their dreams would never be fully realized.

Like the modern metropolis, to whose genesis it was so tied, Progressivism contained within itself contradictory tendencies. On the one hand, many Progressives promoted scientific expertise and technical efficiency as the keys to a more advanced form of society. On the other hand, Progressives also looked to civic ideals that seemed to require a moral and political integration of life which could only be achieved if modern citizens could be educated to a high level of public participation. Were social action and political reform to be conceived as tools wielded by superior experts or as processes of mutual involvement between civic educators and organizers seeking to enlist a broad public? This opposition within the movement was simultaneously being played out in the evolution of the professions as the tension between technical and civic models of professionalism.

PROGRESSIVE PROFESSIONALISM: THE CASE OF LOUIS BRANDEIS

An uneasy tension between reliance upon technical expertise and the traditional civic loyalties of the professions has been one of the enduring legacies of the Progressive era to professional life. More clearly than virtually any other figure, Louis D. Brandeis, the "People's Lawyer" appointed to the Supreme Court by Progressive and former university president Woodrow Wilson, embodied the clashing features of Progressivism. His career and teachings left a considerable imprint on both the bar and the bench. But they also dramatized an interaction and clash between the technical and civic emphases of professionalism on a nearly heroic scale. What seemed to him but two complementary aspects of responsible practice have appeared to later generations of lawyers as more often mutually exclusive directions of the professional enterprise.

One side of Brandeis enthusiastically endorsed the utilitarian quest for "efficiency" in business and government, nearly as a social panacea. This was the Brandeis who used the latest results of social science in his briefs to argue for the desirability of a decision, the Brandeis who thought of law as an instrument for social reform, who sought for "social inventions" designed to make the mechanisms of society less prone to friction. Yet Brandeis also brought to the bar and bench traits of mind characteristic of the practical social intelligence espoused by the pragmatist philosophy of John Dewey. This Brandeis could argue for a "right to privacy" in order to protect the free unfolding of individuality. This Brandeis celebrated the enlarging effects of legal practice on the characters as well as the minds of both clients and attorneys. He could also enunciate and hold fast to legal principle, to the despair of more consistent—or simple-minded—practitioners of "sociological jurisprudence" or legal realism, for whom law was an instrument reflective of its times and no more.[2]

The more technocratic side of Brandeis took classic form in the celebrated Eastern Rate Case of 1910–11. This legal battle over whether the economically pivotal northeastern railroads should be granted a freight rate increase against the united opposition of shippers and consumer interests established the term "scientific management" in the public mind. It was Brandeis's famous brief which proposed that a solution was to be found in the enhanced economic efficiency that would result from the adoption of Taylorite principles of management by the railroads. Applying the "social invention" of scientific management, Brandeis argued, would preserve the railroads' profits while keeping shippers' rates down, allowing a reasonable wage increase for rail workers *and* benefit the public, all at the same time. Thus could enlightened expertise, personified in this case by Taylor, resolve what appeared to be intractable political conflicts among opposing parties.[3] In Brandeis's view a legal process informed by the "facts" was itself the chief means for social progress through reform, as it had been for Bentham and the British utilitarians of the nineteenth century and was for his contemporaries, the intellectuals of the British Fabian Society.

Social engineering from above the conflict, such as he advocated in the Eastern Rate Case, fit with a prominent aspect of Brandeis's view of modern society. He saw society as a complex interplay of frequently blind forces which required the intervention of persons gifted with wide and disinterested intellect to remain in balance. Seen under the corresponding metaphor of a "social invention," law could appear as simply a means for effecting results rather than as a charged medium of connection which shapes both the participants in the conflict and the nature of the ends pursued. Brandeis's view was not as icily technical as the mechanical metaphor might make it seem, however. It also included a large of element of noblesse oblige which Brandeis shared with the patrician reformers of his adopted region, the province of greater Boston.

Born to immigrant German Jewish parents in Cincinnati, Brandeis early acquired an enthusiasm for the transcendentalist culture of New England, which he happily embraced as a Harvard student. He made the New England tradition of patrician reform his own, exhorting a Boston audience to recall "the great heritage of an honorable, glorious past, handed down to us by our fathers."[4] Part of Brandeis looked to the past. He favored a world of middling-size enterprise, protected by government, in which the traditional Calvinist virtues of hard work, probity, and concern for the public weal could continue to flourish under twentieth-century conditions. In other equally central attitudes he anticipated and helped shape much that would characterize liberalism from the New Deal onward: reform from above, but in the people's interests, especially through legal regulation and control.

Brandeis set out his conception of the lawyer's vocation most clearly in a lecture he delivered to prospective law students at Harvard in 1905. In that lecture, titled "The Opportunity in the Law," Brandeis argued that legal practice provides great opportunities for those so motivated to improve social life. Brandeis was arguing in deliberate opposition to another understanding of "the opportunity in the law" put forward by a very different publicly engaged attorney, Elihu Root. It was Root who epitomized the conception of the lawyer as technician of business effectiveness by insisting that it was the lawyer's job to tell the client how to do what the client wanted to do.[5] For Brandeis, on the other hand, the practice of the law works to develop capacities in the practitioners which are of special value in a democratic society.

Brandeis asserted that the lawyer's training and experience "fits him especially to grapple with the questions which are presented in a democracy," questions, Brandeis added, which required a cast of mind different from those of "the scientist or the scholar."[6] Rather, Brandeis argued, the lawyer's practice, if general and not confined to a single specialized area, finally "extends into almost every sphere of business and of life." This range "ripens his judgment" while "his mind becomes practised in discrimination as well as in generalization.... He is apt to become a good judge of men." These qualities, taken together, fit the lawyer for a "position materially different from that of other men. It is the position of the adviser of men."[7] The upshot of all this, for Brandeis, was that the lawyer was both fitted for and obligated to a role very different from a simple effort to advance the client's interest. As counselor, the lawyer was to inject the larger perspective of the public interest as it bore on the matter at hand. Ideally this made the attorney a "lawyer for the situation," as Brandeis put it.[8]

This highly civic conception of the lawyer's calling corresponds to ideas advanced by the idealist philosophers of the previous century, whose thought carried much influence in the Cambridge circles Brandeis admired and frequented. In his celebration of the kind of practical judgment which he saw as the lawyer's best skill, Brandeis was echoing a venerable tradition that ultimately reached back to Cicero and Aristotle. In this view, a good life for individual and society depended less on applied intelligence of the abstract scientific sort than on a trained capacity for judgment which Aristotle called *phronesis*, or as Cicero Latinized it, prudence. Practical judgment results from a kind of reasoning Aristotle called deliberation. Its aim is decision, not simply reflection. "In an unqualified sense," wrote Aristotle, "that man is good at deliberating who, by reasoning, can aim at and hit the best thing attainable to man by action."[9] In Brandeis's rendering, the aim of legal education and practice was to develop professionals expert in this capacity for practical judgment. Such professionals could be trusted to educate their clients and the public at large to see the ethical and civic dimensions of even routine legal matters. They would give living texture to Progressive institutional reforms.

EMBRACING THE WHOLE: TOWARD A CIVIC PROFESSIONALISM

In the struggle of the new middle class for an identity, the organizational professions provided the model. Part of the world of corporation capitalism and at home in the bureaucratic settings of administration, professionals also seemed not entirely of that world. Brandeis, for one, placed considerable store on the prospects of professionalizing business not only because he thought it would improve efficiency but also because he was convinced that professionalization would have a moralizing effect, providing purposes and motives beyond the utilitarian goals of the marketplace. This sense of higher purposes helped steady the nerves of middle class professionals.

Professionals were in the main aware that their lives had to respond to two pulls. On one hand there were the claims of conscience, identification with the values of vocational integrity and a justly ordered polity. On the other, there was essential concern for technical competence and practical efficiency, the components of successful modern enterprise. The challenge—and the need—was to bring these two kinds of concern into complementary relation. Then, conscience, by providing a sense of connectedness, could guide enterprise, while prudent enterprise provided the material basis for ethical life. In this context, the contribution of pragmatic philosophy was vital, especially the highly influential pragmatism developed by John Dewey.

While Progressives such as Brandeis embraced Frederick Winslow Taylor's "scientific management," and Taylor's collaborator Morris Cooke hoped to realize the new metropolis by applying scientific management to city government, others, including Dewey, were drawing from the idealist philosophy of figures such as T. H. Green a broader social vision of progress which could serve as an alternative to the utilitarian notion that progress meant increasing the sum of individual satisfactions. In Britain, by the early nineteenth century, the idealist current had found expression in Samuel Taylor Coleridge's proposal for a new elite of "clerisy," a public-spirited, educational leadership concerned with social and cultural life, supported by institutions independent of government. Similar themes reached a wide public through such writers as Matthew Arnold, so that by late in the century the early crudity of the utilitarian philosophy of Jeremy Bentham had incorporated important features of the idealist politics of conscience into a new middle class ideal of professionalism based on service, responsibility, and the efficient use of resources for the public good.[10]

The British idealists' approach had a formative influence upon the orientation of Dewey's pragmatism. It also had affinities to Tocqueville's argument that a strong social consensus about public aims and the ethical norms to guide their pursuit would be the best way to realize the positive potential of democratic societies. Besides Dewey, in differing contexts Jane Addams and Herbert Croly also worked, from the 1890s through the coming of World War I, to formulate a Progressive public philosophy which provided the rationale for a professionalism with strong civic focus.

Croly, for example, sought to persuade his readers that a modern society needed public commitments broader than simply impersonal rules to guarantee fairness. The old small-town morality, which as Tocqueville had seen was grounded in a fuller moral ecology than mere rules of procedure, was in decay. In its place, Croly had warned, came the growth of an amoral pursuit of self-interest which was blind to the larger whole. The earlier homogeneity of the society was daily receding, "and no authoritative and edifying, but conscious, social ideal has as yet taken its place."[11] Croly proposed that a new spirit of professionalism could become the moral salvation of the individual through membership in a reformed national American society, mediated through occupational and local institutions. An ethos of shared loyalty, well institutionalized, would provide the milieu within which individual achievement could be developed and rewarded. For Croly, it was the task of intellectuals, in the spirit of Coleridge's clerisy, to provoke, inspire, and criticize these developments.[12]

Significantly, Croly, Dewey, and Addams all sought to marry idealist values to pragmatic philosophy, and they did so in trying to come to grips with metropolitan life. It was at the new University of Chicago, located in the most dynamic of the new industrial centers, that Dewey began to develop a persuasive philosophy of education and practical life. In the same city, and also during the 1890s, Jane Addams was developing at Hull House a new kind of urban service institution, the social settlement. During the following decade, Herbert Croly, also influenced by idealist philosophy through Josiah Royce at Harvard, took up editorship of the *Archi-*

tectural Record in New York. Through that journal's particular attention to the problems of building and city planning, Croly began to formulate a new view of American democracy. In 1914, he established a national pulpit for these views as editor of the *New Republic*.

All three thinkers accepted the growing specialization and interdependence of modern society which the industrial metropolis dramatized, but they sought to render its complex functional inter-relationships intelligible and mutually responsive. Providing this intelligibility was for them the professional calling par excellence. By bringing the interdependence to vivid public awareness, they hoped to provoke political action. Aroused publics would then struggle for conscious regulation and planning of what would oth-erwise have remained but dimly perceived, disconcerting develop-ments, benefiting the powerful few but harming the many. Once the public had begun to discover itself in this effort to control its environment, these Progressives reasoned, the possibility opened of turning awareness of interdependence into a cultivated disposition toward mutual trust and solidarity among citizens. Their common political and cultural vision was in this way both optimistic about the potential of democracy under modern conditions and educa-tional in a basic and radical sense.

In the imagination of these thinkers a vision of the reformed metropolis began to materialize. This new city was not conceived as simply a healthier and more efficiently administered marketplace of skills and goods. City life was to be transformed. Not merely an unfortunate economic means, life in the metropolis was to become an end, good in itself as well as in its consequences. The final justi-fication of reform was to make the metropolis a school—and labo-ratory—of democracy. Inclusive of all, open by communications and commerce to the world, sustained by an efficient, professional-ized government, and unified by popular participation and celebra-tion, the metropolis would become a whole greater than the sum of its parts.

An ecology of civic institutions, extending from neighborhood, school, and church through clubs, sports, and occupational associations to libraries, theaters, and museums, would be nurtured as sites at which a diverse body of citizens could develop and celebrate both themselves and their city. As Dewey put it in 1916: "A democracy is more than a form of government; it is primarily a mode of associated living, of conjoint communicated activity." In practical terms, this meant "the breaking down of those barriers of class, race, and national territory which kept men from perceiving the full import of their activity. These more numerous and more varied points of contact . . . secure a liberation of powers" which it was the office of the reformed Progressive school to elicit and harmonize.[13] This description could have served as a vision of the new city as well.

Lawrence Cremin has written that the master purpose at work in this brand of Progressivism was rooted in a long tradition of Western culture that reached back to Plato. It was to "transform all politics into education." This was true of Jane Addams, for example, but it was preeminently true of Dewey. "The Progressive foresaw the responsible and enlightened citizen informed by the detached and selfless expert, the two in a manifold and lifelong relationship that would involve every institution in every realm of human affairs."[14] Dewey's philosophy focused on his expansive understanding of science as a method of social formation which he aimed to actualize on the local level in the school. More than merely one specialized institution among others, Dewey wished the school to take on something of the role the church had once played in Western society: it would be the site where the individual could discover and be grasped by the spiritual current of the age and make it his or her own. For Dewey, science and education, properly understood, contained the creative nucleus of a whole social order, a society which could learn, reflect, and take action in common.

During the 1890s John Dewey articulated this philosophy of what he would later call "creative democracy" at the new University of Chicago. The University of Chicago had been founded through the philanthropic largesse of John D. Rockefeller and its first president, William Rainey Harper, sought to make the new institution a contributor to the city's life through experiments like an extension program and the Laboratory School. There, with his wife Alice Chipman Dewey as director of the Lab School, Dewey presided over an expansive department which combined philosophy, psychology, and education.

If democracy's promise of human dignity and community was to be redeemed in the new conditions, Dewey was convinced that the spirit of reflective inquiry he identified with science had to play a major role in everyday life. As a leading pragmatist, Dewey contended that thinking was itself a kind of doing, a mode of action. It followed that, like any skill, thinking could only be learned and practiced in appropriate social contexts. He concluded that developing a democratic public would require creating institutions within which learning could become a continual practice in all areas of life. This meant reforming existing institutions to offset the narrowness of outlook bred by the pursuit of specialized interests. The institutions to which he looked were those he judged able to foster an informed public: the mass media, voluntary associations and, above all, education. As professionals were becoming crucial to all these institutions, Dewey sought to develop a cultural understanding that would orient professional life there toward public concerns. Through the agency of teachers, social scientists, journalists, and administrators the experimental outlook would spread throughout the society.

Dewey argued that the inherited American individualism, because it denied the dependence of the individual on social nurture and support, had become irresponsible. But individualism seemed worse than useless as a guide to action in the twentieth century because it provided an unrealistic description of contemporary conditions. Society was growing constantly more interconnected, while individuals became increasingly interdependent. Citizens could fulfill their potentials only if they could grasp the whole of which they were part and collectively work toward improving its life for all concerned. As Dewey put it, "the attempt to cultivate it [wholeness] first in individuals and then extend it to form an organically unified society is fantasy." The only way to bring individual purposes to a harmonious fulfillment would be "membership in a society which had attained a degree of unity," and that could be achieved only "through personal participation in the development of a shared culture."[15]

The researcher and the journalist were to act in the larger social context much as the teacher in the setting of the Progressive school. He or she was to define for the other members of the group the context in which they find themselves—and assist them in learning how to take part in that process of defining and problem solving through experiment and interpretation. Dewey was surely too sanguine when he imagined a future of public-spirited experts seeking to assist the lay public in discovering itself, just as the American university would not turn out to embody the public purposes embraced by Chicago in its early days. Had Dewey paid more attention to the power of the tendencies running counter to his vision, he might have better understood the difficulty of the project he was urging.

In the same city, and for a period in collaboration with Dewey, Jane Addams was pioneering at Hull House a more radical response to lives disrupted by immigration and rapid social change. In contrast to the more bureaucratic approaches which came to dominate much of social work, Addams did not emphasize rules and sanctions designed to separate "deserving" from "undeserving" recipients of aid. By integrating her clients into a professionally sustained community of work, education, and discussion, Addams sought to make possible their development as active and responsible family members, workers, and citizens.

Jane Addams had to struggle to forge for herself a public career and identity at the end of the last century, a time when genteel, middle-class women were expected to remain comfortably, if passively, at home. Addams studied at a ministerial college, then tried medical school. In the end, her personal quest for a vocation helped define a new profession. Unlike most of her contemporaries, Jane

Addams saw the settlement house movement as more than a form of charity or moral uplift carried out by the middle classes for the poor. Instead, she conceived Hull House, her experimental settlement of 1889, as a center for community education and organization. Its aim was to enable the impoverished immigrants of the raw boomtown that was industrializing Chicago to become full participants in the life of the society they were joining. Her Chicago was three-quarters foreign-born, and Jane Addams was aware that the old pieties of small-town America were of little value to these workers and their families. What was needed, in her words, was "an institution attempting to learn from life itself." An institution capable of developing a truly metropolitan, democratic sensibility.

In this endeavor, Addams early on enlisted the assistance of interested faculty from the new university, including John Dewey. But better than Dewey, Addams realized that it was difficult to mesh this organic and activist understanding of the work of settlements with even the best of the research university model. "It seems," Addams complained, "as if the men of substantial scholarship were content to leave to the charlatan the teaching of those things which deeply concern the welfare of mankind." Confronted with the fragmenting—and, she thought, often trivializing—effects of specialist knowledge, Jane Addams invoked the medieval clergy as a model for the kind of general understanding she thought most valuable. "The beginner in knowledge," she noted, "is always eager for the general statement, as those wise old teachers of the people well knew, when they put the history of creation on the stage and the monks themselves became the actors."[16] Addams sought a new kind of clerisy, public-spirited and attuned to the problems of new times.

Hull House organized a wide variety of social services for its clientele. It became deeply involved in research and political agitation in support of labor and sanitary legislation. But its heart was in its educational endeavors. Addams aimed to give the young men and women, who were often only a short remove from their peasant origins, an understanding of the industrial metropolis. By providing a sense of the history and nature of the emerging industrial society, Hull House tried to provide for the immigrants a sense of the whole and their particular parts in it. By intellectually grasping the context of their new lives, Addams hoped, the immigrants would also become better able to shape and fulfill themselves in practice. Through experimenting, Addams developed an understanding of the possibilities of social work which was, and continues to be, remarkable, rooted in her vision of a "Christian humanitarianism" whose central tenet was "a deep enthusiasm for humanity, which regarded man as at once the organ and the object of revelation."[17]

Addams was seeking to involve the entire community in an educational effort whose aim was to form active and responsible citizens. She was impressed by the intellectual eagerness of her clients. "A settlement soon discovers that simple people are interested in large and vital subjects," she wrote. "Simple people did not want to hear about simple things; they wanted to hear about great things, simply told."[18] This approach to education led Addams, in an era when American fear of the foreignness of immigrants often took wild and punitive forms, to encourage her clients' knowledge of and pride in their ethnic heritage.

Jane Addams encouraged students in the Hull House English classes to write, in the new language they were struggling to acquire, "some of those hopes and longings which had so much to do with their immigration." She described a young Russian immigrant girl trying to describe the vivid inner life of her relative, an old Talmud scholar. This man had previously appeared to many of the other hard-pressed immigrants, especially the youth, as lazily self-absorbed. "Certainly," Addams concluded, "no one who had read her paper could again see such an old man in his praying shawl bent over his crabbed book without a sense of understanding."[19]

For Jane Addams the settlement was a new model institution, part school, part church, and part community-organizing project, which social work was to staff and develop. But the purpose of the settlement, as of social work, lay beyond itself. Philanthropy had a civic, political, end: the formation of citizens through the repair and promotion of public life. Addams saw her calling as an open-ended responsibility. She was a founding member of the National Association of Colored People, the Progressive Party led by Theodore Roosevelt and, later, a national leader of opposition to America's involvement in World War I.

Characteristically, Addams was often at work developing collaborations of professionals. She involved the architect Allen B. Pond to design new settlement housing, supported Margaret Haley's drive to gain professional status for school teachers, and joined John Fitzpatrick of the Chicago Federation of Labor in promoting workers' rights. Addams, then, understood professional expertise in anything but a narrow sense. She saw professionalism as linked to the broad social vision of participation and trust among citizens which she called democracy. In this she was extending into the world of complex organizations the best ethical aspirations of the free professions. She aimed to help her fellow citizens to see their worlds and themselves, not as problems to be solved, but as participants in developing settings for a life worth living.

If every writer's dream is that life should pay his or her art the supreme compliment of imitation, then Herbert Croly, after turning forty, must have been a happy man. In those heady years of change prior to World War I, Croly had witnessed a meteoric ascent of his fortunes. Croly had gone from life as an obscure architectural journalist and sometime Harvard student to become a sage: overnight he became the inspirer of an influential public and an advisor to the charismatic Theodore Roosevelt. The vision which Herbert Croly presented to the world of 1909 in *The Promise of American Life* was stirring people to action.

Just a few years after his book's publication, Croly was sought out by the well-to-do reformers Dorothy and Willard Straight and given a free hand to organize a journal to spread his ideas. The result was the *New Republic,* and Croly brought together on its first masthead a powerful set of journalistic talents, including Walter Lippmann. The new magazine was soon attracting America's foremost intellectual and literary lights as contributors while it quickly drew a readership which included Woodrow Wilson, Louis Brandeis, Jane Addams, and John Dewey. Its subscription list was a virtual roll call of Progressivism.

The Promise of American Life was at once a sharp criticism of existing American institutions and a plan of social "reconstruction." At the center of that book was the vision of a new type of American hero. America's folklore had exalted all-round individualists: frontiersmen, self-taught yeomen, and adventurers. Often enough, they were represented as holding rather tenuous connections to settled society. But, argued Croly, the social context in which such figures made sense no longer existed in the United States. In sharp contrast, Croly's new hero was to be part of the society, committed to a specific sphere of activity within a complex division of labor. This new kind of citizen was also to be a person of special training and awareness. And Croly's hero would be loyal to a deeper destiny than individual success. The new type of American Croly thought he could discern struggling for self-definition was the civic professional.

These new heroes would still be committed to advancing the national promise of individuality and emancipation. But each would now be "doing his own special work with ability, energy, disinterestedness, and excellence." Croly exhorted his readers to grapple with an apparent paradox: to become truly free, the individual had now to learn that self-fulfillment came through public service in loyalty to a larger purpose. "What the individual can do," wrote Croly, "is to make himself a better instrument for the practice of some serviceable art; and by so doing he can scarcely avoid becoming also a better instrument for the fulfillment of the American national promise."[20]

Significantly, when Croly was asked where he had derived the idea for this new vision, he responded that its source lay in a novel of a decade earlier, *Unleavened Bread,* by the popular Boston writer Robert Grant. In the part of the story which struck Croly, an idealistic young architect intent upon using his skill to address the problems of poverty and distress in New York was undone by his effort to placate his wife's social and financial ambitions while remaining faithful to his own sense of responsibility. By trying to serve two antithetical purposes, the architect lost everything: he paid the price of divided loyalty and died from the stresses of overwork and a bad conscience.

However melodramatic, *Unleavened Bread* hit home to the young Croly, then deeply immersed in the architectural world of New York. Commenting on the fictional architect's situation, Croly later commented, "It struck me as deplorable . . . I began to consider [its] . . . origin and meaning . . . and the best means of overcoming it."[21] What struck Croly was the architect's lack of a "well-domesticated tradition that would . . . make him build better than he knew."[22] What had destroyed the fictional architect was a problem Herbert Croly found endemic in many of the most important areas of American life: the lack of well-institutionalized professional traditions which could support individuals in their quest to serve the public need. Croly had rediscovered the paradox of democracy which Tocqueville had commented on regarding the arts of his day. The problems of architecture in the industrial city provided the organizing insight for Croly's analysis of the deficiencies of American institutions more generally and set him on a quest for a public philosophy able to recover the "promise of American life" through a civic professionalism.

FACING THE CHALLENGE OF THE METROPOLIS: ARCHITECTURE AND PLANNING

It was no accident that it was as an architectural critic that Croly came upon his insight that a civic professionalism, as part of a broad public philosophy, could provide a resolution to the problem of civic purpose in American democracy. Because they so visibly affect the lives of all, architecture and city planning have posed in especially vivid ways the question of professional responsibility in a democracy. In this century the metropolis has served as the supreme symbol and symptom of the emerging global civilization. It was architecture and urban planning which for a time gave the most visible embodiment to the hopes that professional expertise could clarify and uplift the conditions of metropolitan life. The several paths of response to those conditions that we have noted running through American political and professional life attained concretely visible form in the directions taken by the old profession of architecture and the new field of urban planning.

In its origins and the social forces which have directed its development, the modern metropolis has been a great marketplace. It has remained fundamentally the City Economic. Still, in Europe, urban reformers appalled at the conditions generated by the uncontrolled commercial and industrial expansion of the nineteenth century could draw upon a long heritage of architectural thought concerned with the moral and social improvement of cities, and their efforts would have important consequences on the development of the American design professions.

In the old urbanism of Europe, the aim of its architecture had been to imprint a clear sense of center and hierarchical order on the built environment by means of focal religious and civic structures. Thus, European cities were memorable chiefly because of the churches, palaces, guild halls, markets, and government buildings which defined their layout and focused the circulation of people and goods. In earlier periods, their town walls had literally bounded and shaped the visual order of city life. Baroque city planning has been described as trying, generally successfully, to unify "the opposites of order and freedom," by focusing "all movement around fixed points," the monumental structures which came to identify Rome, Paris, and London.

This was a planning tradition which reached back to the cities of the classical world. For Baroque city planning and architecture, it is "the space that governs the design, and the solids are entirely in the service of its dramatization."[23] Such architecture was a visual rhetoric: it represented the primary purposes and values of its society. It aimed to persuade those who encountered it to understand the city from the viewpoint of its sacred and noble centers by placing these in a commanding relationship to the secular, peripheral, and private aspects of life. For this tradition it was indeed true that architecture was the supremely public art, "the total environment made visible."[24] This humanist architecture had, since Vitruvius and Alberti, spoken a confident language of form. Just as in the classical cosmology there could be only one perfect form for each function, so the classical architectural orders and forms were thought to represent a unique, universal rationality. At their best, buildings and urban designs were thought of as microcosms, revealing and celebrating in human scale the timeless rational harmonies of the larger cosmos.[25]

The shock effect of the revolutionary social transformations worked by industrial capitalism ended the plausibility of traditional humanist architecture as a conception of urban design. Fears of incipient chaos, spiritual as well as social, stalked the established cities of Europe as much as the less formed environments of the New World. By the end of the nineteenth century, two major programmatic responses had appeared to the baffling situation in which it was "already the end of the old, humanist, man-centered world with its fixed values—and the beginning of the mass age of modern history, with its huge environments and rushing continuities."[26]

One response had by that time achieved worldwide recognition. This was embodied in the dramatic transformation that the Emperor Napoleon III and his planner Baron Haussmann had worked on Paris. Haussmann had turned the old city, centered on the life of its antique and varied *quartiers* into one vast workshop, market, and showplace interconnected by the most spectacular street design ever constructed: the famous boulevards which have become the trademark of the City of Light. The other, less exampled response had sketched out an opposing direction in which the reconstruction of community life and a sense of the public welfare became guiding principles. In his much-noted work of 1889, *City Planning According to Artistic Principles*, the Austrian architect

Camillo Sitte opposed the open city of traffic circulation with one focused instead on a series of public squares around which the life of the reformed city was to pulsate.[27] Both were to have important echoes in the American metropolis of the twentieth century.

The United States had few traditions of urbanism outside the eastern seaboard. As they spread across the continent, Anglo-Americans had managed in the absence of cities in the European sense of centers of government, religion, trade, and culture. Once beyond the port cities and the ordered towns which survived from colonial New England, the nineteenth-century American landscape had drawn amazed (and usually appalled) comment from Europeans because it seemed to lack meaningful shape or center. Instead, the United States appeared as a series of campsites, in which individuals and families struggled to wrest from nature, machines, or each other the elements of personal well-being. America indeed embodied in its contours its promise as the land of liberal capitalism, with little government, few cities, and apparently limitless individual mobility.[28] But all that changed quickly, painfully, and without plan as industrialization drew millions from all over the nation and the world into ramshackle, swarming concentrations of industry and housing somewhat euphemistically called cities.

With the sudden shift of economic gravity to the cities, the principle of allowing the unguided market to decide how land was to be used was visibly producing intolerable conditions. The well-to-do fled to new railroad suburbs beyond the smoke-belt, but the more farsighted among even those fashionable refugees realized that something had to be done, if only to make their place of business less revolting to prospective customers and clients. Thus was born in the metropolitan middle-class public, and particularly among physicians involved with public health, social workers, architects, and social scientists, a movement for reform. Women were often conspicuous as leaders in these efforts, which provided new possibilities for service outside the middle-class home. The reformers sought public sanitation and order, but they also desired appropriate physical forms to civilize the new forces of market and machine. In this process the aesthetic visions of European critics of industrial life such as Camillo Sitte, John Ruskin, and William Morris found resonances in the work of Americans such as Frederick Law Olmsted, the creator of New York's Central Park and a pioneer in designing a new urban environment.[29]

SHAPING THE THINGS TO COME: A PROFESSION FINDS A MISSION

Architecture in America was then just at the point of establishing itself as a profession. The generation of architects who came into prominence at the turn of the century, including Stanford White, James McKim, Louis Sullivan, Daniel Burnham, John Root, and Frank Lloyd Wright, differed profoundly among themselves about the direction architecture should take. But they were all acutely aware that they were breaking new ground and creating the visual forms for a new America. Their style of professional practice, too, expressed this sense of excitement and mission.

Following the lead of European-trained master H. H. Richardson, with whom a number of them had apprenticed, these architects at first modeled their offices on the cooperative *atelier* system developed by the French architectural academy, the Ecole des Beaux-Arts, the leading exponent of the classic style. The *ateliers* of the Ecole were in effect design studios in which students apprenticed with masters in a heady atmosphere of mentorship and camaraderie.

As American architectural schools developed and the scale of building finance and construction grew, this early heroic moment was superseded. In the growing centers of commerce the nature of the architects' clients was shifting as the scale of the work demanded began to grow vastly larger and more complicated. Banks and large corporations demanded different kinds of expertise than private clients wishing a new residence. In place of the *atelier*-style office, large new architectural offices appeared, organized not as collaborations among artists but, like business firms, as task groups of specialized experts, often mixing engineers with architecturally trained personnel.[30]

The leader in this transition from small office to large, businesslike architectural firm was the Chicago architect, Daniel Burnham. Perhaps not so coincidentally, Burnham was also the originator of the first city planning movement in the United States. Through the last decades of the nineteenth century the architectural firm of Burnham and Root prospered in the new Chicago which rose after the fire to become the nation's second metropolis. The firm's prosperity derived in at least equal part from the engineering background of Root and Burnham's extraordinary capacity to provide eloquent architectural metaphors to express the needs and desires of their clients. Burnham was like many of his generation in having had no formal architectural training. He developed his considerable gifts through a series of apprenticeships.

Burnham and Root helped pioneer the great architectural and engineering innovation of the age: the skyscraper office building. From their service to the business needs of the rising prairie metropolis, the partners prospered. In order to handle the surge in commissions efficiently, Burnham innovated organizationally, dividing the firm into effectively specialized units which handled the complex tasks of design, construction, and supervision. In this work Burnham and Root were not alone. Among their chief rivals was the equally innovative firm of Dankmar Adler and Louis Sullivan. Sullivan has remained famous as a precursor of the later modern style and the mentor of Frank Lloyd Wright. Louis Sullivan could see in the new skyscraper, in whose design he was a master and which was in one sense simply the epitome of the commercial urge to economize on space, "in some large elemental sense an idea of the great, stable, conserving forces of modern civilization."[31] Sullivan had only contempt for what he saw as Burnham's Philistine preoccupation with adapting historical forms as decoration for the new technologies that were transforming both building and cities. Yet, like Burnham and other Chicagoans of his time, such as John Dewey and Jane Addams, Sullivan wished passionately to construct a context within which modern persons could orient themselves toward a robust democratic community life. Yet, what should be the guiding norms for this enterprise, now that traditional norms could no longer serve naively as a source of aesthetic and moral order and unity?

THE CITY BEAUTIFUL

Burnham was less original an architect than Louis Sullivan. Yet he was considerably more than simply a business or professional innovator. He thought of himself as an artist, and in his midforties Burnham found the great opportunity of his life. He was retained, together with his partner Root and the already-famous landscape architect Frederick Law Olmsted, by the commission planning the Chicago World's Fair of 1893, the enormously successful World's Columbian Exposition. The result was the famous White City which was destined to have such enormous impact on the future of American cities—and which Louis Sullivan, though a contributor, would later describe as a backward-looking disaster for American architecture. It was the first large-scale project of unified social and aesthetic planning to be undertaken in the United States. In the White City's grand plan of neoclassical civic architecture, boulevards, parks, fountains, and vistas, Burnham first developed the conception of urban planning which he would apply to Washington, D.C., Manila, San Francisco, and to the city of Chicago itself. It would be known as the City Beautiful ideal, and it became a feature of Progressive Era hopes. In its style it pleased both many Progressives and a segment of the business elite for whom its classical allusions provided a welcome international symbolism that proclaimed their sophistication and status as urban benefactors.

While Burnham certainly saw no ultimate conflict between the market economy which supported his work and his civic goals, Burnham moved in a direction which coincided at many points with Progressive reform. Like the Progressives, he sought "to restore to the city a lost visual and aesthetic harmony, thereby creating the physical prerequisite for the emergence of a harmonious social order."[32] A little over a decade later, the young architectural journalist Herbert Croly enthusiastically endorsed Burnham's comprehensive plan for a new San Francisco, again linking social advance and "national aesthetic aspiration."[33]

The sensibility which Burnham sought to embody in his vision of the City Beautiful was perhaps best portrayed in his own interpretation of his purposes. "While the keynote of the nineteenth century was expansion," he wrote, "we of the twentieth century find that our dominant idea is conservation." This observation, which paralleled Sullivan's search for forms appropriate to the "great conserving forces" of the age, led Burnham to the classic questions which link economics to the ends of politics. "The people of Chicago," he observed, are now asking: "How are we living? Are we in reality prosperous?" Burnham saw that these concerns about the quality of life were grounded in economic considerations of whether the city was a convenient business site and whether it was a "good labor market" in which "labor is sufficiently comfortable to be efficient and content?"[34] But the economic considerations did not wholly determine the ends of the City Beautiful.

Later critics would point out that City Beautiful proceeded from the point of view of the great new fortunes of a booming Chicago and the mobility of modern capital, considering the needs of other classes only paternalistically from above. Burnham was vividly aware that good planning could be sold to business leaders because it raised land values. He certainly grasped the rhetorical appeal of planning, as in the famous quote attributed to Burnham to "make no little plans. They have no magic to stir men's blood."[35] He also understood the mass appeal of the visual "production values" of his neoclassical visions, an idea which would be elaborated into a hugely successful "Magic Kingdom" by the son of one the laborers on his White City project, Elias Disney. But Burnham's interest pointed beyond the concerns of a good business climate to questions of the kinds of character and social fabric the city's arrangement would form and attract: the classic issues of political philosophy.

The kind of happy symbiosis between art, commerce, and civic morality which Daniel Burnham sought to embody in his great city plans was to prove elusive. Yet, Burnham had intuitively hit upon a professional role very like the sort of civic professionalism which Croly advocated in theory. Unlike Frank Lloyd Wright, who solved the problem of the lack of secure cultural standards by overwhelming his clients with sheer charismatic power, Burnham's appeals to civic leaders and organizations were significant gestures toward building social consensus for a public vision of the city. In this process, the architect's role was that of advocate as well as the artist who could give vague aspirations evocative form. Burnham had gone beyond providing a desired service to clients and, by redefining the city's needs in a strikingly attractive way, actively brought into being a new public as his "client."

The City Beautiful ideal, however, like many of the disparate features of the Progressive movement, failed to sustain the mediation it promised or to gather sufficient public support. Business was often wary of its costs, and reformers, concerned with urban poverty and health, worried that the monumental improvements would deflect resources and attention from urgent social needs. During the 1920s, the planning impetus would continue, though in the form of "metropolitan planning," a mode of thinking which took the expansion and economic development of the cities as unquestioned goals, seeking to enhance the business climate while providing the growing middle classes with housing. In the tradition of metropolitan planning, architecture continued to adapt to the corporate world, while the evident need to coordinate overall efforts gave rise to a new profession: the scientific urban planner. In that vision the architect was closely yoked to the engineer in the search for economic and social efficiency. On the other hand, after World War I, a new approach to urban planning appeared, calling itself the regional vision. For the regionalists the architect was one of a group of craftsmen-professionals who would serve as guides and pedagogues in the transition to a new ecological vision of civilization.[36]

A METROPOLITAN ECOLOGY: THE REGIONALIST VISION

In the 1920s a group of intellectuals representing several professions, including architects Clarence Stein and Benton MacKaye along with the young generalist writer Lewis Mumford, formed a small organization they somewhat grandiosely styled the Regional Planning Association of America. Their common belief was that the industrial era that had concentrated population and machinery in the great urban clusters, with all the resultant pathologies by then long familiar, was past its prime. The new technologies of electricity and electronic communication were opening the possibility of a new form of life both healthier and more humanly fulfilling. Those possibilities could only by grasped by a more holistic approach to the problems of economics and politics, one rooted in a new awareness of the connections of city and countryside. They would call these connections, by analogy to the newly developing subfield of biology, ecological.

The import of this vision was conveyed by Lewis Mumford, who came to maturity just after World War I, when he described the "essence of the art of building cities" as guided by the realization that "life has, despite its broken moments, the poise and unity of a collective work of art." The office of the city was "to create that background, to achieve that insight, to enliven each individual capacity through articulation in an intelligible and aesthetically stimulating whole."[37] Substitute "professional" or "architect" for "city" and one has a new statement of the ideal of civic professionalism.

In his treatment of the status of the architect in the developing corporate society, Mumford epitomized the new regional planning movement's critique of the direction in which the profession had developed. "Cut off from his true function to serve and beautify the community," Mumford complained that the architect had come to be "made an accessory of business itself, like the merest salesman or advertising agent." Given this reality, it was no wonder, according to Mumford, "that the architect speedily lost his leadership; and that the initiative went once again into the hands of the engineer."[38] For Mumford, architecture was first and foremost a social and cultural achievement. It "sums up the civilization it enshrines, and the mass of our buildings can never be better or worse than the institutions that have shaped them."[39]

The regionalists were scathing critics of the modern city's total subjugation to real estate values and business enhancement. They criticized the class order and inequalities of capitalism while also strongly attacking the forms of state coercion then appearing in communism and fascism. But the regionalists' primary concern was constructive rather than critical. They sought to reshape the human habitat so that cities, towns, and their regions would become schools of responsible democracies, able to live in harmony with the natural and larger human world. Drawing on precedents such as Ebenezer Howard's regional "garden cities" proposals, their goal was environments in which modern individuals could recognize their unique possibilities and appreciate their common destiny. And they believed that in this project the imaginative artist, especially the architect, had a special creative role to play.

For the regionalists the architect did not act alone. The architect's calling was a collaborative one, to share the formative and educational function in society. Architecture was the art of designing environmental forms to enhance the full development of all society's members. While socially radical, the aims of the regionalists were also deeply continuous with the classical Greek and Roman roots of architecture—and the democratic tradition. Thus, Mumford could write that one must ask what functions the city performs in order to know what the architect and planner must do. Like Aristotle, Mumford insisted that the city is formed, "not merely by the agglomeration of people, but by their relation to definite social and economic institutions." The purpose of "community planning," then, was "to express these relations clearly, to embody them in buildings and roads and gardens in which each individual structure will be subordinated to the whole." The regionalists' scope was even wider. They insisted that the city had developed as the integrating node of an interconnected region that included a variety of habitats, natural and social. The aim of regional planning was to recapture for its citizens this life-sustaining web of interconnection, to render legible their present position in the environment and in history. Why, then, should all this be the special concern of architects? Because, Mumford argued, the modern architect, "cut off though he is from the actual processes of building," still remains the "sole surviving craftsman who maintains the relation toward the whole structure" which had once been typical of all craft workers.[40] Like Burnham, Mumford too saw the architect by training and tradition as a potential mediator, a figure able to grasp interconnection and render it physically as well as intellectually visible.

Modern individuals could only act freely and responsibly, argued Mumford, if they could grasp the whole context of their lives, including the linkages between home, work, and public life. Architecture and city planning were to make these linkages less abstract and render them obvious. Like John Dewey, Jane Addams, and Herbert Croly, Mumford and the regionalists were searching for forms of democracy appropriate for the urban and technological era. Much in the regionalist conception of human society recalled the idealist philosophy of the nineteenth century and, through it, the classical tradition. For the regionalists, as for Aristotle, the city was above all a public place. The chief goal of city building in this tradition is well described by Hannah Arendt when she speaks of the function of great works of art. To provide a "home for men during their life on earth," a "world," Arendt wrote, "the human artifice must be a place fit for action and speech . . . the measure can be neither the driving necessity of biological life and labor, nor the utilitarian instrumentalism of fabrication and usage."[41]

Mumford's sense of the overriding value of the city as an intelligible social whole, and of the purpose of practices such as architecture and the other crafts, echoed the Greeks. Arendt argued that the public realm needs artisans in their "highest capacity," the "help of the artist, of poets and historiographers, of monument-builders, or writers because they alone can provide, through works of art, enduring expressions of the ends that give focus and meaning to the story of a society's life."[42] Mumford and the other regionalists certainly wanted the architect to take on this office, and for similar reasons. They knew, however, that they were struggling against the utilitarian drift of American society in the twenties. Where was the institutional structure needed to support these aims to come from? Where was the public to sustain and vitalize this conception of collaborative professional activity? No more than the Progressive advocates of the City Beautiful were the regionalists to find a lasting institutional home for their civic conception of artistic and professional identity.

The Limitations of the First Effort at Civic Professionalism

The figures we have surveyed lived through a key moment of national restructuring. The pragmatist Progressives made it a visionary moment. They proposed a vision of how an industrial, metropolitan United States could develop its democratic potentials beyond the local communities of the nineteenth century to become a more inclusive and unified national society. With their differing emphases, Brandeis, Croly, Dewey, and Addams sought to unite scientific progress with humanistic institutional reform. They looked toward a society of skilled, specialized groups working collaboratively to render conditions more like those depicted in the new city and regional plans. The pragmatist Progressives were confident that it would be possible to educate experts in scientific inquiry who were also attuned to matters of equity and inclusion in an increasingly interdependent yet ethnically pluralistic society. Their models of such collaboration came from the great causes of their era, such as public health in which physicians and nurses had worked with social workers, engineers, educators, and journalists to create new standards for city life and the administrative agencies to protect them.

Their moment did not last. American entry into the Great War brought big business and the national government together, a collaboration which marked the triumph of a different version of the national society. This was a system in which the organizational professions, working in vertically structured enterprises, would set the dominant model. The mechanism of the market, guided by corporate and governmental management, would order priorities and the terms of collaboration. So, while many of their ideas found incorporation piecemeal in the maturing national society, especially after the New Deal and World War II, the pragmatist Progressives' synthesizing vision of civic cooperation was not sustained. Fellow-traveling critics of the "pecuniary values" of the new industrial order such as Thorstein Veblen despaired of reform.[43] Their cultural heirs among the younger generation who came to maturity in the twenties, including Lewis Mumford, found few political embodiments for their own hopes, and adopted instead the stance of cultural critic, while refusing to place trust in either the market system or the growing federal government.[44]

What was the weakness of the pragmatist Progressives' vision? Part of the answer lies in their diagnosis of the American situation, while the other part concerns the kind of response they made to that diagnosis. Succinctly, thinkers such as Brandeis, Croly, Dewey, and Addams saw the nineteenth-century democracy decomposing into a series of fragments under the impact of the uncontrolled market and the industrial system. The old moral core of American democracy, centered on the town, the church, and the household seemed to be giving way. On the social level, this meant the breakdown of the controlling moral order which had guided America's provincial communities, especially the household order, releasing women as well as men into a wildly uncertain marketplace.

Instead of the generalist Independent Citizen, who was

expected to play a variety of roles in society and was judged by similarly general notions such as reputation and "character," the new economy demanded specialists. And specialists came to exalt competence as judged by their professional peers above the old moral norms. At the level of the individual, this decomposition liberated new possibilities but also threatened moral and psychic chaos. Thus, Walter Lippmann, one of the younger Progressives, could comment during the twenties that "the modern man is unable to think of himself as a single personality, so that . . . morality thus becomes a traffic code designed to keep as many desires as possible moving together without too many violent collisions."[45] It was inconceivable to the pragmatist Progressives that so vast a transition could be negotiated without recourse to a new synthesizing public philosophy. Here they showed themselves the spiritual, if more secular, heirs of liberal Christianity and idealist philosophy.

As we have seen, the pragmatist Progressives attempted to popularize just such a mediating, synthesizing public philosophy. While embracing science and modern metropolitan conditions, it nevertheless taught the need to achieve a measure of wholeness, a rational harmony among life's ends, in the organization of society as well as in individual aspirations. Thus, while they criticized the narrow cultural homogeneity of the nineteenth-century society, and particularly those who wished to confine women to permanently domestic roles, these thinkers also disliked the tendency of the industrial order to split life into separate worlds of work and leisure consumption without providing a moral mediation between the two. Accordingly, the pragmatist Progressives focused on the development of a revitalized sense of the public and civic life. Their more cosmopolitan civic culture aimed to enable specialized groups and free-lance individuals to grasp their interdependence. Such a civic culture would give rise, they thought, to new social institutions, such as professional communities of function, through which an awakened public could find itself amid the complexities of modern life.

By the 1920s, however, metropolitan opinion was changing.

With immigration cut to a trickle and the economy surging upward for nearly everyone but the farmers, intellectuals worried less about social and moral fragmentation and more about a stifling provincial conformism they felt to be endemic in the broad American populace. This change of focus was symptomatic. It marked a growing chasm between the metropolitan culture of expert competence and those provincial worlds which still adhered to the inherited moral ideals of character. That opposition set off a series of cultural-political conflicts during the 1920s, in the struggle over repeal of Prohibition, the Scopes trial, the rise and fall of the Ku Klux Klan. These cultural cleavages signaled the failure of Progressive hopes for successful democratic mediation between elite and popular understandings, a development which would return to haunt enlightened American opinion at century's end. With the eclipse of the Progressives' mediating vision went hopes for reorganizing professional life on civic principles.

Instead, the institutional order stabilized in the form which the corporate reorganization of the economy had given it at the turn of the twentieth century. In this order, work was a part of the "public" realm, carried out in specialized enterprises aiming at efficiency and guided by market and government. The logic of the organizational professions fit this pattern. Professionals, at least in the leading metropolitan centers, became specialized experts who advanced knowledge by subdividing tasks and applying the results according to formal procedures. As much as possible, government, the management of public services, even politics were reshaped to accord with these norms. This rationalized world of work and enterprise contrasted sharply with the "private" sphere of personal life, supported by a widening variety of consumer goods. There, enlightened individual choice in the pursuit of happiness was to prevail over restrictive small-town morality.

In the decades after 1920, the cleavage between metropolitan and provincial lives and attitudes was not so much mediated as stabilized. Metropolitan professionals, in contrast to their locally bound peers in the provinces, embodied a secular consciousness and led the way in experimenting with new permutations among the available options for happiness in personal life and relationships. The national news media, staffed by metropolitans and sponsored by the corporation economy, brought these attitudes into provincial life. Despite frictions, however, the result was less overt conflict than gradual accommodation, with local life slowly coming to reflect metropolitan models. Economic growth, which brought more Americans into the national system of corporation employment and consumption, proved a remarkable lubrication system. Education, especially the research universities, also provided a continuous route for mobility upward from the local to the national networks of business and professional life.

This process was first slowed by the Depression and then greatly accelerated by World War II and the explosive postwar boom. These developments muted questions about the relation between professional expertise and civic life through the middle of the century. However, just as the contemporary "culture wars" between traditionalists and modernists (and postmodernists) have suddenly reactivated the fault lines separating metropolitan from provincial moral orders, so the collapse of steady economic improvement has reopened the pragmatist Progressives' concern for mediating philosophies and civic renewal. As we shall see in succeeding chapters, the return of those repressed elements of the early twentieth century national debate is also reawakening interest in the nature of professionalism and its desirable location in the national life.

4

NO CENTER TO HOLD:

The Era of Expertise

"Thus in the beginning," wrote John Locke, "all the world was America."[1] Locke was referring to the Americas before the European conquest, when he imagined an abundant nature appropriated by native peoples unencumbered by civil government. However, Locke also believed that labor, the willingness and ability to turn nature to productive use, established a right in property for the industrious and the able. Locke thereby installed the conquest of the world through tools and work, together with the individual's secure appropriation of the resulting abundance, as the basis of human happiness. This idea has been an essential aspect of the spirit of the United States throughout its life, but at no time more centrally than during and after World War II.

At that time it would have been only a slight exaggeration to say that all the world wanted to *be* America. Even her enemies envied the undeniable prosperity and strength of the United States. At that zenith of power and prosperity, which lasted a quarter of a century, from 1945 into the early 1970s, the nation seemed Locke's

97

vision updated, a uniquely modern and successful society, built on the basis of heroic labor in the form of advancing technology. America's ingenuity, its ability to "roll up our sleeves" and "solve problems," had triumphed over the ideological fanaticism of the Axis powers. Victory had gone not only to the more virtuous cause, but to the more resourceful and flexible kind of society.

In postwar America, expertise took on a charismatic power. To possess it, to be linked to it, simply to bask in its wonderful effects, made life sparkle with promise. The radiance had been signaled by the triumph of American scientific and organizational know-how in the war. Aircraft engineering, radar, computers, the world's greatest industrial output and construction projects which dwarfed the pyramids, the atomic bomb: these were the visible tokens of a people's power and pride. Beyond the military gains of the war, science and engineering daily demonstrated their capacity to control nature for human benefit. Advances in military medicine drastically improved the odds of survival outside the battle zone for combatants and civilians alike as wonder drugs such as penicillin loosened the grip of pestilence. Medicine, now firmly anchored in the research institute and teaching hospital, went on to achieve such stunning breakthroughs as the eradication of polio, promising successful future wars on the old enemies of infirmity, mental illness, perhaps mortality itself.

Not only technology, but systems of social control and management appeared to have taken a quantum leap as a result of the prodigies engendered by the wartime marriage of science and administration. At the climax of the postwar era, the space program of the 1960s would provide the world with its most attractive symbol of Promethean technology: the astronaut out for a walk on the surface of the moon. Accidentally, that same mission would also provide a reminder of the fragility and connectedness of the human world, our "spaceship earth," through the stunning scenes of an "earth rise" broadcast live from space. That image, itself the direct result of rocketry and electronics integrated through modern management techniques, helped touch off a powerful reverberation of concern about the effects of those systems of technology and organization on the human habitat.

But those sentiments grew strong only toward the end of that postwar era. Its predominant tone was captured in the advertising copy of Madison Avenue and television. There American industry, more and more guided by expert management, was translating scientific knowledge into the marvels of synthetic materials, while automobiles and jet aircraft delivered new opportunities of mobility. By the 1960s, in a kind of parallel to the technological glory of the space age, the destructive business cycle seemed to have been tamed by expertise, banishing depressions and opening hope that long-standing social problems such as poverty and racial discrimination were on the verge of solution. Under the banner of expert problem solving, the professional knowledge class seemed to have at last come into its own.

War is among the most revolutionary agencies in human experience. By focusing the energies of a population upon the single goal of victory over the enemy, war can generate a profound sense of common destiny and purpose. World War II instilled in the American population at large the belief that its national purposes embodied moral righteousness in an invincible collective power. At the same time, war also brings to the fore instrumental rationality in all its sublime, ruthless power. Instrumental thinking concerns itself with means rather than ends or final values. It asks, relentlessly: How well is this approach working? Could it be improved? What kinds of improvement will be most effective for the least cost?

The achievement of a balanced and sustainable form of cooperative life, if not collective purpose itself, can only coexist tensely with the indiscriminate pursuit of instrumental rationality. The latter, as modern experience has shown, often works to undercut the former. The use of war and preparation for war as a unifying strategy is thus for any nation a dubious and dangerous strategy over the long run. Without the overwhelming pressure of mortal threat, most societies have striven to contain the inherently disruptive effects of unrestrained instrumental thinking within constraining customs, the social equivalent of the lead shields in which American technicians learned to shroud atomic reactors. War may or may not be the "health of the state," as social critic Randolph Bourne put it. But for the United States it certainly proved an ideal forcing-house for instrumental thinking and its near kin, technical, problem solving rationality.

In World War II, the practice of "total war" demanded the mobilization of the resources of whole continents, human and natural. This process accelerated the economic and technological trends which had long been pushing the world's leading nations toward a new kind of human society, one which conferred historically unprecedented importance on figures who could combine a high level of technical expertise with organizational skill.

These global developments also set the stage for the postwar American achievement of historically unprecedented prosperity. This context, in which enormous economic growth and technological progress took place against the backdrop of actual or "cold" war, was both the cause and the consequence of an enormous expansion of the professions. It brought professionalism, with its capacity to deploy technical and organizational ingenuity in the defining and solving of social problems, to the top of the agenda.

Already during the war, governmental and business leaders were busy discussing and planning the basic direction American society should take after victory. Their immediate motive was the prevention of another massive economic downturn on the scale of the Great Depression following the sudden demobilization of the economy and population which victory would bring. Not surprisingly, then, the focus of the discussion was almost entirely on economic issues in the narrow sense. What emerged was remarkably clear-sighted about the economic and technological features of the postwar world. But the experiences and challenges of American city planning had little impact on that historic discussion.

The dominant postwar conception of the good society would prove very different from the vision of twentieth-century democracy which had been proposed by the pragmatist Progressives Jane Addams and Herbert Croly, drawing on the pragmatism of John Dewey. Their vision of a metropolitan nation had rested upon developing the social capacities by which interdependent but dispersed and anonymous citizens could recognize each other and themselves as members of a public and so organize for action to achieve a rich, shared form of life. Professionals, in that vision, were to assist and support the nascent publics in developing the understandings and institutions which could make the modern public viable.

By contrast, postwar reality defined professionalism in predominantly technical rather than civic terms, as rightly concerned only with improving the means by which individuals and groups could pursue their opportunities in an expanding economy. Rather than the civically active metropolis of the pragmatist Progressive vision, there emerged a dispersed, suburban America in which the good life was remarkably uniform yet narrowly individual and private in orientation. The increasingly influential patterns of professional life were organizational in form, and focused on the application of technical knowledge to the material environment, as in engineering, or the human, as with medicine and management.

Consider, for example, the Sunbelt of the southwestern United States, including California, Arizona, New Mexico, and Nevada. Beginning with the Hoover Dam on the Colorado River during the New Deal, and increasingly during the war, the region became the beneficiary of vast federal outlays for military installations, weapons plants, water projects, highways, and other features now called infrastructure. (These infusions of governmental subsidy continued throughout the postwar era, especially through the close government-industry cooperation practiced in the defense-oriented aerospace industry.) During the war years a report by the Pacific Southwest Office of the National Resources Planning Board, a New Deal institution later scrubbed by a hostile Congress, noted that "technological progress," by promoting an "ever widening flow of employment opportunities," had enabled California and nearby states to absorb "huge population increases decade after decade." After the war, the Council predicted, "a new frontier will be awaiting exploitation—an economic frontier opened by technology."[2]

The report stressed the role that private enterprise would have in exploiting this new frontier, though it also highlighted the needed partnership between industry and government which the wartime experience had fostered. The report concluded with the prescient observation that the region needed to prepare for a long-term decline in the proportion of the workforce employed in agriculture and industry, with growth in the service and distribution areas. These admonitions were taken to heart, with the key role to be played by private industry in generating the new jobs, and government working to provide the needed assistance. The institutional patterns which emphasized private enterprise and individual mobility were mostly taken for granted, even as they generated the dispersed suburban workplaces and automobile suburbs (with decaying older cities), segregated by race and social class, which have become the American norm. The long-term effects of these patterns on the land and on quality of life were hardly imagined or considered.

The society envisioned amid the stress of war and later etched in the physical and institutional structure of the nation contained three major components. First, as the emphasis on jobs in the Pacific Southwest Region's planning report indicates, it was a society focused, beyond all other values, on the provision of economic opportunity for individuals. For most Americans this meant two interrelated but increasingly distinct spheres of life: work and leisure. Jobs were instruments, providing the means. The goals for economic activity were set by the expectation of a rising level of comfort and consumption. On the macroscale, this relationship was echoed in the economists' preoccupation with keeping demand high so as to provide a continuing incentive for expansion in the provision of goods and services, and therefore expanding opportunities for profitable investment. As the planners' reports indicated, the progress of technology was the key to this system, and in practice this came to mean large private and public outlays for education, research, and management of the whole process.

Second, this was the economy of corporation capitalism in its mature form. It was an institutional order in which the great corporations and their investors played the starring role, with a vital but ancillary role for government, a legacy of the bitter experience of the Depression. The social philosophy of the New Deal was by no means universally embraced, but government was confirmed in its role of regulator and honest broker, whose task it was to insure that as the economy expanded, its opportunities and benefits continued to spread as well. The postwar period saw the highest proportion of the workforce ever organized by unions. Not coincidentally, those decades were marked by high wages and a steadily rising standard of living. Buoyed by great increases in productivity, the era was also characterized by a great expansion of administrative regulation and governmental intervention throughout the society, which worked to finance housing for returning veterans and college education for the children of wage earners, and aided tendencies toward greater equality, helping finally to enfranchise African Americans as full citizens. Often working in government or institutions associated with it, professionals came to be valued instrumentally, as key enablers of this vision of progress, which in fact they often were.

The third feature of postwar society involved the maintenance of the larger context within which the intermeshing corporate and governmental arrangements flourished. The postwar era saw a great burst of institutional creativity, as the United States took the lead in establishing the United Nations, the World Court, the World Bank, and an international currency regime guaranteed by the American dollar. Here both private and governmental agencies played important roles, but the major hand was that of the state. For the first time in its history, the United States found itself not only inextricably tied into the international order, but the single dominant power. A sense of historical mission to accompany this new role had already been enunciated before the nation entered World War II in publisher Henry Luce's famous declaration of the "American Century."[3]

These beliefs could launch great constructive enterprises such as the Marshall Plan of 1947. They were also easily pressed into service to sustain the long period of mobilization against the Soviet Union which came to be known as the cold war. This permanent, partial war economy ensured that the instrumental bent of war planning would continue to exercise a powerful, and in the long term distorting, influence on all sectors of American life. Everything from educational expenditure to the gigantic interstate highway program were justified on the basis of "national defense." These developments created a need for broad policies for managing so vast an enterprise, and for the expert personnel who could conceive and implement them. It was precisely the moment for the forceful touch of an expert elite.[4]

This core institutional order linked the corporation economy closely, though not necessarily smoothly, with government at every level. Though the United States was the giant of the postwar world, in many ways the successor to the power of the British Empire, it did not stand in isolation. The smooth functioning of the postwar order depended on maintaining a favorable balance in its interactions with both wider global economic and social forces and with the cultural and political life of American society itself. The system also depended upon the natural resources and physical conditions of the nation and its partners in trade. At the beginning of the postwar era, the balance of power and benefit in each area was highly favorable to that corporate order.

By the late 1960s, the very success the American order had engendered in Europe and Japan had nurtured mature economic rivals in some ways more efficient than the United States itself. The cost of sustaining the united front against the Soviet menace continued to rise, especially thanks to the Vietnam War, putting the squeeze on the nation. That is, the patterns of interchange had turned seriously against the good functioning of the postwar order.

In domestic affairs the Civil Rights, student's, and women's movements; in natural resources, rising prices and the beginnings of environmental protest; in international affairs, the Vietnam War, consequent inflation, and the weakening of the dollar all produced serious dysfunctions that ate into both the economic growth and the social confidence which had been the mainstays of the affluent society of the postwar decades. With these sea changes there would also begin a corresponding erosion of confidence in the professional enterprise.

THE ANATOMY OF A PROFESSIONAL SOCIETY

At the height of American postwar success, social investigators began calling attention to the consequences of these developments for the basic structure of the society. Many believed they were witnessing the rise of a new social formation. It was characterized as the organizational, information, or service society, but most lastingly, as the postindustrial society. By the early 1970s, social analyst Daniel Bell succeeded in making the term popular when he announced that the nation had reached take-off into a new kind of society, one based less upon the extraction of natural resources and the "fabrication" of goods typical of the industrial era than upon "processing," a society in which the key to wealth is knowledge, the command of the techniques by which things and people can be shaped and reshaped.[5]

Bell's abstract generalization described what was different about the new industries and services of the postwar society, as compared to the smokestack industries of the past. The new economy relied upon expert knowledge and skills of social communication to a vastly greater degree than any previous social system. Compared to the establishment of the corporate capitalist order at the turn of the century, the "knowledge class" of professionally trained workers had doubled as a percentage of the American workforce. By the 1970s, the proportion of professionals in the labor force had risen to thirteen percent and Bell was forecasting a further increase, approaching a full twenty-five percent by the year 2000. And the numbers understated, if anything, the influence of these workers due to the range of their involvement in all sectors of society.[6]

In Bell's account, the success of the postwar society marked nothing less than a new phase of social evolution. This change of phase was being heralded by the momentous change from goods production to "services" and the new practical value of theoretical knowledge. The kind of knowledge produced in universities and scientific institutes had become the key source of innovation, as in the electronics industries, and was, in the social sciences and management, the key resource for governing an increasingly complex society. Bell went on to locate four distinct "estates" within the "professional and managerial class." First came the pioneers of innovation, scientific researchers. Then came the technological estate, peopled by those who applied scientific knowledge: engineers and health care professionals. These were followed by the administrative and managerial professionals. Fourth and last came the "cultural, artistic, and religious professionals" whose major concerns were with the elusive but critical goods, value, and meaning.[7]

For Bell, the crux of the issue posed by the coming of postindustrial society was that this growth in the number and technical quality of professionals was not in itself enough to make so complex a social order viable. (He was, after all, writing in the wake of the troubles of the late 1960s.) The very scale and complexity of the new society would make it imperative to "define some coherent goals for the society as a whole and, in the process, to articulate a public philosophy which is more than the sum of what particular . . . social groups may want."[8] In saying this, Bell defined the need without, however, suggesting how it was to be filled.

Recently, British historian Harold Perkin has described the long-term evolution of Great Britain toward what he calls Professional Society, one which shares many features with Daniel Bell's conception of the postindustrial society. In Perkin's account, as in Bell's, this new social form is gradually succeeding the early capitalist order based around the undisputed power of the property owning class. This order is market-oriented and class remains an important shaping power, but it is no longer all-pervasive. Instead of a horizontal organization by class, Perkin argues that modern nations have come to resemble the Giant's Causeway in Northern Ireland. Rather than a field of class polarization, the social landscape is dominated by many competing hierarchies of power, each jealous of the others and each based upon a distinctive and unequal combination of ownership (class power) and expertise (professional power).

A cultural formation that Perkin calls the professional social ideal has come to provide a corrective to the dominance of specialized, technical processes in modern societies. Perkin argues that this social ideal, almost a kind of public philosophy, has during the twentieth century been spreading throughout modern societies, though at different rates and to different degrees. While class society has been permeated by the "entrepreneurial ideal based upon active capital and competition," professional society is characterized by a rival emphasis upon human capital "based upon trained expertise and selection by merit" and exercised through cooperation.[9] In the conflict among social ideals, Perkin notes, the professional ideal has tended to displace the old working class ideal of common labor and cooperative endeavor, though certain features of professionalism, especially its concern for serving the community, also resonate with working class solidarity in a way entrepreneurialism does not. The professional social ideal prizes mutual service, the efficient use of resources, and responsible use of knowledge for the larger good. It also has some considerable "fit" with postindustrial trends, and suggests a way to humanize the austere qualities of most depictions of the postindustrial world.

The larger implications of the professional social ideal received powerful restatement in the postwar period in Britain in the work of T. H. Marshall. In a famous essay of 1950, "Citizenship and Social Class," Marshall argued that, while the dominance of entrepreneurialism had weakened the old notion of social solidarity implicit in the idea of the "body politic," public provision of important goods, such as health care, education, and culture could be used to offset the power of money in order to nurture a more integrated society, one which guaranteed a civilized life for all its members.[10]

The British debate over the welfare state, which took place at roughly the same time as the postwar planning discussion was proceeding in the United States, forms an interesting contrast which emphasizes the strongly technical and utilitarian quality of the American professional era. The British debate, focused by the report of the Beveridge Commission, was explicitly about the moral requirements of citizenship and the social goals of a victorious, postwar Britain. In the United States, not only was the discussion in almost exclusively technical economic terms, with little or no moral criticism, but the whole process was far less unified and focused. There was simply less real discussion and debate. The American plans for a postwar order were far less examined and debated than Britain's and ours rather than theirs were more decidedly couched in nationalistic, even imperial terms, as in Henry Luce's famous declaration of the coming "American Century."

In the 1960s, many of the worldwide developments which Perkin describes were affecting thinking in the United States. In one of the most influential books of the decade, *The New Industrial State*, economist John Kenneth Galbraith hailed the consolidation of the "new industrial state," with the judgment that ". . . power has, in fact, passed to the association of men of diverse technical knowledge, expertise, or other talent which modern industrial technology and planning require." Galbraith explicitly noted that the expert-guided economy was weakening the traditional appeal of labor unions to solidarity in favor of individual upgrading, leading workers to urge education rather than joining the union upon their children.[11] The professional social ideal was perhaps about to be extended and realized in the world's most advanced industrial nation.

THE UNIVERSITY AT CENTER STAGE

The American confidence in technical expertise echoed Louis Brandeis's Progressive Era enthusiasm for scientific management as the key to resolving social conflicts. Unlike Brandeis, however, the most vocal proponents of organizational professionalism rarely combined this technical emphasis with attention to the practical and moral dimensions of professional intelligence. But this was largely because they could still feel supreme confidence that the moral foundations of American society were secure and effective in guiding the events of their time. Those moral foundations, they tended to assume, once laid by the religious and civic authors of American culture, formed a kind of inexhaustible resource of hope, moderation, and fairness which could be counted upon tacitly to undergird social progress. The confidence that many Americans felt in the nineteenth century that their system of laissez-faire economics would lead to automatic progress still clung to the national imagination.

This moral confidence, combined with an enthusiasm for scientific and technical progress, was extended by sociologist Talcott Parsons to the professions. From an influential position at Harvard University, Parsons articulated the professional enterprise in a way that summed up the hope and confidence postwar America placed in professionalism. Parsons was emphatic in stressing the central importance of professional expertise. He called the "professional complex" the most important single "component in the structure of modern societies," going on to declare that it and not "the special status of capitalistic or socialistic modes of organization" was the "crucial structural development in twentieth-century society."[12] What led Parsons to so strong and striking an evaluation of what he knew was a "set of occupations which has never figured prominently in . . . ideological thinking?"[13] It was his conviction that the modern professions represented an evolutionary social advance in the direction of a greater rationality in human affairs.

The professions, according to Parsons, gave special prominence to the intellectual component of cultural life, a quality he termed "cognitive rationality." By emphasizing formal training in technical thinking, professional education produced experts who could bring greater efficacy in suiting techniques to advance goals. These capacities were certified by educational testing and state licensing. But professional life, particularly the modern organizational professions, had also developed the "institutional means of ensuring that such competence will be put to socially responsible uses." That was to say that through the professional complex, the United States had solved the moral problem posed by the differentiation and inequality induced by the division of labor: professionalism was advancing the technical efficiency of particular social functions while it simultaneously directed that efficiency into socially beneficial channels. The spearhead of these developments, in which Parsons suggested the United States was leading the world, was the modern research university.

There, in the universities which were expanding enormously thanks to government expenditure of unprecedented scope, Parsons described the cultural generator of these advances. It was the graduate school of arts and sciences, increasingly well-funded and dedicated to pure research, on the analogy of technological progress through scientific investigation. In these faculties, Parsons noted, "the typical professor now resembles the scientist more than the gentleman-scholar" of the older American college, and the researcher is motivated by the need to achieve a "reputation in a national and international cultural forum" rather than relying upon "locally defined status."[14]

Thus, specialization and differentiation of function enabled technical rationality fuller application, freed from the constraints of the more "diffuse social responsibility within a collective system" which traditional academics, like their clerical progenitors, carried. To balance the situation, Parsons noted that this older, more diffuse culture of responsibility was actually being extended as more preprofessional students had to enroll in undergraduate college programs.

The concrete meaning of all this became clear when Parsons described how the new system worked. He took medicine as the pioneer in "marrying the university to professional practice and education," citing the Flexner Report of 1911 and Johns Hopkins as the key points at which medicine developed, through the teaching hospital, a flexible vehicle for "working out the application of research to practice."[15] The same model was being extended, Parsons noted, to field after field. Thus, law, the venerable agency for implementing the moral consensus of the society, had since Oliver Wendell Holmes and Louis Brandeis come to center its own thinking around the university-based social sciences. Similarly, education, social work, and psychotherapy were becoming branches of applied psychology, while engineering found its equivalent of the teaching hospital in industry and the military. Management, from guidance of the national economy to control of local organizations, was similarly the application of the social sciences and the new information processing field of cybernetics.

The common theme was that the university and credentialing system allowed American society to specialize more functions, improving each of them through the application of technical rationality, while making them work in concert toward both a better material life and a society of greater inclusiveness and fairness. There runs throughout the discussion the presupposition that somehow the basic moral values of individual opportunity, fairness, and social harmony will prevail throughout the increasingly differentiated professional system. For Parsons, as for most American liberals of that era, there was little need to worry about nurturing that basic moral matrix. Shrill calls for "moral rearmament" could be left to benighted conservatives.

This peculiar moral optimism showed up in Parsons's claim that the clergy, though they were recognized as the distant progenitors of professionalism, could not be considered professionals in the full modern sense. The problem, for Parsons, was that they lack a specific technical competence and held "diffuse social responsibility within a collective system." Artists and intellectuals (those concerned with general social understandings as opposed to specialized sciences), were similarly disqualified because of their rootedness in social interests outside the research university.[16]

By contrast, no question was raised about how the progress of technical rationality, the assimilation of the university to the paradigm of scientific research and the practitioner to the role of technician, might affect the value orientation of the professional complex itself, not to mention its implicit moral base. The organizational society was institutionalizing the professions as ever more efficient extensions of the purified, specialized technical rationality of the research institute into the messy world of daily life. What neither Parsons nor other proponents of the new order questioned was whether this development was compatible with the long-run social purposes the professions were expected to serve. Was, in fact, the professional enterprise, seen as the cutting edge of the whole society's line of development, humanly sustainable? Or did it rest upon seriously flawed intellectual, moral, and institutional premises? The events of the late 1960s made such questions harder to avoid, as they made the benign confidence of the previous period hard to sustain.

Crisis of the Professional Era

If any one figure summed up in character and career the shocks and tragic turns taken by American society during the climax of the postwar era, the decade of the 1960s, it was perhaps Robert McNamara. During that fateful period, McNamara rocketed to fame as standard-bearer of the capacity of expert management to solve problems. He served as Secretary of Defense in the Kennedy and Johnson administrations, and was a chief architect of the American strategy in Vietnam, a strategy which was in many ways designed and executed according to the most technically advanced theory of expert control then available. The disastrous outcome of that strategy for the nation, both abroad and at home, stand to this day as the most poignant symbol of a turning point in contemporary history.

McNamara's career was, like so many other American leaders of that time, given effective direction by the events of World War II. Early in the war, Robert Lovett, a Wall Street insider who had generously responded to the call to government service, recruited McNamara from his teaching post at Harvard Business School into his operations planning group in the Army Air Corps. This operation was an experiment, designed to test the potential of the emerging field of statistical control techniques for improving the combat-readiness of American air power. McNamara arrived confident in the power of advanced statistical techniques to give managers a new level of command over the factors of production, human as well as material. It was simply a matter of adapting and fine-tuning the powerful new techniques of systems theory.

With the aid of early data processing machines just becoming available, McNamara helped Lovett's team to calculate precisely the life expectancy of its air crews and even how many planes could be counted upon each day in each theater of the war. *Fortune* magazine played up the new operation, describing this achievement of modern systems thinking as the application of "proven business methods to war."[17] After the war, McNamara and his associates were recruited in turn by Henry Ford II to turn around the floundering automotive giant. As the "Whiz Kids," they were to reapply those same methods to reproduce at Ford Motor Company a dramatic, much-imitated reorganization and turnaround into profitability.

In 1960, McNamara responded to John F. Kennedy's call to Washington to join his new administration. That administration had pledged itself to "get America moving again" by revitalizing the nation's sense of purpose. Here all the themes of America's postwar development reached a kind of crescendo. McNamara was to be a leading player in this development. He quickly became the star on the New Frontier's team of university-recruited experts, the then-celebrated "best and brightest." As Secretary of Defense, McNamara's application of proven business methods to war fit well with the administration's confidence that expert thinking could lead to improved control over events. McNamara proved a great innovator. He extensively reorganized the Department of Defense and the procedures of the military services around the sort of Whiz Kid principles which had so catalyzed Ford Motor. Where possible, the theme was to substitute procedure for individual judgment and quantitative measure for personal assessment.

This policy was to have dramatic, and fateful, consequences on the conduct of the war in Vietnam. One effort sought to bypass the usual methods of subjective assessment by military and intelligence officers in the field. Instead, during the war McNamara's staff developed a complicated and sophisticated set of quantitative indicators such as "body counts" and "kill ratios" in an ill-fated effort to quantify and so objectify judgments about the progress of the fighting.

The organizers of the new procedures, however, overlooked the propensity of the human parts of the system to modify their behavior to accord with their own interpretations of the directives handed down in apparently "objective" form from above. In time, commanders of combat troops began to organize their field activity around the indicators themselves, as distinct from traditional military objectives. From there, the forces in the field slid into manipulating or even falsifying their data. Promotions and whole careers came to depend upon the quantitative measures demanded by the new systems of control. The outcome was that military operations were often directed toward fulfilling strategically meaningless but "objectively" important kill and body count goals. The results, of course, were both monstrous and tragic.

McNamara's program was designed to modernize the organization of the military services themselves, to bring them into line with the latest management theory and practice. The goal, that is, was to recast the military profession as something more like, and more amenable to, civilian management on the business model. However, by establishing a new system of quantified incentives and assessment, the program worked to play down or extirpate just those structures of tradition, loyalty, and esprit de corps which had given the armed forces their distinctive ethos and much of their effectiveness. With bitter irony, those efforts to "rationalize" warmaking contributed substantially to the breakdown in military effectiveness suffered by American forces in Indochina through their unintended but quite devastating effects upon morale. In short, the systems approach ran afoul of just those aspects of human society which its proponents ignored or believed could be reduced to formula and procedure.

In the end, despite the disaster of Vietnam, as a citizen and as a professional Robert McNamara showed himself to be better than his theories. When he had concluded that his judgment about the Vietnam War had been tragically wrong, he resigned in early 1968 from the Johnson administration. To his credit, McNamara later reentered debate over defense policy by arguing that nuclear deterrence was a counterproductive policy at a time when it was not popular in Washington to say so. Still, the moral of the tale is the one which a professional military officer become Secretary of State preached at the beginning of the era of American predominance. George C. Marshall, when urging support for his plan to aid war-ravaged Europe (and in the process our own economy), had argued eloquently that there is finally no way to ensure success through pure technique, and that the chief threat to any successful people is always its own hubris.[18] In the American case, this proved to be above all else the hubris of technique.

The self-inflicted wounds suffered by American government and society during the Vietnam conflict posed, for thoughtful Americans, disturbing questions about the premises of the whole postwar structure of expertise. Could that order of affluence have raised expectations it could not fulfill, and which it in fact seriously undercut? For many troubled citizens it seemed for a moment that American society in general, and the university-centered professional complex in particular, was chiefly producing, in a way ironically different from Marx's famous adage, its own grave diggers.

The '60s was indeed a time of major questioning of the direction in which the nation was moving. During that decade a powerful polarization began to divide the previously broad "consensus" about the generally benign course of American development. On the one hand, there were many determined to press ahead with the postwar agenda, eager to continue the patterns of economic and technological expansion, culturally powered by utilitarian individualism and nationalism, which had proved so successful for nearly two generations. Questioning and protest, however, stripped the veil of moral innocence from these hopes. By the end of the '60s, the leadership of this tendency passed from the consensus-seeking establishment figures represented in the postwar administrations of both political parties to more contentious representatives of the ambitious economic powers of the Sunbelt states who, though themselves major beneficiaries of governmental intervention and subsidy, strove to recall the nation to a banner of renewed anticommunism and laissez-faire.

This ideology by no means prevented the enactment of reforms in the areas of civil rights, occupational safety, and environmental quality—all areas of administration in which professional expertise played a central role. The inclination of these predominantly Republican leaders and their supporters, however, took a rather hostile stand toward the earlier equation of social progress with the prominent role of university-educated experts. By the 1970s, influential intellectual pundits styling themselves "neo-conservatives" would single out the professional experts as a New Class, responsible for sowing seeds of amoral skepticism about national purpose.[19]

The other great tendency of the times proved no more friendly, though for quite different reasons, to the professional complex Robert McNamara embodied and Talcott Parsons had praised. This tendency sprang directly out of the moral idealism of the New Frontier and the burgeoning movement for Black civil rights, that was taken up by the Great Society of the Johnson years. Particularly attractive to the young, the religiously liberal, and the university-educated, this movement sought to lay claim to core values of the American moral center that had been overwhelmed by the rush to affluence, especially justice and social responsibility. The upsurge of '60s idealism, like that of the Progressive Era half a century earlier, criticized virtually all institutions, but while like its Progressive predecessor it was generally critical of big business, its sharpest attacks were leveled at the very institutional sphere in which it came to self-consciousness: the university.

Talcott Parsons had been right to emphasize the new centrality of educational institutions to modern societies. He seriously misjudged, however, the pedagogical effects of the postwar system of education on the nation's youth. As student movements erupted across America's campuses, starting at the University of California in Berkeley in 1964, the themes of civil rights, equality, and opposition to the war in Vietnam mingled with a generalized outrage at the kind of specialized, achievement-oriented education which had settled into place in school and campus. As the postwar university was being expanded and rationalized to become a more integral component of the economic growth system, the nation was undergoing great social change. The student population, though greatly expanded compared to anything in previous history, was still overwhelmingly upper-middle class, male, and white, with a preponderance of native-born Protestants. They were typically the children of the expanding professional middle class. The social movement set in motion by these "privileged" students, however, greatly accelerated efforts to open higher education to women, minorities, and the less privileged. The generation of '60s students themselves proved to be suffering not only from bad conscience about their privileges, but also from a severe case of one of the most characteristic disorders of modernity: alienation.

The era of the "multiversity" and the affluent class- and income-segregated suburbia, from which the students mostly came, was beginning to make a series of very discomfiting discoveries about itself. That was the time when "the organization man" was criticized as a cultural ideal by claiming that organizations were the enemy of genuine individuality.[20] It was also the time in which "juvenile delinquency," the "identity crisis," and widespread poverty were "discovered," while the "feminine mystique" came to define the life of postwar suburban housewives, alone all day with the kids. Above all, it was the time in which the injustice of racial discrimination and the drama of the civil rights struggle was brought into the living room through television. In this climate of generalized self-questioning, the university seemed to many students to represent a suddenly obsolete culture of smug obtuseness. The culture of the specialized graduate and professional schools was spreading throughout the undergraduate curriculum, ousting the older humanistic culture at nearly every turn. This institutional ethos of the university provided the students with a permissive context in which to experiment, yet seemed, and in many ways was, closed to their deeper doubts and ideals.

The American research university embodied a faith in specialized, scientific, secular reason and was as ill-suited as the liberal political order to addressing issues involving fundamental matters of identity and purpose. At Berkeley, Clark Kerr, the chancellor of the University of California system, was hailing the "knowledge industry" as society's most valuable instrument for "the production, distribution, and consumption of knowledge in all its forms."[21] Against the utilitarian emphases upon competitive success and individual achievement which were the typical working values of the system, the students raised their banner of self-discovery and general understanding, of individual empowerment and social solidarity. It would prove a heady though unstable mixture. New prophets such as social critic Ivan Illich attacked the whole professional system as a threat to the nurturing of "autonomous individuals" which was subjecting them "to the domination of constantly expanding industrial tools." The result, Illich wrote, was that "people tended to relinquish the future to a professional elite."[22] The very tendencies which the proponents of the professions had been celebrating, the "antiprofessional" critics demonized and damned. An older populist suspicion of experts and elites lived again, now on the political left, as it would rise shortly on the political right in the neoconservative attacks on the New Class.

The tragedy of the times was that neither the romantic world of student rebellion nor the professional ethos of the technically oriented universities proved able to provide the needed imagination or commitment to invent a better form of life. The desire of the idealistic young for a life marked by wholeness, authenticity, and community collided with the widely perceived social fragmentation and personal conformism of American affluence whose sources lay in the narrowness of the division of labor generally and the technical focus of so much of the professional life more specifically. Yet, the modernity which the students protested as "alienation" and "dehumanization" also opened new possibilities. But it proved beyond anyone's capacity at the time to grasp these in coherent ways.

The reforms of that era began to correct some of the worst inequities of the postwar order, especially in regard to race and sex, but the criticisms of fragmentation and alienation went largely unaddressed, while the postwar marriage of private consumption and a militarized economy continued. The increased emphases upon social justice and individual fulfillment helped promote a growing concern about the quality of life, as opposed to a merely economic standard of living, paving the way for the rise of "postmaterialist values" such as concerns about the natural environment.[23] However, the postwar economy had grown beyond the moral patterns of the family firm and local community. The informal controls of the old gentry ethic in the professions was being superseded by the bureaucratic structures of organizational settings. The suburbanized, postindustrial social patterns provided few integrating practices to replace the old ones. The substitution of rule and procedure failed to provide the desired sense of orientation and participation.

For a time in the early 1970s, the country saw efforts to translate some of the concerns of the movements for reform both into national legislation and into the professions themselves, as some theorists of the student movement had been urging. Finally, however, while the basic structure of the postwar order held, there was too little institutional experimentation and reform to revitalize the nation's self-confidence about the future. The abiding result was that most established ways of life lost legitimacy. Regrettably, though predictably, the consequence has been a rising tide of cynicism, within as well as about the professions, plus ever more bitter "culture wars" fought over the unresolved divisions which surfaced during the turbulent '60s.[24] That cynicism about institutions and those cultural conflicts soon acquired massive power due to economic and social changes which began to engulf the United States during the 1970s.

PROFESSIONALISM UNDER STRESS

Beginning in the early 1970s, the dynamic stability which had characterized the postwar economic picture was replaced by a series of rapid and often violent shocks. Whole occupations, industries, and regions suddenly found themselves overtaken by foreign competitors and made obsolete overnight. Economic security became a subject of everyday worry and anger, creating the perception of rising stress throughout the population, including the momentarily secure. The root cause of these distressing events was the increasing disorder of the international economic system, a disorder which reverberated domestically with the breakdown of the informal social contract that had underpinned the interest-group bargaining typical of postwar politics. In that climate the fragile social contract which had led labor and business to moderate their demands on each other reverted to a sharply oppositional stance. A similar tone of suspicion and hostility spread through much of American society.

During the years of these changes, the 1970s and 1980s, professionalization continued to grow in the United States, but the distribution of that growth shifted markedly. Resources and applicants shifted away from the public-sector fields which had flourished before 1970, such as education and social services, toward fields directly related to business, military, and technological institutions. These shifts were partly due to conscious governmental policy and spending, and partly resulted from changes in society itself, such as the educational effects of the decline in the number of school-age children. Professional growth occurred mostly in areas where the technical understanding of professionalism was least likely to be broadened by the intrusion of moral and political concerns. Again, the causes and the results were mixed. Thanks to governmental policies of affirmative action to correct past patterns of discrimination, professional education became far more open to women and minorities than it had been. At the same time, professional life within such economic and social circumstances itself became more competitive and constrained to focus on economic success, or at least survival. The expansive professional era of previous decades did not return.

Within the tightening squeeze of economic pressure, work life, even for the professional middle class, became increasingly constrained by the imperatives of economic efficiency and organizational growth. This forced to the margins the traditional professional concern with the intrinsic purposes of work. The focused life seemed more than ever a luxury to be indulged in during leisure time. This period saw the increasing assimilation of medicine and law, the core free professions, to the model of organizational professions. Law firms found themselves under increasing pressure to emulate the standards of businesses. The ever more complicated and expensive world of high-technology medicine slowly catalyzed government and third-party insurers to take steps to bring physicians increasingly under the control of large health care corporate entities.

There was more at work in these trends than ideology. As the economy found itself exposed to unexpected shocks from abroad, the social bonds which the conflicts of the 1960s had strained began to give way. During this time the American economy found itself in an intensifying competition with Europe and Japan. The apparent prosperity of the nation during the 1980s was largely funded by massive military spending, the last gasp of the cold war era which abruptly ended with the collapse of the Soviet empire at the end of the decade. During those years, American business was finding itself pressed to compete effectively in the now global economy. In the press, major organizational citizens from banks to corporations to public agencies defaulted on long-standing bonds of trust with their workers, with their clients, with communities, and the public at large. The result was an interdependence without mutual trust: the precondition for generalized hostility and fear. All sectors of the population which had the means sought to defend their newly perceived vulnerability by organizing in their own interest.

This strategy of secession from the social contract was pursued most aggressively and successfully by the affluent groups, including the professional middle class. In an economy which no longer enjoyed rapid productivity growth, the advance of some now had to occur at the expense of others. The prediction that the nation was becoming a "zero-sum" society was, by the 1990s, confirmed.[25] While the "culture of contentment" enjoyed by the rich and the professional middle class improved in gratifying ways, the economic misery of the many worsened.[26] The postwar institutional order was in tatters and, with it, the good conscience and social esteem of professionalism.

The appearance of the yuppie phenomenon during the 1980s gave these large-scale social trends an immediate and none-too-lovely human face. The young, urban professionals of the acronym were "discovered" in 1984, their reality certified by a *Newsweek* cover story and a great deal of additional media attention. Like so many social "discoveries," this one called attention to a certain style, a way of putting life together, more than it described a clear statistical category. The term referred to a lifestyle concentrated upon occupational success, often in the recognized professions and particularly in fields tied to business, which sought the proper reward for hard work in the private acquisition and display of status goods.

In outline, the yuppie phenomenon simply advertised the basic goals of the postwar economic order in heightened and streamlined form. What made the yuppiedom of gentrified urban neighborhoods stand out against typical American middle class life was the apparent willingness of yuppies of both sexes to subordinate all other life goals, including family and child rearing, to career success and consumption. The yuppies were, as Barbara Ehrenreich put it, "exemplars not of their generation but of their class, the same professional middle class that had produced the student rebels."[27] Alienation had not gone away. Instead, a new generation had found another, less publicly oriented promise of a cure.

Beneath the envy and moral indignation stirred by the preening of yuppyism lay the continuing, unsettling presence of economic disorder. And the most powerful and affluent professions had become very much a part of the sclerotic condition of American society. This situation emphasized the often contradictory results of earlier efforts to amend the postwar order. For example, legislative reforms of the early 1970s had opened political campaigns and the regulatory process to more direct public involvement. They also allowed, if unwittingly, well-organized and highly funded "publics" to assemble smaller versions of the powerful lobbying arrangements President Dwight D. Eisenhower had dubbed "the military-industrial complex." A medical-industrial complex soon grew up, along with specialized law firms whose entire clientele consisted of one or another agency of the federal government. In these highly politicized organizational contexts the old client-centered, paternal-istic ethics of the free professions proved less than adequate guides to maintaining professional integrity amidst severe economic strain.

By the 1990s, the wracking changes in the economy were undermining old conceptions of professional identity and responsi-bility. In an era of radical economic instability, when investment capital shifted rapidly around the globe seeking the highest return, organizations themselves began to implode. In a mad effort to attract or retain investors—or to prevent hostile takeover from out-side—business firms intensified their efforts to squeeze more out of their employees, professionals as well as others. The technical focus which had dominated postwar professionalism now tended to blur into a self-interested economic strategy for taking advantage of shifting market winds. In this swirl of uncertainty, the "casino capi-talism" of the United States in the 1980s, whole new professional enterprises were born: the rise of consultant firms.

While the established professions were becoming domesticated for organizational life, the consultant firms adopted, as often as not, the swashbuckling outlook of old-time entrepreneurial capitalism. The organizational push for predictability and efficiency has long worked to isolate technical proficiency from concerns with institutional responsibility. The intensified economic focus of the professional consultant reduced the civic dimensions of professionalism still further. The combined effects of these developments, however, has been sadly similar. They have weakened integrity of function and public service which were the special attributes of professional occupations. This at a time when the entire economic order was suffering from a breakdown of mutual confidence, the systemic consequences of pushing self-regarding instrumental rationality to the limit.

Under these circumstance, Tocqueville's democratic paradox has returned with a vengeance. Observing the more dispersed and far less integrated civil society of the nineteenth century, Tocqueville had stressed that the long-term viability of free institutions, and thus of individual freedom, required some means whereby the intrinsic values of activities essential to the common welfare could be protected from meltdown into the cash nexus.[28] At a moment when the unregulated cash nexus of the market threatens to implode upon the social order it should serve, the reinvigoration and institutionalization of the ideals of integrity of function and public responsibility which professionalism represents would fill an essential need.

We need a new professionalism adequate to the changed circumstances of American life. The first step toward this reinvention of professionalism, however, requires that professionalism be understood as a public good, a social value, and not the ideology of some special interest. To make good on this claim, the positive features of professionalism must be extended to all work in the modern economy. By combining the dignity and security of occupational identity with the integrity and competence of social function, professionalism can be a major resource for rebuilding not just a dynamic economy, but a viable public order as well. The chapters which follow are concerned with reinventing professionalism as a civic art, in order to reform the professional enterprise and extend its goods more broadly while helping to spark the renewal of the larger society. The succeeding chapters will argue that, while it may seem idealistic, this cause will in the longer run prove the most realistic strategy by which to address not only the crisis of professionalism, but the problems of work and meaning.

5

REINVENTING

PROFESSIONALISM

Few moments in history are more disconcerting yet so exhilarating as times of interregnum when an old order of affairs has ceased to operate but no new pattern is yet clearly in place. In the history of the sciences we have become used to calling such moments revolutionary.[1] In social and political affairs it is perhaps more accurate to call them periods of historical discontinuity. At such times, specialized knowledge and routine functioning, which contribute both progress and stability in more settled periods, can become menaces rather than blessings. Then the need is for criticism, but even more for reflective rethinking which can imaginatively conceive emerging novelties as a whole situation.

When an era ends, as for example when the age of European world dominance ended after 1945, the effect is sudden, often unpredictable change. Europe, which had been at the center of world power, was suddenly reduced to one of several areas con-

127

tested between the United States and the USSR, powers which were viewed by many Europeans as alien and dangerous to the values of a now dwarfed European culture. Today, that conflict of superpowers, the cold war which had been the central organizing fact of the past half century, has itself come to an abrupt end. Since the dissolution of the Soviet world before an astounded global television audience, it has become clear that we have today entered another such moment of historical discontinuity.

If taken as suggestive rather than precise examples, well-chosen historical analogies can ease the anxiety of such moments of change and provide the perspective and orientation necessary for effective response. For the United States today, the signs of major discontinuity are manifold: the evident breakdown of the once-successful postwar economic order at home and the uncertainty which hangs over the international economic scene; the resulting conflicts between suddenly unrestrained local interests which have followed the cessation of the cold war; the destructive effects of an anarchic instrumental rationality at work in technologies and organizations with uncertain social mooring; the rising tide of cultural division in American life, accompanied by a frightening dissolution of the social fabric. The nation has not merely entered a period of readjustment in which the basic institutional order can be taken as sound; this is a time of massive decomposition. The only adequate response has to be an equally massive movement of criticism and reconstruction.

The last comparable moment in American history was neither the 1960s, despite the apocalyptic rhetoric of the time, nor 1945, nor the trauma of the Great Depression. These were times of major readjustment, but they could and did assume the basic adequacy of the economic, social, and political structure then prevailing. The scope of today's challenges rather suggests the period stretching from the 1880s until World War I. During that time the United States restructured itself from an insular and dispersed, racially divided, dominantly Protestant, agrarian-commercial society into an industrial giant and world power, whose strength lay in a national economy centered in great cities with multiethnic populations.

Through that tumultuous period, immigrants, Catholics, Jews, women, and African Americans began aggressively to seek equality and full participation in American life. The nation's life was itself reshaped through a whole set of new institutions ranging from the corporations to regulatory government to the university-led education system, all staffed by the new type of organizational professionals. This was the period of massive national restructuring, described in Chapter 3, which provided the context for the rise of the organizational professions.

During that time of discontinuity a century ago, Americans discovered they were living in a new world which presented important challenges to the nation's inherited, if still limited, dedication to democracy. Today's challenges are no less sweeping and unprecedented: how to invent a new global order while seeking to enhance the national well-being; how to adapt to technological change humanely while striving for ecologically sustainable economic growth with equity and inclusion. The efforts of the pragmatist Progressives such as Herbert Croly, John Dewey, and Jane Addams to bring civic concerns to bear on the rationalizing tendencies of technological society may be our most valuable analogies for making our way in this moment of historical discontinuity.

Herbert Croly's thought and career seem especially suggestive for this effort at reconstruction. Like Addams and Dewey, Croly had frequent recourse to the idea of reconstituting an active public.[2] Responding to a moment of historical discontinuity which seemed to discredit the older American values of democratic civic life, Croly put forward the idea of the public as a new kind of civic community. He sought to promote a new process of social learning and moral deliberation. Croly understood, before most of his countrymen, the problems of interdependence which the new corporation capitalism posed for civic community in the United States. He insisted that the sine qua non of a complex, interdependent modern society was to make the growing differentiation of skills and social position an asset rather than an obstacle to democratic life. To guarantee that specialized expertise be employed within a wide horizon of common needs and aims, Croly sought a new equivalent for the declining local civic communities.

Professionalizing work was to be a key part of this project. Finding individual scope and recognition, even within large organizations, through craftlike dedication to public standards, professionalization would enable citizens to depend upon each other for the common goods of modern civilization. Educated middle class professionals were to provide leadership in the opening technological, organizational era.[3] Croly looked to them to mediate between the often-closed domains of the emerging national economy and the provincial worlds in which most Americans felt most at home. In this way, professionals could provide models of how to use knowledge for the general betterment, as exemplars of a democratic community appropriate to the twentieth century.

At that past moment of epochal social change, Croly also insisted that functional expertise and interdependent cooperation could be sustained only if all the participating groups recognized each other as sharing a common destiny, and raised cooperation to the status of a conscious social value. This was the core meaning of his proposed "new nationalism." Croly's national purpose was to make concrete what his teacher Josiah Royce had called the spirit of loyalty to a cause, that moral sense which Royce had argued was the necessary foundation for justice and social trust. In this conception, the trendsetting middle-class professions were to become standard-bearers leading the process of institutionalizing civic professionalism as a common social value. As we have seen, however, while Croly was proved right about the nation's need for a sustaining public purpose, it would be imposed from above for purposes of meeting emergences and preserving military strength instead of growing through interaction between leaders and participants in common civic projects.

Ours is a new moment which will test whether American democracy can develop new ways to advance its historical commitments. But social projects, like individual purposes, must be worked out in the context of historical contingency manifest in the actual state of economic development, the institutional order, and the sphere of culture. These conditions, as we have noted, are in many ways today characterized by decomposition, as the once-successful patterns developed during the period of postwar American supremacy prove less and less functional. Reconstructing professionalism, no less than other key projects of reform, must begin from a sober assessment of the actual state of the professional enterprise and the way in which professionals understand their own lives.

THE DISINTEGRATION OF PROFESSIONAL INTEGRITY: A CLOSE-UP

Contemporary professional life continues to be lived along parallel but unequal lines, the provincial practitioners and the metropolitan professional elites. Provincial practitioners, although usually trained at metropolitan institutions, find their most significant connections and purposes within localized settings. There, long-standing features of American civic life, especially the importance of public cooperation, moral character, and local community service, temper the allure of pure technique, the rewards of wealth, and the expanded personal options available within the metropolitan context. The vastly increased integration of national markets and aspirations has steadily overshadowed those provincial loyalties, however, creating an undertow which runs against the viability of loyalties to place and local culture.

The same dynamism of the national economy and trendsetting metropolitan organizations and opinions pull professional ambitions toward high-status national institutions. Metropolitan professionals typically work at the center of their fields and live within geographically dispersed networks of peers. They are often closely identified with the workings of national business, government, or professional organizations. They are far less tied to local civic milieus and naturally identify most closely with their careers and the settings of metropolitan life. It is not surprising, then, that it has been among metropolitan professionals that most condensed symptoms of the stresses of historical discontinuity have appeared. The yuppie syndrome is perhaps the most disturbing manifestation of tendencies which, in more buffered forms, have affected professionals, and indeed, virtually all parts of the American population.

The lifestyle adopted by the young urban professionals of the past decade compactly expresses the tensions underlying professional life. The yuppie, it should be noted, confounds much accepted cultural wisdom. Contrary to the supposed contradiction between a sturdy work ethic and hedonistic consumerism, once argued by Daniel Bell in *The Cultural Contradictions of Capitalism*, these urban professionals work very ambitiously while also consuming commodities and stimulating experiences with equal energy.[4] The problem of the yuppie life does not seem to be conflict between work and hedonism, but the discovery that both success and pleasure are often capricious and without significance.

The ethos of yuppie life is characterized by a high level of material security and a vast number of opportunities for personal exploration and fulfillment. It is also a life of intense competitive pressure and little free time. Yuppie life is thus riven by harsh dichotomies. Competence and adaptability are the presiding values in work. This cult of competence is at the same time curiously detached, engendering few lasting ties to employers, coworkers, or organizations. The yuppie must travel light, emotionally as well as physically. The demands and stresses of highly competitive work are expected to be balanced or at least relieved in the intimate realm of personal life. Yet, even there, relationships, including marriage and family, are sources of enormous anxiety and, often, severe disappointment. The often conflicting demands of such a highly segmented life require a strategy for managing it all and, finally, soothing the hurts of an inevitably wounded self. Metropolitan professional life is therefore marked by massive consumption of professional services, from personal financial management to child care to psychotherapy. These further the fragmentation of existence,

132

threatening to transmute the effort to live well into an exhausting battle for psychic survival.

This dichotomy between the harsh demands of the marketplace and the private sphere of personality is familiar to many of the metropolitan professionals' fellow citizens. It is rooted in the characteristically sharp differentiation Americans now experience between the public and private spheres. Our economic as well as public institutions have become increasingly governed by instrumental and utilitarian standards, pushing workers to narrow their concerns to technical competence and self-protection. In other capacities, however, as consumers, members of associations, and private persons, Americans expect a different logic to apply, one which gives expression to individual yearning and the desire for a satisfying life.[5]

While many Americans become "gradgrinds" at work, bent on improving efficiency and payoff, in the recesses of private life, where they believe they can be themselves, they often seek compensation as "Bloomsburies." They find themselves emulating the Bloomsbury set of Edwardian Britain who, finding little meaning in the public culture of their time, sought fulfillment by cultivating a romantic sensibility tinged with terminal irony. The consumer economy provides essential support for this private quest, especially in its marketing of the nostalgic delights of an upscale, autumnal hedonism. Not only metropolitan professionals, but most citizens of modern societies, even self-described postmodernists, must negotiate a compromise between these two ways of living, sometimes adopting the no-nonsense seriousness of a gradgrind, while now and again affecting a Bloomsbury style of aesthetic detachment. This division of life into contrasting spheres of value was what Max Weber identified as the modern fate. Earlier, it had seemed to G. W. F. Hegel a description of alienation, a state of unhappy consciousness.

Louis Auchincloss's *Diary of a Yuppie* takes its readers into that ethos via the world of corporate law as practiced in the go-go financial scene of New York in the late 1980s. The novel tells the story of attorney Robert Service and his wife Alice. Both in their early thirties, the book takes them through the near-ending of their marriage while Bob bounds from conquest to conquest, playing the casino world of corporate takeovers in which the manipulation of financial assets had displaced the nurture of enterprise. The story provides a chance to observe close up a character type, a moral philosophy, and also the deformation of old-time blue chip law firms into unprincipled competitors for clients in the world of business services. The old gentry ethic of the free professions has here been ousted by the purely strategic orientation of finance under conditions of reduced governmental regulation. A blatantly mercenary professionalism has evolved as a response to an increasingly dangerous and bellicose economic scene. The vehicle for the tale is the private journal of Bob Service, over whose shoulder, as it were, we are allowed to peek as the events unfold. Like Alice, a former literature major at Columbia, Service's literary heroes had been aesthetes, especially Walter Pater and his ancient Epicurean alter ego, Marius. Like Pater's Marius, Service is incapable of profound loyalties, but unlike Marius he insists that he is fundamentally like everyone else, except that Bob Service can accept this fact in sangfroid, without illusions.

Bob Service harbors no illusions about the law, either. He sees his superior realism setting him apart from both Alice and his professional mentor, Branders Blakelock. "The trouble with you," Service instructs Alice—and through her Blakelock—is that she doesn't grasp the "moral climate in which we live today. It's all a game, but a game with very strict rules . . . but there is no particular moral opprobrium in incurring a penalty."[6] Bob Service's great talent is his ability to manipulate, as it is his peculiar character flaw that he cannot distinguish manipulation from genuine persuasion. Service insists, however, that his view is not exceptional, only exceptionally honest. Thus he is not surprised later in the story when his own protégé turns on him. Neither is he surprised when Alice, who has all along deplored his cynicism, at the story's end apparently accepts not only him on his own terms, but also the possibility that he may be right about humankind. Service—an ironic cognomen to be sure—fits well into a time when the educated middle class sees discontinuity all around: in the breakdown of professional and personal mores, in the loss of any sense of calling beyond a financially successful career.

Service can move easily between the harsh world of business and the softer climate of the personal sphere because for him these transitions involve no differences in principle, only changes in modulation. Service's ability to modulate his presentation of self to charm or force the other to his will serves him well in the venue of corporate law. This, of course, is precisely Auchincloss's point. Service literally refuses to credit any other way of relating to the world. Yet, Auchincloss's novel gains its savor from the reader's belief—or at least hope—that there is a richer moral world, though an alternative to its protagonist's invincible cynicism casts little shadow in the book.

The yuppie strategy, as pursued in Auchincloss's tale, is a relentless organization of life in instrumental terms. Its social consequences are suggested by the wrecked relationships and broken trust which Robert Service leaves in his choppy wake. But this approach to living is revealed as failing even on its own terms. The private satisfactions of winning, having, and achieving fail to stem an anxious agitation which, like an addiction or an obsession, presses on toward yet more struggles. Service cannot achieve a stable and satisfactory form of life. The instrumental life is seen to implode upon itself.

Robert Service is a literary creation. However, achieving a meaningful, satisfying life while gripped by a devouring orientation toward career success is a very real and widespread problem in contemporary life. In the absence of an ethic of calling, the quest to "become one's own person" through instrumental achievement cannot, for most, support satisfaction in practicing a profession over time. In the absence of social confidence in the value of the work done, ambition must become paranoid and even self-destructive.

Without shared confidence in the value of the task, there can be no secure recognition for individual achievement, leaving individuals endlessly anxious, having to validate their self-worth through comparative ranking along an infinite scale of wealth and power.

When winning isn't possible, or its personal cost becomes too high, or when one's career has plateaued, the instrumental orientation toward success reveals its poverty. It fails to provide an enduring sense that life is worth living and even, ironically, that this would-be imperial self has value.[7] Then begins the search for authenticity in expressive identity or the secretion of a hardened shell of cynicism which are such prominent features of today's society.

By contrast, a professionalism which unfolds as part of a cooperative civic culture provides an escape from this unhappy consciousness by focusing the person's energies outward, engaging the challenges presented by social reality. But such a professionalism depends upon certain kinds of institutional development which sustain the intrinsic values of professional work while connecting professionals with other citizens. Without such institutions professional morale must wither, and with it the objective dependability of those professional functions so vital to the life of modern societies.

THE UNDERLYING PROBLEM: NEGATIVE INTERDEPENDENCE

The entropic forces tearing away at metropolitan professionals point up the paradox of global interdependence. As the units of the global system become more tightly linked, the prosperity of each depends upon close cooperation with the others. Yet, this very interdependence seems to generate intensely distrustful, competitive, and hostile responses. We might describe this condition as one of negative interdependence. That is, interdependence turns negative in its outcomes when it is inescapable yet is neither acknowledged nor taken as a shared responsibility by those involved.

In an interdependent situation marked by uncertainty and limited trust, participants with dominant market positions or political power will be tempted to resist those cooperative activities which imply immediate costs to themselves, despite their recognition that it would be generally beneficial if all complied. Similarly, individual social actors will be tempted to seek unilateral advantages, even when they realize that all would suffer if everyone did the same.[8] But whatever their short-term benefits, these strategies inevitably increase social entropy, with negative consequences for the individual participants as the social environment on which they depend erodes and finally collapses. In even the moderately long run, no purely individual strategy can overcome the underlying logic of interdependence. Either the actors learn to cooperate, regulating and sharing responsibility for the collective effects of their individual actions, or they continue to suffer the downward spiral of negative interdependence.

Consider the contemporary consequences of the decomposition of the postwar order of national economic regulation. As we have seen, it has set off a suspicion-driven strategy of increasingly desperate, unregulated competition among nations as well as among interest groups within them. By intensifying the pressure toward instrumentalizing relationships, unmediated competition makes loyalties hard to sustain, undermining the moral infrastructure of civilized freedom. Among the secure, the result has been the cultural fragmentation characteristic of the yuppie syndrome. But among the urban poor, as Cornel West has shown, the consequence has been a far more immediately destructive nihilism.[9]

Neither is unregulated competition likely to prove economically sustainable. The era of the Great Depression witnessed a particularly vicious cycle of negative interdependence. Then, firms who sought to shore up their market position by the familiar tactic of shedding workers to lower costs discovered that what appeared individually rational turned out to be collectively ruinous. What lightened the costs to individual firms also depressed the collective purchasing power of their markets. Only the governmental management of the national economy which sustained postwar growth

137

proved able to compensate for the disastrous logic of negative interdependence. It should not be forgotten that even then, this solution had to be imposed over the loud protests of some of the very firms which were thereby rescued from oblivion.

The contemporary metropolis, as we have seen, shows similar tendencies toward destructive negative interdependence. The flight from the compact industrial cities into the suburbs was promoted by both government and business in the postwar decades as the opening of another American frontier, a technological return to a pastoral golden age. Nearly half a century later, however, that vast experiment is producing increasingly negative results. This is the case not only in the depressed and crime-ridden central cities, but also in the stressed-out, overextended "edge cities" where mounting infrastructural costs, social problems, and consequent demands for services continue to exceed the citizens' capacities to cope—or willingness to pay. Interdependence again seems to have overtaken the uncomprehending individuals whose lives depend upon it.

The scope of the contemporary challenge of interdependence has been graphically laid out by Robert B. Reich in *The Work of Nations: Preparing Ourselves for 21st-Century Capitalism.*[10] Reich places his analysis within a longer narrative which reminds the reader that America's postwar middle-class society, unlike the more state-directed and cooperatively organized European social democracies, was very much the consequence of an expanding consumer economy ruled by the great corporations. The key change of the past quarter century has been the end of the nearly self-contained American national economy.[11] This new world spanning web of enterprise no longer gives competitive advantage to the massive, hierarchically controlled corporation which once ruled the marketplace.

The new unit of enterprise focuses on "high-value" products and services, pursuing fast-changing specialized market niches, the competitive targets of profitability. It has no need "to control vast resources, discipline armies of production workers, or impose predictable routines." Instead, the high-value enterprise, like a centrifuge, is rearranging the once-familiar contours of the workforce. The nerves and sinews of the new enterprise are "problem-solvers, problem-identifiers, and strategic-brokers."[12] Such enterprises must be unencumbered by bureaucracy. They depend upon speedy information flows and the timely application of expertise to shifting problems.

These trends set the context for the increasing importance of expertise, but expertise which can be flexibly deployed through collaborative activities. Today's economy is increasingly divided into three occupational groups. Reich calls these the "routine-producers," the semiskilled and unskilled workers who were the backbone of the high-volume economy; "in-person servers," among whom are found a disproportionate number of the women in the workforce; and the new and dynamic factor, the "symbolic analysts." Among these latter Reich clusters researchers, engineers, bankers, lawyers, consultants of all types, systems analysts, journalists, "and even university professors." What they have in common is symbolic analysis: a set or sets of "tools for doing conceptual puzzles." Symbolic analysts now make up about twenty percent of the nation's workforce but reap half the total income. More than raw materials or simple labor, the symbolic analysts are the key resource for high-value production. Their particular skill is to "solve, identify, and broker problems by manipulating symbols."[13]

Much of *The Work of Nations* is given over to discussing the education, work styles, and social organization of symbolic analysts, these human counters in the economic game of the future. The surprising upshot of Reich's argument is that these developments are rendering obsolete professional life as it is now structured. Reich sees the traditional professional career, based upon certified training in a fixed body of knowledge and progressing through a fairly fixed occupational ladder, as passing away with the bureaucratic organization. Along with the corporation economy of the past century, Reich is forecasting the demise of the narrowly specialized, technically oriented, organizational professions.

In the new economy, Reich argues, the important thing is not mastery of a body of knowledge—that can increasingly be obtained through a few strokes of a computer key—but "the capacity to effectively and creatively *use* the knowledge." Practical, multisided intelligence, that is, will become more valuable than narrow technical capacities. Or rather, the two are being combined in new ways so that the practical and general orientation often has the upper hand on the technical and the specialized. However, Reich also calls attention to disturbing features of the emerging culture of the "symbolic analysts" which tend to reinforce the fictional picture of yuppie culture sketched by Louis Auchincloss. "The symbolic-analytic mind," Reich summarizes, "is trained to be skeptical, curious, and creative."[14] Indeed, symbolic analysts increasingly carry over their strategic and instrumental thinking from their work to their social and personal lives. The result is what Reich calls "the politics of secession."

Reich descries the appearance among the ascendant symbolic analysts of "the darker side of cosmopolitanism." He writes: "Without strong attachments and loyalties extending beyond family and friends, symbolic analysts may never develop the habits and attitudes of social responsibility. They will be world citizens, but without accepting or even acknowledging any of the obligations that citizenship in a polity normally implies."[15] Reich fears that such people will resist any calls for common sacrifice and commitment based on justice and fairness, ideals they may find to be "meaningless abstractions." Reich concludes his gloomy coda with a hope that somehow a "sense of national purpose" might arise to rescue us, and especially the losers in the ruthless game of global high-value capitalism, from the devouring logic of unfettered problem-solving, problem-identifying, and strategic-brokering.

Toward Positive Interdependence: The Civic Alternative

The alternative to worsening social entropy is positive interdependence. The outcome of interdependence becomes positive where the interacting parties develop the breadth of understanding, skills of cooperation, and willingness to share responsibility which enable them to turn the situation to their advantage. They learn to increase the complexity and stability of their environment rather than to deplete it. In other words, positive interdependence is the result of the successful application of capacities for civic cooperation. The viability of every society, as of the emerging global economic and political order as a whole, is now highly dependent upon the ability to manage the strains of interdependence toward positive outcomes.

Embedded in Reich's analysis is a vivid example of the difference such cooperative cultures can make, even within the near-anarchic conditions of contemporary global capitalism. This is in his description of the "symbolic-analytic zones," special "geographical pockets" which have become the not-easily duplicated sources of American success in technological innovation. Places such as Silicon Valley, California, or the Research Triangle in North Carolina, it turns out, function as "learning communities" in which proximity and ease of informal contact, in symbiosis with large formal organizations such as universities and private and governmental support, prove crucial to creative work. In contrast to the symbolic codes with which they work, "the cumulative shared learning on which such ideas are based is far less portable."[16]

What these places show, even though their genesis and position in the world economy are too special to permit wide generalization, is that even the new economy depends upon intensive networks of human interaction focused within cities and surrounding regions. That is to say, these centers illustrate what is wanting, and wanted, in the current disorder: the stabilizing gravity exerted by shared social purposes and adequate institutions. The one-sidedness of Reich's diagnosis in this regard is corrected and suggestively filled out by economist Lester Thurow. What Thurow has said about the larger economic order suggests the direction in which the reform of professionalism should proceed as well.

In *Going Head to Head*, a survey of the relative situation among the advanced economic nations, Thurow reminds us that the global economic system is very much a *political* economy and is becoming, if anything, even more so.[17] The units and structures which will shape the new economic order, however, are also in flux. The system of national economies, presided over by the United States, is giving way to a quite different one. From now on national economies will count, but they will find themselves interlocked with entities of supranational scope, such as the European Community or the North American Free Trade Area, which will become the crucial agents who will organize, with and through specifically economic institutions such as firms and cartels, the coming world economy. At the same time, local regions, including trading cities such as Singapore, have come to the fore within these larger systems as the specific sites of innovation and development.

The new situation is forcing all economic actors to change their mode of operating. In the present global economic context, "countries cannot watch out for their narrow economic interest all the time."[18] They must take interdependence more seriously into account. Like citizens in a democracy or enterprises within a national economy, nations may want their immediate self-interests gratified, but they are faced with the need to "play in a competitive-cooperative game, not just a competitive game." This means that, although "everyone wants to win," if the game is to be played at all, "cooperation is also necessary." If individual players fail to do this, "no system can sustain itself." In a context where no single power can play the role of manager of the world economy as the United States once did, leadership becomes more important than before, but it now must be a leadership able to derive much of its power from the building of consensus.[19]

A reformed professionalism fits logically within this general perspective. In order to achieve the dependability and creativity in economic and social functions upon which everyone's prosperity increasingly depends, the individual "players," organizations and individuals alike, must cooperate as well as compete. But they can do so only if they are able to sustain a stable consensus about where their common interests lie. They must also learn to recognize that upholding standards of excellence and reciprocity is a common necessity. For this, consensus-building leadership, and active participation in sustaining a shared enterprise, is needed at many levels of modern organizational life.

The restructuring process will demand the civic virtues of political imagination and institutional citizenship. In these circumstances, professionalism with a civic orientation could go a long way toward fostering the core virtues needed to revitalize institutional citizenship. Even in its present state, the professional spirit provides one of the most widely understood languages and conceptions of functional integrity, a language used by most of the professional middle class which heads and operates most of the society's central institutions. It is one of the most potent and widely spread understandings capable of being reshaped to articulate the contemporary needs of building a new institutional order. The important question is how professionalism can be reconstructed to respond better to the imperative of positive interdependence.

RECONSTRUCTING PROFESSIONALISM: A PRAGMATIST APPROACH

Reconstruction is a term of art in American pragmatist philosophy. It was popularized by John Dewey and invoked by other pragmatist Progressives such as Addams and Croly. As a critical approach it is especially apt for social and cultural questions about which no one can pretend to a totally objective viewpoint but which demand serious and responsible efforts at understanding and response. As a species of practical reasoning, reconstruction is a modern descendant of the "practical philosophy" developed by Aristotle for dealing with ethical and political questions. Reconstruction is thus implicit in every exercise of critical intelligence. This is the core insight of pragmatist philosophy.

Reconstructive practical reason aims to better attain goals inherent in a practice that has become "problematic," that is, lost, confused, or self-defeating. Reconstruction proceeds by taking apart the components of the problematic situation in order to reassemble the components in a new form so as to unblock the constricted or dissociated patterns of activity. Reconstruction, then, is intelligence at work to better fulfill the purposes implicit in a certain practice. It proceeds by seeking a more successful way of understanding or acting toward the goals of that practice, thereby realizing more fully its potentialities.[20]

Reconstruction always involves interpretation, in the sense of a construction of the situation in terms of an imputed purpose. But the truth-value of the interpretation is always provisional. The proof of its validity is itself always subject to further challenge and amendment based upon future experience. The judgment that the defining purpose imputed to a situation has been sustained is a complex reflective process. Its most important indicator, though still a provisional one, is that the new understanding permits thinking or activity to go on in ways which restore or augment the complexity and coherence lost to the practice in its formerly problematic condition.

In its present problematic state, professional life is a ripe candidate for a reconstructive effort. Its aim will be both to better understand the intrinsic purposes of the professional enterprise and to suggest the lines along which the enterprise needs to move if it is to reclaim those purposes in more vigorous and coherent ways. As starting point, we can begin by summarizing what our survey of the historical evolution of the professions suggests about their purposes. Professional life is concerned with the application of trained intelligence to the business of modern life. It is also about bringing the intricacies of technical processes within the sphere of moral meaning and social purposes. Professionalization is not, then, simply a reflex of the expanding division of labor. It is also an active social response to it. As new knowledge grows, and new instrumental systems expand, every society needs to restructure itself not only for efficiency but to improve equity, to reweave the bonds of trust and responsibility so that they encompass the emerging areas of human activity. Professions thus stand on the boundary of interaction between systems of technical capacity and the moral and political processes which aim to integrate these powers into humanly valuable forms of life.

Professionals take part in the commercial life of civil society. Like other workers, they make their living by trading upon their capacities in the labor market. However, professionals enter the labor market with credentials, and sometimes state-certified licenses, which establish them as the owners of a marketable type of property, a kind of human capital. This capital is the result of their development of skills and acquisition of knowledge in institutions designed for that purpose, especially the university. Like physical capital, professional capital is appropriated by individuals and negotiated in the market. In this way, the possession of professional credentials confers a measure of independence upon its possessors, giving scope for their individual potentials.

Professional credentials do this in two ways. In the external sense, the professional degree or "shingle" provides for social recognition. It confers upon its possessor a socially significant identity, a standing from which to advance a career "open to talent." In an internal sense, too, the professional's acquired knowledge and skill open possibilities for finding challenges and satisfactions in applying these capacities to situations in resourceful, even innovative ways. Indeed, one of the distinguishing marks of professional life is the expectation that the practitioner will not only dependably carry out routine functions but is able to contribute to improving the practice of the field. One expression of this norm is the requirement of original research for the Ph.D. degree. In other words, by possessing their peculiar form of human capital, professionals gain both dignity and opportunities for creativity, thereby enhancing opportunities for self-realization.

The security and negotiability of the professional's human capital exists, however, only as part of the public order of civil society. Even more than most other kinds of property, professional capital depends upon civil society's structure of legal procedures and reasonings. For example, the law benefits professionals by regulating the market for their services; it protects society by defining enforceable standards of practice. Professional status is in principle open to all, regardless of social origins. Yet, individuals can garner the benefits of professional credentials only by joining a corporate group defined by moral expectations as well as standards of technical competence. As is vividly the case with physicians and clergy, by becoming professionals individuals integrate their personal identity in important ways with a collective project, and find themselves held publicly accountable for the reliable performance of services according to prescribed procedures.

Entering a profession, then, does more than open up opportunity. It also makes the individual dependent upon the disciplines and control of a quasi-corporate form of life. Without this, the individual is in a far more precarious market position. In a sense, professional "property" is shared property. In order to be able to make individual use of professional capital, the individual must be licensed by a professional community. This demands of the individual a demonstration of the character as well as the expertise that defines being a doctor, lawyer, accountant, scientist, or teacher. To extend the economic metaphor, we can say that the professional's human capital can produce effects only within the network of "social capital," the expectations of competence, trustworthiness, and honesty generated by a community of practitioners through sustained cooperation.[21]

There is significant tension between these two features of professional life. The first feature, the freedom to employ one's human capital to maximum advantage and personal satisfaction, strains against this second feature of dependence upon a demanding, collective enterprise. On the other hand, professional freedom of opportunity is only realized through the individual's acceptance of responsibility for the purposes and standards which define the profession. Individual initiative and collective loyalty depend mutually upon each other and yet pull in opposite directions. This tension is inherent in any interdependent situation, but it could be argued to be a particularly salient feature of modern societies based upon an extensive division of labor. That this is heightened in professional life only indicates how representative the professions are of the larger social world of modernity.

For professionals, this tension is heightened by the fact that the negotiability of professional "capital" is highly dependent upon a third, civic or public factor: the public legitimacy of professional services. These services, after all, are often beyond lay ability to understand fully or to judge. There is thus an inescapable relationship of trust between practitioner and client involved in any successful professional enterprise. In the United States, this has meant both implicit civic compacts between particular professions and the public, such as exists in higher education, or the development of explicit charters of relations between public and profession in the structures of the bar, medical boards, and various kinds of certification.

The third, civic dimension of professionalism thus emerges from the fact that professional capital is so visibly a social and political artifact. In a democratic society professional legitimacy is always precarious because it can only be secured so long as a general balance is maintained between the kinds and degree of professional privilege and the public's perception that professional services contribute significantly to the public welfare. The importance of recognizing this third, civic dimension to professional life becomes apparent from the consequences of its neglect, when professionalism is viewed in abstraction from its civic context of negotiated interdependence. Then, professionals find that their enterprises appear either as fixed features of society whose legitimacy is taken for granted—or as strikingly successful monopolies which have exploited public credulity to manipulate legislatures into granting them outrageous privileges and power. Neither view holds out either reason or hope for constructive engagement with the serious tensions outlined above.

By contrast, this effort at intellectual reconstruction has construed professionalism as a still-incomplete project whose eventual outcome remains unclear. It has, however, uncovered three constituent features of professionalism—(1) that professional skill is human capital that is (2) always dependent for its negotiability upon some collective enterprise which is itself (3) the outcome of civic politics in which the freedom of a group to organize for a specific purpose is balanced by the accountability of that group to other members of the civic community for the furtherance of publicly established goals and standards.

Through this process of reflection, professionalism's implicit aim has begun to emerge into some clarity. That aim is to organize the conditions of work so that workers can develop and express their individual powers, by engaging them responsibly in ways that assure individual dignity through being recognized as contributing to enterprises of public value. This purpose links expertise, technical innovation, and freedom of enterprise to individual fulfillment through the responsible discharge of socially recognized tasks. Its chief enabling condition is the practice of social cooperation, both within the community of practitioners and between them and the other members of the public.

As disclosed by this intellectual reconstruction, professionalism's inherent logic addresses a central problem of modern life. This is the question of meaning, much discussed in some circles today. Meaning refers to the sense of value persons experience when they understand their own lives to be linked in a significant way with the larger processes at work around them. It has both an inner and a public face. To discover meaning is to find a point to living by recognizing oneself as a participant in a worthwhile enterprise whose accomplishment calls out one's energies and whose purposes define and vindicate one's having lived.

To live with meaning is to have discovered the secret to fulfillment. In the modern world, the sources of meaning are plural, a significant advance over the narrow possibilities offered to most persons in traditional societies. This is in part the result of the extension of freedom to ever greater sectors of the population, enabling women, the young, and ethnic and racial minorities to begin defining their own lives. Meaning, then, can lie not only in work but in family life, in religion, the nation, in friendship, the arts, knowledge, national and global concerns. In modern societies with a highly differentiated yet relatively open division of labor, however, work plays a key role in providing the means by which individuals can develop their capacities and express their individuality. Work is also a key source of solidarity through the pursuit of shared goals and values. In its broadest sense, the value of professional life resides in its having served as a continuing collective experiment, or series of experiments, in devising an answer to the question of how meaning can be institutionalized in work.

MAKING INTERDEPENDENCE WORK: CIVIC PROFESSIONALISM

The professional enterprise represents, in varying degrees across its many forms, so many institutions of civic cooperation planted within the workings of economic life. The vital mission of professional work is to infuse economic activity with opportunities for individuals to develop themselves through contributing to public values. At its best, professional life models this aim in practice. When successful, the professionalization of work is not only a means toward intense individual satisfaction, but a source of integrity which helps unify and justify personal effort. Civic professionalism means becoming more conscious of these defining values. Its achievement will require sustained, long-term effort at the project of reconstruction.

One key to that project lies in grasping the importance of institutions. As the enduring patterns of interaction through which human beings live, institutions are the most common and most powerful of educators. Thus, American society's heavy reliance on market mechanisms to allocate opportunities and essential services in areas ranging from skills to health care teaches its youth effective lessons about the need to get ahead and the disgrace of failure. Professionals, too, have been educated to very different understandings of their work in different historical moments and within various social contexts. The more closed moral cultures of regional society have inculcated the civic qualities associated with the traditional free professions. On the other hand, the organizational professions taught the superiority of meritocratic promotion and bureaucratic classification in formal organizations to untidy negotiations among professionals, employers, and clients. Institutions can have these deep effects upon attitude and character because they structure attention and provide sanctions to reinforce the dispositions appropriate to their ends.[22]

Institutions are the entering wedge through which moral meaning comes to affect technical and instrumental activities. Institutions "moralize" the performance of instrumental functions by embedding them in networks of social expectations.[23] Institutions are thus key generators of social capital, resources of trust upon which individuals can draw as they pursue their own purposes and to which they contribute by practicing their occupations in responsible ways. Thanks to institutions, the tasks of making a living or solving technological problems, practicing the arts, or figuring out how to live together can become foci for enriching character, friendship, and self-transcending loyalty. These processes in turn provide vital social energy upon which civic culture can draw.

Professionalism, we can now see, is itself a protean institutional form. It can give moral significance to the instrumental functions of work in ways which allow its participants to control and take responsibility for their actions as free persons. But the reverse is also true. The professions will not fulfill their promise, nor will the positive qualities of professional work reach more persons, unless professionals can reconceive their roles within enhanced civic interaction. Especially in the case of the "symbolic analysis" occupations which are proliferating among and outside established professional fields, the fluidity and instability which has resulted needs to be turned into positive interdependence. This will require serious efforts to reconstruct professional work and the relations among providers of skilled services. That task requires leadership, since it is unlikely that purely routine performances will be enough to correct the dysfunctional state of many professional enterprises.

Leadership for reconstruction is inconceivable without a common language and frame of reference within which to make sense of the current situation and through which to articulate strategies for achieving positive interdependence. A key means toward this end is the articulation of a public philosophy. The aim of a public philosophy is to bring into view the human possibilities and goals tacitly presupposed in the society's day-to-day life. A public philosophy aids the practical work of reconstruction. It interprets institutions by giving an articulation of their purposes and of the values they aim to sustain.[24]

By making purposes explicit, a public philosophy does not just idealize or celebrate these purposes and values. It also generates discussion and debate about those supposed purposes by focusing critical attention upon them. In this way, public philosophies serve to frame social discourse, creating common ground for discussion where varying understandings can strive to make sense of an intricate and equivocal, yet shared social life. Articulating a new public philosophy which can describe the possibilities of stronger civic cooperation is no detached, theoretical matter. It demands the development of social partnerships which embody positive interdependence in practice. Forging those relationships is the work of professional leadership. Its work is integral to the larger effort toward professional, and social, reconstruction.

THE CHALLENGE OF CIVIC PROFESSIONAL LEADERSHIP

The renewal of professionalism through reconstructive leadership is perhaps best illustrated by the work being done today by trailblazing civic professionals. At first glance, the grisly epidemic of violence among the nation's young minority poor would not seem a likely catalyst toward such revitalization. Yet, at least one contemporary professional argues persuasively that, properly understood, it could be just that. Deborah Prothrow-Stith, M.D., is a dean at the Harvard School of Public Health and a former commissioner of health for Massachusetts. She is also author of an unusual study of teenage violence, *Deadly Consequences: How Violence Is Destroying*

Our Teenage Population and a Plan to Begin Solving the Problem.[25] The book describes the situation of poor, inner-city minority youth, one in which the effects of the loss of social capital are tragically apparent. It is a world in which the breakdown of trust and mutual accountability have proceeded to a terrifying point whose consequences are all too well-known: unemployment, drug addiction, premature pregnancy, and violent, often deadly, crime.

This is a situation which has proved, by tragic negation, that interdependence is an inescapable feature of modern societies and that nurture of the integrity of family and community matters desperately. For the urban poor, particularly the African American poor, the familial and institutional networks they had once constructed with great courage under considerable hostility and assault have shattered. In America's devastated urban areas, the mutual accountability upon which civic life depends been has been unraveling for decades, and the major institutions of our cities have proved unable or unwilling to prevent the slide into despair and violence of young men born to those among the poorest of the poor. However, the book also documents the widening eddies of destructive violence, now turned inward, manifested by the rising rates of teenage suicide among the white, the suburban, and the middle class.[26]

In the usual division of professional labor, violence is an affair for the criminal justice system and perhaps social work, but not medicine. Yet, as Dr. Prothrow-Stith points out, "more violent crimes show up in the emergency rooms of our hospitals than make it onto the police blotters."[27] Indeed, it was during her medical residency at a large northeastern medical center that Prothrow-Stith first encountered the enormity of the problem of youth violence. It was, she reflects, "a shocking contrast to my previous understanding of young male life" gathered during her African American upbringing in the South. This contact propelled her to search for an adequate professional response to the problem. The search led her toward a more comprehensive understanding of the missions of public health and medicine, and toward action to reshape professional education and practice.

Deadly Consequences begins with the story of that search. For Dr. Prothrow-Stith, it turned into the gradual discovery that the technical orientation and organizational structure of today's professions are inadequate to their common purpose, which is to provide a first defense against the unraveling of the social fabric. From the typical expertise expected of physicians, that of being technically good at specific medical interventions, Prothrow-Stith moved to ask what might be done to lessen the need for treating the bloody results of street violence. Her first thought was that prevention might be sought through the criminal justice system, with its several component professional groups, law enforcement personnel, lawyers and judges, social service providers. But here, too, she encountered a tendency similar to what she found typical of medicine: to define the problem in terms of the field's favored methods. Here was positivism in action.

"There is," Prothrow-Stith reflects, "a self-perpetuating industry built around putting people away, just as there is around various forms of acute care provision in medicine." What makes this purely technical approach troubling is that soon increased use and effectiveness of the intervention itself comes to be seen as progress toward solving the problem. Thus, more people in jails is touted as controlling crime, just as a better survival rate from heart surgery is identified as progress against heart disease. But in fact, comments Prothrow-Stith, "we are gradually coming to see that our major diseases today, such as heart disease, a typical 'modern' affliction, are caused by environmental and, often, behavioral factors such as diet, stress, lack of exercise, and so forth." Thus, she argues, public health is a more effective long-term response to the problem of disease than any amount of medical intervention after disease is already advanced.

From criminal justice, Prothrow-Stith moved to the mental health fields as possible sites for developing a more comprehensive approach to preventing youth violence. But here, too, she was disappointed, and for broadly parallel reasons. The technical orientation of psychotherapeutic intervention, whether by means of drugs or dynamic therapies, focuses principally on the individual. She found that mental health professionals were reluctant to shift their focus, in either clinical practice or research, from the interesting, and often lucrative, problems of acute individual malfunction toward a strengthening of social bonds which could make these malfunctions less likely and less destructive. She found psychiatry in particular to be busily extending the typical medical focus on biological research into the realm of behavioral disorders, usually with minimal reference to factors in the social and cultural environment. Once again, the problem was not that these approaches were valueless, but that their exclusive dominance in the profession made a grasp of the complex sources of the problems they were trying to treat nearly impossible.

It was, then, virtually by process of elimination that Prothrow-Stith settled upon public health as the professional and institutional context in which to pursue her concerns. Public health, like the related, less well-established fields of community or preventive medicine, has remained an essentially interdisciplinary effort. While a large portion of public health professionals are drawn from medicine, as well as nursing, Prothrow-Stith argues that it is far more attentive to practical concerns with social well-being than medicine. Research and teaching in schools of public health is not only more interdisciplinary than in medical schools; it is also less driven by purely academic concerns and more interested in the interrelations between the biological sciences and human social life. It is to public health, then, that Prothrow-Stith urges we should turn to pursue the problem of removing the scourge of youth violence through a major commitment to prevention.

A strengthened, emcompassing field of public health could function as a useful catalyst toward wider professional reorganization. Thus, Prothrow-Stith notes that law enforcement agencies have come gradually, and often not very willingly, to recognize that beyond higher arrest rates and better electronic surveillance systems, partnerships between enforcement agencies and communities which emphasize enhancing community responsibility—like Town

Watch—are ultimately needed to handle crime. Similarly, she believes that "medicine is coming gradually to pay more attention to behavior and education."

These parallel developments, Prothrow-Stith argues, are widespread today. What is still inchoate is awareness of what is common in all these areas: the need to strengthen civic connectedness by developing partnerships between professional schools and organizations and other vital institutions of civil society. Like law enforcement, ". . . the problems of family viability, education, and much of medicine demand an approach that could be called preventive, one that focuses upon the whole context of the problem in order to find solutions."

What is bringing such approaches to public attention is economic necessity. The existing methods, which define solutions in terms of technical repairs, are simply so expensive that, with today's proliferating manifestations of breakdown, they cannot be paid for much longer. Here lies an opening for the civic orientation to prove its value in a variety of professional fields, including some parts of medicine. "We have almost no choice but to change," muses Prothrow-Stith, yet "we need what amounts to a change of ethos, away from a system geared to intensive, acute care toward a much greater concern with prevention and maintenance." A change of such magnitude is not necessarily to be expected. To succeed, it will need validation from the traditional core fields of the technically oriented professions, like medicine. The change will go forward, according to Prothrow-Stith, if and when these fields "see themselves as part of the answer rather than the whole solution."

If such changes begin to succeed, and new intellectual linkages grow in the professions, these will encourage more comprehensive organizational connections. If these institutional innovations take hold, professional education will change and new attitudes will result. The meaning of such a change in ethos will include broadening the working definition of health care from acute care to include prevention; moving from a professional fixation upon individual achievement to a concern for collective responsibility;

6

WHAT IS PROFESSIONAL KNOWLEDGE?

Expertise and Professional Education

CRISIS OF THE MERITOCRATIC UNIVERSITY

The spirit of professionalism grew up in the key institutions of industrial America which made their appearance a century ago. The corporation, the hospital, governmental administration charged with economic and social function, the educational complex, especially the university: these have been the professions' natural homes. Today, while some of these institutions face new global competition, others are in serious dysfunction or have become the objects of intense public scrutiny. Through its enormous expansion during the intervening years, the university, as the common training ground for most professional occupations, has until recently been successful in resisting changes to its basic structure and organization.

Now, however, the nation's universities face mounting public worry, and often hostile legislative scrutiny, about their functions. Yet, they have been curiously slow to mobilize effective resources

159

for either defense or reform. According to Derek Bok, the former president of Harvard, the decline of sympathy for the institutions of higher education among the shapers of opinion and public policy stems from a perception that universities have failed to promote purposes of public value. Instead, many universities are perceived as having turned away from their public mission to concentrate narcissistically upon their own inner life and advancing their organizational advantages. Even through the trials of the student revolts of the 1960s, Bok notes, universities received public support because they were seen as actively engaged in two great social tasks. One was opening up access to careers, especially in the professional fields, for newly aspiring groups beginning with the returning GIs of World War II and extending to minorities and women. The second task was the production of useful research to build prosperity and progress. Bok believes that the objectives were achieved, and that these achievements remain "unequalled anywhere."

Bok argues that universities today need new ways to serve the public but, he notes, they do not have them. Nor do they seem able to "embrace goals around which a new alliance can be forged."[1] Bok concludes that to "reclaim the public trust" higher education has to reorganize itself to respond to some of the challenges which currently worry Americans about the nation's future. He chooses three such national challenges to which the university, in particular the professional schools, have much to contribute. The first is the improvement of the public schools, to which Bok would like to commit faculty not simply from schools of education but from all across the university to work in partnership with teachers and administrators and the public. The second challenge is making better health care available to all. Here he notes that, while the university trains all the medical personnel, it has reinforced rather than criticized or corrected a system which has produced serious and very expensive misallocations of resources, personnel, and expertise. The third is the modernization of American business, to which business schools have, as Bok wryly notes, contributed far less than the painful force of Japanese and European competition.

Bok says important and reasonable things about each area, but his Whiggish celebration of the university's postwar progress causes him to overlook an even more striking point. He does not ask why the postwar goals no longer suffice to give higher education sufficient public legitimacy. Nor does he seem to notice the profound contrast between the new goals he proposes and the university's postwar mission. Higher education's postwar achievements were essentially utilitarian and meritocratic in nature. Through scientific research the university contributed materially to national military power and helped keep the nation's industrial, consumer economy the envy of the world. By expanding and diversifying its student body and fields of study, the university vastly expanded the pool of national talent which could enter the middle class.

Neither of these projects involved any fundamental change in the organization of research and teaching as these had crystallized around the turn of the century. The university pursued an internal logic, a guiding and absolute faith that the "cognitive complex" based around scientific research was the sufficient as well as necessary condition for human betterment. By contrast, the three areas of contemporary challenge which Bok singles out—education, health care, and business and the economy—suffer from problems rooted in profound dislocations in the American social and moral fabric. They will not be resolved simply through the application of new instrumental techniques, as many in the universities thought poverty could be resolved during the 1960s. Instead, these problems concern the malformation of institutional structures as well as frayed moral bonds. Addressing them requires grasping their historical dimensions, and their ultimately cultural and moral nature, hence the centrality of replacing the relative isolation of the university with new relationships between it and education in its many dimensions, health provision, and business and the workforce.

This change demands greater mutual understanding and trust. But it also requires a shift of academic attention to the moral-practical dimensions of learning. Bok makes a strong case for refocusing the university's attention, especially the attention of the professional schools, outward. What Bok does not see is that such a massive change in focus, because it runs counter to much of the existing understanding and organization of not only professional knowledge but of the paradigm of academic thought which grew up with the research university, will require a corresponding reform of the priorities and structure of the university as a whole.

The postwar university of which Derek Bok is in many ways justifiably proud functioned as the apex of what has been termed a "national personnel system." Indeed, Harvard, under Bok's predecessor James Bryant Conant, was the trendsetting model for this development.[2] The system provided a new level of career mobility during the postwar decades and, for increasing numbers of Americans, including far more women and minorities than ever before in national history, college and postgraduate education formed a reliable route toward professionalized, white-collar occupations. The university thereby continued, with greatly augmented impetus, on the course it had been pursuing since the beginning of the century, toward credentialing a new class, the "meritocracy" whose claim to leadership is based upon merit, especially the talent demonstrated in academic achievement. Overall, it was a loose system which contained vastly disparate kinds of colleges and universities, a few truly national in importance, and many which supplied the provincial middle class with localized occupational mobility. At the system's core, formal schooling and testing functioned to make "routine the eternal unruly American obsession with personal ambition."[3] Less flatteringly described as "credentialism," this meritocratic system was greatly spurred by the nation's success with manpower channeling through the draft in World War II.

This meritocratic professional system is heir to the utilitarian social engineers in the line of Frederick Winslow Taylor, who have sought to combine equality of opportunity with efficiency in the management of social resources for economic growth.[4] It has also served as the major bridge institution between provincial America and the national networks of the metropolitan society, typically a one-way bridge over which talent has traveled from the former to fertilize the latter. As never before, however, this whole system has come under question. The crisis of confidence in the university stems from the weakening of coherence and legitimacy in the meritocratic system.

The meritocratic ideal has justified itself on the grounds of its social utility. This has meant that leaders who advance to power through the system of credentialism must offer proof of their merit by providing both increased opportunity for others to emulate them and, whether they are political or business leaders, show that they can spur economic growth. However, many of the key instruments of the meritocratic system have become suspect or eroded: standardized testing and college admissions processes, public schooling as a pathway to advancement, and access to the best education regardless of wealth. At the same time, the presumed relationship between academic achievement and actual performance has been seriously challenged, not least in the professions. For many, the system has been failing on its own terms.

To these criticisms, Derek Bok has added his own in *The Cost of Talent*.[5] Bok found that since around 1970, the end of the postwar boom, professional compensation has become more and more radically skewed toward leading figures in the private sector. In the United States, the rewards earned by an elite among business executives, physicians, and lawyers are two to three times greater than those earned by their European counterparts. Their rewards are also much greater than those enjoyed by most of their colleagues in their own fields. By contrast, professionals serving the public sector, such as teachers, civil servants, and social service providers, earn significantly less and enjoy far less social prestige in America than do their peers in Europe and Japan. These tendencies, Bok argues, harm the nation's long-term interest in a balanced distribution of skilled professionals among a variety of professional fields. The disproportionate channeling of rewards into a few areas of the private sector tempts talented young people to oversubscribe those fields, to the detriment of overall social efficiency and often individual happiness.[6]

163

As Bok points out, the background for the crisis of the university and the meritocratic system is the uneven performance of the economy over the past two decades, with the concomitant fraying and weakening in the social fabric of communities and families throughout the society. The animating idea behind the postwar meritocratic system was effective training and the selection of talent.[7] As the heir to Conant, it is perhaps fitting that Bok should assume throughout his analysis that talent is an inelastic natural resource which may be "selected" or "wasted," but cannot in any significant sense be developed. But there is also a significant change in strategy for making the system work. Where Conant sought to give the meritocracy a broad cultural base through the encouragement of general education as a support for specialized study, Bok wants to make the meritocrats more socially responsible by expanding their sights outward toward areas of social need.

Resolving the problems of education, health care, and the effectiveness of American business, however, involves more than the selection of the competences necessary for achievement. It requires that academic professionals and their students develop new capacities beyond technical skills through communication with a far broader range of groups and issues in the society. Meritocratic leaders, however, have relied on the "objective" superiority of expert opinion. They have been very reluctant to engage in reasoned public judgment of the kind that matters to most Americans, discussions which consider the moral as well as technical aspects of life. This orientation, common among metropolitan professionals, has fueled the popular perception that the meritocratic leaders are mere technicians, self-interested ones at that, who lack moral bearings, so that the nation's vast intellectual capacities somehow fail to serve the common good.[8]

On the other side of the social divide, among those seeking entry into the educated middle class, there is the increasingly painful awareness that many of their fellow citizens are growing up incapable of emulating these trendsetting models of achievement. The income gap between the college-educated and the rest of the population continues to widen. Yet, many American young people leave secondary school with little preparation for more advanced study. At the same time, others fear that, even if sufficiently prepared, they will lack the financial resources needed for entry into metropolitan educational institutions. The big worry is that these developments may be connected: that the same economic and social processes which account for the rise of the technically oriented meritocrats have also helped disintegrate the moral sources of personal character and community cohesion necessary for developing educational self-discipline, while a growing proportion of the youth population, even among the middle class, sinks deeper into relative poverty.

Given these social problems, the anxiety surrounding higher education today is comprehensible. Demands for multicultural education, whatever their intrinsic merits, certainly reflect the worries described above. Yet the underlying problems of social decline and economic polarization are less well understood and certainly harder to control by formula and procedure than the simple expansion of meritocracy. Where the postwar university largely confined its sense of mission to the promotion of skills in the detached sense of techniques for acquiring or generating information, the new problems bring to fore educational themes once thought to have been relegated to the past—or at least lower levels of formal education—themes such as the nurture of character and the purposes of knowledge. Attention to the social and moral sources of ability breaks down the wall between theory and practice, as it focuses attention on the social capacities of families and communities. These new concerns require the university, especially its professional schools, to broaden its meritocratic agenda to embrace a concern with the purpose and social organization of knowledge. Without such scrutiny, it is unlikely that the university will develop effective responses to the new conditions.

The dimensions of the challenge become clearer as we ask what stands in the way of effective response. The answer is disturbing, though manifest. Beside, or rather behind, the inertia of entrenched interests there is also an ideal and a regime of knowledge which is strongly resistant to the stance of social engagement and moral inquiry demanded by today's challenges. This is the epistemic regime of positivism. It has been central to the university for a century. It lay at the core of Conant's idea of a national educational system guided by a scientific elite, and it has to date successfully resisted all efforts to displace or change it. The continuing hold of positivistic dogma over the thinking and practice of higher education is a key problem which must be confronted by anyone who concludes that the needs of our time demand a reshaping of professional knowledge as well as the way professional life is organized.

EPISTEMOLOGY AS IDEOLOGY, OR THE POWER OF POSITIVISM

The ideal type of the modern university, as we have seen it described during its heyday in the 1960s, sharply distinguishes facts from values as it segregates the generation of knowledge from its application. In organizing itself around these distinctions, the university embodies the basic features of the idea of positivist civilization enunciated in the early nineteenth century by the "prophet of Paris," Auguste Comte. Although positivism in the technical sense as a theory of science, or in logical positivism, as a philosophical theory of meaning and language, has been successfully criticized many times, its power as a kind of ideology or understanding of life retains great influence. In significant part this is because that ideology valorizes scientific and technological rationality and certifies that their application to the human world can be unproblematic.

Comte projected a vastly influential picture of the progress of civilization. According to Comte, humanity was struggling to pass beyond its early immaturity, which had led to the invention of divine protectors to explain a terrifying world, into a mature outlook which could confront and master the human as well as the physical world by the unaided power of scientific reason.[9] In the Comtean picture, the remnants of the primitive "theological or fictitious" level of knowledge were due to pass off the historical stage, as were their motley successors, the "speculative or metaphysical" notions such as the soul, under the triumphant impact of scientific or "positive" knowledge. In this culminating stage of human cognitive development, exact measurement and application of the principle of cause and effect were enabling modern scientists to render the world predictable. They were thereby able to extend human capacities to control the workings of physical nature and, Comte hoped, the evolution of human society as well.

Neither Comte nor his followers had use for the concern with character formation which had been central to the inherited educational system centered upon the ancient classics. Rather than reshape that inheritance, Comte simply moved to abolish it. The advances in knowledge and power which Comte expected were to result from methodical intelligence working on carefully defined problems in specialized fields, an intelligence which was to be completely detached from moral or cultural understandings. The final achievement, positive knowledge, was to be a unified system of physical and social laws which would make good on positivism's promise of human betterment.

This, with modifications, is the program upon which the modern research university was founded a century or more ago. Of course, the American university has never been a pure type. It has in some places uneasily tried to incorporate the older tradition of the liberal arts college, whose emphases have been at odds with positivism. The universities have also had to respond to the demands of their contributors, their markets, and government as well. These demands have usually been for more directly useful outputs rather than pure science. Still, it has been the idealized Comtean program which has inspired the university's core development ever since.

Positivism's protagonists have been amazingly successful in installing the basic features of Comte's new cognitive complex at the center of industrial civilization. Comte's purpose was to make the new kind of knowledge and the expertise based upon its application the central shaping force of the future. In many ways, his disciples succeeded in fulfilling their master's hopes. However, Comte also realized, as his epigones often have not, that the regime of positive knowledge would make exceptionally austere demands. While science described how things worked, it could not answer the old religious and metaphysical questions. It could not say what the world really was and indeed the desire for such knowledge was one of the chief renunciations demanded of humanity's new "maturity."

Positive knowledge provided facts but carried no values. It approached the world as a set of processes to be neutrally mapped and, if possible, elucidated through the generation of explanatory laws. The secret to the success of modern natural science, the positivists grasped, lay in its stance of objectivity, a deliberate distancing from the observer's interests and beliefs as well as from the world. Following a succession of early modern philosophers, the positivists identified reason exclusively with this methodically detached stance. Viewed in this way, observable processes could be comprehended and, as technology advanced, manipulated to serve human purposes. Hence the close connection between natural scientific knowledge and its instrumental application in technology, the scientific-industrial complex which powers the modern political economy. But the ends for which they were to be manipulated, ends which presumably had something to do with the scientific observer's interests and beliefs, could not themselves be probed rationally.

Ends and meanings were, by definition, the products of something other than reason. In other words, according to Comte's austere picture, science could provide no larger meaning for life. Values could be studied scientifically, their forms and development mapped. But values could not be rationally assessed nor debated. Humanity would henceforth have to find solace through the cultivation of emotional expression, which is all positivism could make of the arts, morality, and religion. The notorious split between the two cultures of the sciences and the humanities, the one the generator of useful factual knowledge, the other the curator of emotive values, remains the enduring legacy of positivist dogma.

It is instructive that Comte thought his discovery too bleak for human consumption in its unalloyed form. He proposed balancing his austere system of knowledge with a consciously constructed religion of social morality. His "religion of humanity," complete with equivalents for most Christian rites, was to replace the old creeds which scientific truth had, he believed, rendered incredible.[10] The aim of Comte's religion of humanity was to calm human anxiety in the face of a meaningless universe and to prevent moral backsliding into self-absorption by building a solidarity upon shared feelings. Its moral expression was to be service to humanity.[11] However, since all values derived from feeling, which was by definition nonrational, Comte found himself having to justify the proposed new religion on grounds of its social utility.

Comte was quite clear about who should provide direction in modern society. That role was to devolve upon the positivistically enlightened savants, engineers, and industrialists Comte saw as the shock-troops of advancing modernity. This has certainly provided a flattering self-portrait for university faculties, among others. The unresolved problem he bequeathed was whence this expert elite were to derive their purposes and values. Nevertheless, positivists have been right in emphasizing the differences between the progress in instrumental knowledge which has come to us from the formal methodologies so prominent in the natural sciences and the interpretive activities typical of other areas of cultural life which do not seem to make "progress" at all. This distinction rests in part upon the institutional differentiation between the processes of markets and technological production which are guided by criteria of instrumental efficiency, on the one hand, and the human activities organized in civil society which aim at very different goals, such as moral agreement or cultural consensus.

The consequences of the scientific and technological triumphalism of modern civilization were well set out by Max Weber in his theory of the progressive "rationalization" of life. By ratio-nalization Weber meant primarily the spread of instrumental means-ends reasoning to ever wider areas of society, a process whose ideal end-point he famously characterized as the "Iron Cage." "The idea underlying the division of labor," according to Ernest Gellner, "is that if you do one thing at a time you do it bet-ter; and moreover, that one 'thing' is to be defined by one criterion, for only then can you tell whether indeed it is being done better or worse."[12] This pattern of thought is what ballistics has in common with genetic research and both have in common with inventors toiling at a better mousetrap—or business strategists trying to undersell their competitors. Once organized within the institu-tional settings of the market or the bureaucratic organization, means-ends thinking improves effectiveness by encouraging the frequent obsolescence of means in the pursuit of goals.

As Gellner notes, however, even highly rationalized societies cannot get by on instrumental automatic pilot. While rationalized organizations may try to minimize human judgment by operating by formalized rules or computer programming, when decisions are to be made at the top they must use a very different kind of think-ing. Where what matters is integration among several goals or kinds of activity, or where overall policy must be considered and evaluated, or where general purposes must be translated into spe-cific judgments in particular contexts, "decisions cannot be effec-tively disaggregated into separate, single-aim issues."[13] In these sit-uations, goals must be compromised as they are blended with other values. Such balancing has long been one of the most prized abili-ties in jurisprudence and statecraft, as development of capacities of holistic, practical judgment was taken as the supreme task of humanistic education. Needing to maintain orientation amid rapid storms of change, modern societies have more rather than less need of these capacities of practical as opposed to technical judgment. In this important way, the ideological triumph of positivism, especially in the university, does not serve us well.

We have seen in earlier chapters how professionalization arose as both a consequence of this enormous expansion of differentiated functions and as a response to the tensions generated by the conflicts among these functions and groups over their interests and goals. Economic efficiency does not automatically produce social justice and peace, nor does military power establish political legitimacy. Modern societies must continually engage in the complicated, ongoing effort to balance their several social processes, some technical and some moral and cultural, from whose interaction the unique freedoms and potentials of modernity arise. That is the task of civic democracy, to which professions can contribute only if they see themselves as parts of an interacting public discussion of these problems. Civic democracy demands the ability to think in terms of complex balances rather than the maximization of effectiveness as measured by a single objective. Unfortunately, this more complex task and vision is obscured by positivism's naive, nineteenth-century faith in an automatically unfolding progress. This unexamined faith is the source of both the narrowness of much of the academy and its nearly invincible self-righteousness.

What, then, must happen if the limitations of the reigning dogma are to be transcended and professional knowledge is to be organically connected to the historical needs of our time? The critical step in this direction lies in the rehabilitation of nonformal modes of rationality which do not screen out the practical, moral, and historical standpoint of both the subjects and the objects of knowledge. That means the rediscovery and expansion of the idea of practical rationality. As Stephen Toulmin has argued, this step enables us to recover the full promise of modernity, a promise at once less grandiose but more humane than the rationalistic conquest of nature pursued by positivists.[14] The second step will be a serious analysis of the social factors which inhibit the potential of practical rationality for transforming professional life. Finally, we will need to develop more effective ways to promote and diffuse such knowledge, within the university, the professional schools, and in the reform of the institutions of professional life.

of technique, the technical model is impotent. But neither is it helpful for establishing such contexts. That requires that the confused, problematic situations of everyday life be somehow transformed into solvable problems. What the technical account leaves out is what Schon calls "problem setting, a necessary condition for technical problem solving." But problem setting is "not itself a technical problem . . . it is this sort of situation that professionals are coming increasingly to see as central to their practice."[18] For example, in medical diagnosis ends are identified and means of treatment are devised only through the interpretation of symptoms as caused by a problem of this or that sort, or because the symptoms respond to some particular regimen.

The kind of skill which makes it possible to appraise situations so that they can be defined as a particular type of problem lies outside the ken of technical rationality. This integrative, practical knowledge is the indispensable prerequisite for both science and technique, though it has always been ignored by positivism. While instrumental reason has posed as the Archimedean point of human action, it is in fact thoroughly dependent upon its much-denigrated complement, practical rationality. Schon's project is to articulate the features of practical rationality in such a way as to place it at the epistemological center of professional expertise.

This alternative account is what Schon calls "reflection-in-action." Once we set aside the dominant model of technical rationality, "which leads us to think of intelligent practice as an *application* of knowledge to instrumental decisions," he argues that "there is nothing strange about the idea that a kind of knowing is inherent in intelligent action . . . that the know-how is *in* the action."[19] Schon provides examples of knowing-in-action which do not require any reference to thought-out rules or theories. He takes his examples from the realms of sport and the crafts, but especially from in-depth analyses of professional work.

From these case studies, a general picture of expertise emerges which is at considerable variance with the positivist view. A good practitioner is indeed a specialist who has learned the rules and

174

basic techniques of a field. He or she "develops a repertoire of expectations, images and techniques" as long as conditions of practice remain fairly routine; over time the practitioner's skills becomes habitual and largely tacit. However, the full dimensions of expertise are only revealed when a professional must respond to new, less defined situations. Here the practitioner's habitualized techniques may be put in play, but now as facets of a holistic capacity to appreciate the novelty of the situation and to redefine it through experiment. For the expert practitioner, these experiments are not simply trial and error. Schon notes that in reflection-in-action, the practitioner "does not keep means and ends separate, but defines them interactively as he frames a problematic situation." Neither does the practitioner separate "thinking from doing, ratiocinating his way to a decision he must later convert to action . . . implementation is built into his inquiry."[20]

Reflective practice, conversation-with-a-situation, is a practical activity, at once a learning and a doing. As a description of professional skill, reflective practice reopens communications between the technical and the practical dimensions of expertise which the technical model of rationality had broken off. This analysis opens to question the long-standing dominance of pure over applied knowledge in the universities and professional schools. This is a particularly baneful institutional residue of positivism. As that account of practice is shown to be seriously flawed, the apparent necessity of this bifurcation of theory and practice is also weakened. One need not be naive about the difficulties involved in such a fundamental institutional change. But one of the most hopeful possibilities such a reform would open up is the development of a far more intimate involvement of the moral-practical dimensions of the humanities and social sciences, as well as the expertise of nonacademic practitioners, within professional education. It also suggests a professional education in which practice is recognized as a potential source of knowledge and cultivated as such rather than relegated to second-rank status as simply an application of independently derived theory.

Beyond Schon's analysis, there is another important implication. The relevant unit of investigation is often not the individual practitioner facing a situation. Especially in the modern organizational professions, the way the larger enterprise is organized plays a crucial role in determining how expertise will be applied and understood: whether in a truncated technical manner or with the full energies of reflective engagement. Because individuals work out professional identities in relation to the organizational contexts they actually encounter, importantly including their formal educational situations, it will be the values operative in these settings which will determine to what degree reflection-in-action actually becomes established in practice. That is, the way organizations institutionalize their practices—and the climate of social interaction in which these organizations operate—is a highly important determinant of the level and quality of professional expertise in any field.

From this institutional perspective, consider a case of "organizational learning" which Schon has detailed. It makes concrete the problems attendant upon extending practical rationality into the contemporary world of the organizational professions. The situation is a business firm making consumer products. The livelihood of the firm and all its employees, as well as its investors, depends upon effective and timely product innovation. This process is organized in a three-level hierarchy of general manager, whose responsibility is to make innovation serve the firm's profitability; the product managers, who seek to develop successful new products; and the technical professionals, who do the actual design work and experimentation. The work is very high stress, which has led to frequent problems of personnel "burn-out" as well as to a disappointing number of wasteful design failures.

The problem did not lie in either incompetence or lack of reflective practice on the part of the professional technicians or managers. Instead, Schon discovered a too-frequent destructive pattern, which went like this: The general manager sought, for reasons of career advancement or even survival in the internally competitive environment of the firm, to devolve as much responsibility for mistakes as possible onto the project managers. They, in turn, were doing the same with the technical professionals. The lower-level workers, then, had a strong need to conceal problems from superiors as long as possible. This led to late "discoveries" of problems by management, followed by too-hasty efforts to correct problems, with everybody trying to protect his or her reputation, which often further slowed and clogged the development process. All the players understood what the problems were, at least from their point of view, but they also knew that these issues could not be safely discussed openly in the firm because it would be read as an admission of timidity or incompetence on the part of those who went public.

The core issue was that the organizational structure, with its system of internal hierarchy and competition for power, impeded extending reflection-in-action from the level of individual professionals confronting their tasks to public analysis and discussion of what was interfering with successful product development. The negative relationships had themselves been established as responses to pressures to maximize competitive individual performance. The chief victims were not only "burned-out" workers but the sense of trust among colleagues in a common enterprise, a trust whose lack was costing the firm dearly in its own competitive struggle. The collective learning capacities of the firm were being actively short-circuited by social and moral, not cognitive, factors, especially the zero-sum, adversarial relationship between higher and lower levels of the firm's hierarchy and among coworkers.[21] These problems had, however, remained invisible from the point of view of formal organizational theory.

In other words, the firm was suffering from self-inflicted negative interdependence. To escape this problematic situation, the firm needed to reform structurally so that the de facto interdependence created among those working together on projects could be recognized and supported to produce positive outcomes. Effecting this change would not be without costs. It would require instituting more job security, flattening the hierarchy of control, and setting up a team-oriented rather than individually focused system of competitive rewards. In addition, the managers would have to reorient their activities to promote mutual trust through continuous sharing of information. All these developments require not only a cognitive advance in organizational learning capacities but a qualitative change of attitude throughout the organization. These advances in collective learning could be expected to pay off by avoiding bottlenecks in product development and burn-out. To work, however, the reorientation would at the same time require the firm's top management to act in good faith with its employees, by entering into relationships as a fully accountable participant rather than as a distant controlling force. One could hazard the prediction that whether management will actually effect these changes is very likely to be decided by their sense of the surrounding social climate: whether it is stable and cooperative enough to allow the firm the time and space it would need to institute such far-ranging reforms.

The pragmatic model of reflective practice, then, opens beyond technical competence to moral and social issues of trust, equity, and civic cooperation. It calls attention to the often vicious interplay of technical rationality and self-defeating organizational logics of the kind displayed by the consumer products firm. The problem often lies in the faulty institutionalization of professional practice in organizations, setting up a squeeze play in which instrumental pressures to maximize technical or economic efficiency weaken professional autonomy. The dominant language of technical rationality only compounds such problems by obfuscating this larger social context.[22] Surmounting this squeeze play will require a new institutional balance between the instrumental aims of economic efficiency and the fostering of habits of non-zero sum cooperation in reshaped organizational contexts. This, in turn, depends upon the organization's social context, which is a much larger and more complex, but nonetheless crucially influential environment.

Genuine professionalism thus requires engagement with moral

and civic purposes as well as technical means, and competence in mutual understanding and compromise as well as knowing how to maximize the attainment of a single goal. Some features of the new economy, such as those trends which put a premium upon innovation and organizational learning, seem to open new possibilities for expanding the scope and importance of practical intelligence in the workplace. These developments could provide the underpinning for a significant expansion of the qualities of professional work, especially initiative and responsibility, much farther in the new workplace. But there are also ominous countertrends at work. Can the new technical possibilities be developed in this way to serve the human and social, rather the purely technological or economic, welfare? A positive answer to this vexing question is closely bound up with the future of reflective practice as the successor to the positivist understanding of professional work.

REFLECTIVE PRACTICE IN THE NEW TECHNOLOGICAL ECONOMY

The question of the future of professionalism in the emerging economy is troubling because of the ambiguities of the new information technology. Among experts in the field there is major disagreement as to how the application of information technology is affecting the worlds of work and business operations and how it can be expected to do so in the near future. Some observers are frankly pessimistic. They note the great potential which the new technology holds for increasing the dominance of capital over labor, on a global as well as local basis, thanks to greatly enhanced capacities to monitor and control workers, effectively restricting the need for skills and discretion to a numerically small elite. They note the long-term decline in the number of workers needed for both manufacturing and clerical functions as technology provides ever more efficient replacements for human labor.

Other observers have made an opposing case. They have emphasized how the new technology and the rapid circulation of capital around the globe are enhancing the importance of skills, especially the cooperative and innovative capacities we have noted above, and the value of settled, well-educated workforces, blurring the contrasts between owners and workers, mental and manual labor.[23] The difficulty is that both pessimists and optimists offer credible arguments. The trends they are debating are both visible but hard to assess, and still developing.

More importantly, much of the outcome hangs not on deterministic forces but on political decisions concerning how the new technology will be integrated into institutional forms and what ends will guide those processes. The important questions concern whether the reflective dimensions of engaged practice will be augmented in the new workplace, and whether we can expect reflective capacities, should they expand, to develop in ways that recognize the full ethical and civic dimensions of modern work.

In the Age of the Smart Machine, by Shoshana Zuboff, provides a close-up look at these ambiguities in the lives of workers, managers, and technical professionals in a variety of industries. Zuboff asks how the new information technology is influencing patterns of work, as well as how existing relations of custom and authority constrain the possibilities inherent in the technology. Zuboff found that the institutional contexts of work, particularly forms of managerial authority which derive from earlier phases of industrialization, have major influence. These social contexts determine whether the new technologies can realize what she sees as their potential for humanizing work, or are mobilized as additional tools to foster existing patterns of control.[24]

To emphasize the alternative developmental paths which she thinks now confront all developed economies, Zuboff distinguishes two ways in which information technology can be used. She contrasts "automation" with "informating." Automation is the familiar application of computers "according to a logic that hardly differs from that of the nineteenth-century machine system"—replacing the human body with a technology that enables the same processes to be performed with more continuity and control. The alternative is something radically novel and discontinuous with the older machine technology. Zuboff calls this informating. Because data control processes generate information about "the underlying productive and administrative processes through which an organization accomplishes its work," this technology makes these operations more visible than ever before.[25] We could say that it opens the possibility for extending reflection beyond individual practices and skills to the organizational context itself.

Because the medium of this enhanced visibility is the interactive electronic network, extraordinary new possibilities result. The information which was once reserved for managers and executives (if it existed at all), can now be fed back into the electronic network, thereby giving workers new potentials for initiative and cooperative involvement in achieving the organization's goals. The same heightened visibility, however, also gives managers far greater power to monitor—and control—workers, thus illustrating the divergent possibilities inherent in the new technology.

Zuboff is sensitive to Donald Schon's point about how much of what we call intelligence is embodied, practical know-how. This was obviously true for the craftsmen de-skilled by the Taylorite organizers of mass production. But she points out that studies of executives reveal that most of their expertise is likewise implicit and bound up with the embodied, public contexts of their work.[26] The history of both factory and office has been one in which whatever tasks could be routinized have been hived off and mechanized, or automated. In many industries, this has produced a workforce composed mostly of semi- or unskilled workers and clerks supervised by managerial staff and executives. The logic of automation simply extends and tightens this system. Its consequence has been an imprisoning workplace in which morale is a persistent problem. Corporations have responded to these difficulties with a variety of efforts to improve the quality of work life, though worker suspicion and resistance has often remained high.

The potential of informating technology, as Zuboff observed it in a variety of contexts, seems importantly different. It works to blur lines separating control from production, and management from workers, making for a more horizontally structured workplace. This is the organizational vision which Zuboff advocates. At the center of the informed enterprise lies the "electronic text," the interactive electronic network in which the internal and external activities of the organization become jointly visible to its participants. Such team-like organizations, Zuboff argues, will be the ones best suited to compete in a global marketplace which rewards, and demands, value-added innovation. This kind of work organization is also far more conducive to the professional style of work than the Taylorite system. It is less obsessed with who controls what, more interactive, more experimental and playful in tone than the old workplace.

The informed workplace also displaces skills, however, from the tacit, embodied knowledge cultivated in shared action contexts to the highly explicit, abstract mode of thinking which is encoded into electronic processing systems. This displacement affects managers and professionals as well as production workers. To function well in the informed enterprise everyone needs what Zuboff calls "intellective skills." These emphasize explicit knowledge, even for those skilled workers and executives who had previously relied mostly on tacit, action-centered knowing. Zuboff illustrates this imperative by showing how electronic machine-controlled systems displace knowing from face-to-face interaction to abstract representations on screens and in data bases. Manipulating, questioning, rearranging these representations requires a high degree of abstract reasoning.

Even executive and professional communication, as it becomes increasingly mediated through the interactive electronic text, becomes more detached from the immediately sensed environment into a highly mediated world of symbols and "information." But this is the realm of the "dark side of cosmopolitanism," those detached symbolic analysts described with apprehension by Robert Reich, the de-contextual "culture of critical discourse" criticized by Christopher Lasch.[27] At this point in the scenario, although Zuboff does not note it, the informed organization begins to appear less different than its automated alternative than it at first seemed. The informed workplace threatens to restrict any culture of reflective practice into the narrow channels of instrumental rationality.

It is therefore appropriate to ask if reflective practice can be expected to survive in the informed organization. As Zuboff's own research shows, the abstract languages of the electronic text have considerable affinities for the stern instrumental logic of economic competition. Zuboff presses her analysis no further than the world of productivity and work, though at points she clearly recognizes the distinctive and essential claims of the moral-practical realm. Is there an institutionally effective way by which practical reason can encompass the detached, intellective thinking enforced by the electronic text? The key issue lies in how the information technology is understood and the context in which it is placed. If it is seen as somehow replicating or replacing practical expertise, then it becomes another agent of technical rationality, out to overtake struggling, imperfect homo sapiens.

That has become the usual understanding of these matters. But there is also a persuasive body of thinking, consistent with the pragmatist understanding of reflective practice, which argues that information processing is not only qualitatively different from embodied intelligence, but is in fact ultimately parasitic upon it. Therefore, the potential of informed organizations lies in using machines to facilitate and amplify the expertise embodied in reflective practice, rather than imagine that one could replace it.

This is the argument Hubert and Stuart Dreyfus make in *Mind over Machine*.[28] Drawing on both the phenomenological philosophy of Heidegger and experience with artificial intelligence and systems engineering, they argue that computer intelligence can be at best a kind of routine competence. By following a hierarchy of rules which define which data or features of the environment to give priority to, the competent human—or machine—can seek goals and achieve purposes. Thus, a competent driver learns to ignore a green traffic light when a pedestrian steps into the vehicle's path. Computers can be programmed to behave in such competent ways, and they may greatly aid in the efficiency of routine functions. But competence is still different from human expertise.[29]

Expertise, as contrasted with competence, can only be achieved in embodied, practically engaged know-how. It cannot be reduced to specified rules and procedures since experts operate holistically, so that "when things are proceeding normally, experts don't solve problems and don't make decisions; they do what normally works."[30] After the fact, an expert design or decision can, of course, be analyzed and reconstructed as a set of procedures. However, the progression from competence to expertise is not to be described as simply a step-by-step build-up of the lower functions. That assumption is the root error of technical rationality. Instead, the progression is "*from* the analytic behavior of a detached subject, consciously decomposing his environment into recognizable elements, and following abstract rules, *to* involved skilled behavior. . . ."[31] At the level of expertise, thinking involves the unconscious recognition of situations as similar to whole remembered ones; it proceeds holistically, by analogy rather than by algorithm. These skills cannot be captured by using rules and explicitly described features, though routine competence can be so described and reproduced.

These reflections hold startling implications for the informated workplace which force us to qualify any purely positive assessment of its potentials. One implication is that to the extent that workers come to see expertise as a function of large knowledge bases and masses of inferential rules, they will fail to progress beyond the level of competence and so diminish the "social intelligence" available to an organization. Without a strong culture of reflective, expert practice, we can now say, the leap beyond competence to expertise will be inhibited. The designers of the electronic texts and the leaders of informated enterprises "may ultimately discover that their wells of true human expertise and wisdom have gone dry."[32]

LIMITS TO THE EXPLOITATION OF EXPERTISE

If this line of argument is correct, engaged expertise at work in reflective practice turns out to be central to the core technologies of the new economy. But the significance of the rediscovery of practical rationality is far wider than simply the critique of positivism or even of models of formal rationality. Most importantly, the appreciation of practical rationality reveals the linkage between the technical and the moral dimension of expertise. Skills depend upon embodied intelligence. This intelligence, however, is itself embedded in the character of human agents. But neither are these characters atomic bits. Rather, human intelligence and character develop within specific kinds of social context which are shaped by shared aims and values. Human agency, that is, grows out of an ecology of institutional life in which agents embody, modify, reject, or further develop common repertoires of skill, understandings, and purposes. The rediscovery of practical reason thus leads us to recognize the need to protect and foster human social ecologies as well as natural ones. And that recognition includes an awareness that, precisely as free agents, all are implicated in both the nurture and the instrumental exploitation of these ecologies; that we are all interdependent. The question is whether we, especially those with professional expertise, can render that interdependence positive: whether we choose to become citizens.

The point can be made in economic idiom, a language which typically assumes, in the image of the "rational actor," that human motives are reasonable only if their aim is the satisfaction of individual preference. It is now widely recognized that in the new economy, physical capital, the means of producing wealth, is increasingly dependent upon the cultivation of human capital, the skills and capacities of a workforce. This is part of what Daniel Bell and others have called the transition to a postindustrial economy. What is less obvious, but which follows from our argument, is that this human capital is a resource which can only develop in the right social environment, a fact which limits the applicability of purely instrumental strategies, even for economic growth. Nurturing social capital in the form of viable families, schools, and communities, recent research by James Coleman and associates suggests, is the sine qua non for the development of human capital or skills as measured by educational achievement.[33] One might then argue that a viable modern economy cannot be sustained without considerable social investment in the social capital of families, schools, and communities, especially for the most vulnerable members of society. Or, as Robert Putnam's studies of Italian regional governments revealed, "The social capital embodied in norms and networks of civic engagement seems to be the precondition for economic development as well as for effective government. Development economists take note: civics matters."[34]

The alternative to thoughtless exploitation of social capital is not a rejection of instrumental reason or technological progress—these are among the most valuable of all human achievements—but rather a different way of relating these human capacities to the historically and socially embodied life of persons and communities. Trust, the primary coin of human capital, is analogous to what economists call a "public good." All need to draw upon it to accomplish individual ends, but contributing to it does not primarily benefit the individual donor. Rather, as a public good, trust confers its benefits on all. Maximizing public, as opposed to private, goods requires operating in different ways, asking how to best organize technique to support valuable practices and the institutions which give the instrumentalities their focus and continuity.[35]

Within the professions themselves, practical reasoning needs renewed articulation as part of the recovery of the civic dimension of professionalism. In the field of health care, for example, it is the goods of care and benevolence which have traditionally been intrinsic to healing that enable expertise to realize its full potentials, not just treating interesting technical problems but restoring real human lives, with histories, needs, fears, and purposes.[36] While articulating this alternative view is not in itself enough to reorient entrenched practices, it is nevertheless vital to the recovery of professionalism as a moral source, and of the moral sources of professionalism as well.

DIRECTIONS FOR REFORM

Reconceiving professional expertise according to the notion of reflective practice reveals the importance of experience and service to the professional enterprise. It also expands the idea of the career open to talent beyond what seemed possible during the era of the organizational professions. The new understanding needs to be incorporated into the system of selection and certification for professional competence either by making service and experience prerequisites for admission to professional programs or by making these activities integral to the process of professional education itself.

Modern interdependence requires that specialization be integrated more by teamwork than by centralized direction. The desirable change is from stiff organizational hierarchies bolstered by amassed credentials toward partnership networks in which demonstrated competence confers authority. A more permeable and flexible organization of the professions is the logical extension of those developments, and the university needs to be a critical participant in these developments.

Because real expertise is never entirely separable from communities of practice, it is never fully purified of social and moral engagement. Thus, its contemporary institutional expression will be partnerships among organizations united in efforts to respond to the problems and possibilities of the society. This kind of cooperative approach necessarily promotes practitioners and the affected communities into a situation of dialogue with theorists in the academy. But students in professional schools, as they become involved in theoretically informed participation in these cooperative efforts, also need to appreciate both the practical nature of expertise and their own responsibility to the enterprise they have joined.

This reorientation, however, requires that faculty and practitioners develop mutual trust and share jointly in reshaping the professional disciplines away from fixation upon rigid bodies of established knowledge into more supple interactive networks of investigators. The internal structure of disciplinary organization and rewards must be restructured accordingly. To facilitate the transition from the technical to the practical understanding of expertise, it is especially important to articulate and strengthen informed, synthetic thinking in professional school curricula and professional continuing education. In the positivist era, the method of the mathematical and natural sciences was the one model which all inquiry sought to approximate. The postpositivist university is likely to be more pluralistic yet more interactive, requiring more reciprocal understanding and flexible cooperation among participants. In this context, the humanistic disciplines, cast as media and traditions of communication, reflection, and judgment, become greatly more important to the success of the entire enterprise.

Suggestions for how such a reformed system of professional education might look are partially available in some European nations. Germany, for example, has gradually developed a highly effective national system for producing well-trained technicians in virtually every area of the economy. Coordinated nationally, orchestrated by regional governments, but administered and paid for by a collaboration among local government, business, and labor unions, Germany provides high quality academic training plus intensive mentoring on the job for virtually all youth. The system has built-in flexibilities in allowing for changes of field while its academic rigor provides a basis for subsequent retraining. Interestingly, in contrast to the rigid separation in American industry between professional and nonprofessional work, a third of German engineers have first had apprenticeship experience and then gone on to higher educational experience, typically while in the employ of the same firm.[37]

In the area of educational reform, the European systems are not models ready for imitation. They typically emphasize only academic technical knowledge and practical job skills. But within this obvious limitation, they demonstrate the value of a broad ethos of social partnership, showing how effective education today depends upon a high level of public cooperation among the key sectors of society. Bedeviled as American culture is by the twin obsessions of individual mobility and the technical fix, Americans have often placed their faith in either the market or government regulation, switching angrily from one to other after inevitable disappointment, while giving relatively little attention to the development of social cooperation beyond the local level. However, as we have seen, in education as in expert skills, the key to success has to do with civic capacities, especially proficiency at supporting long-term cooperation among divergent groups.[38]

That kind of cooperation only works among participants who can learn to understand the situation and orientation of others, citizens who recognize that they nevertheless share long-term interests. The most serious obstacle to this kind of public cooperation is the nation's unhappy heritage of racism. As W. E. B. Du Bois noted at the beginning the century, racial prejudice and oppression engendered a "double consciousness" among those African Americans who aspired to full citizenship and participation in national life. Even today, the long-lingering effects of racism can distort and inhibit the reciprocities of understanding which civic democracy demand, making it hard for minority professionals to develop that "better and truer self" celebrated by Du Bois which does not eliminate the facets of doubleness but unites and affirms them in the wider civic identity of the democratic promise.[39]

American history can provide hope but no clear conclusion about the nation's capacities in this regard. But if the United States proves able to fulfill its democratic aims, it will be because Americans have committed themselves to the long-term task of nurturing civic capacities among all groups in the society. This effort provides the raison d'etre for a civic professionalism. One potentially encouraging development in this direction is the growing interest, among practitioners and the public at large, in the ethics of professional life.

7

CONFRONTING
MORAL AMBIGUITY:

The Struggle for Professional Ethics

"One bad ethical decision," warns the ad copy for a new professional newsletter, "could destroy your career." But for the low subscription price of $148 the informed professional can "forestall costly lawsuits, avoid unnecessary conflicts with patients, and minimize the time spent with institutional review boards." Taking care to be ethically correct, from the professional's side at least, can signal simply canny self-protection. Indeed, everywhere the message to professional practitioners and aspirants is to focus on self-interest in the narrow sense. The lay public seems less and less to look to the doctor or lawyer for wise counsel. Today the concern is whether the professional's malpractice premiums are paid up.

The evident worry among physicians that ethics is somehow about self-protection seems to confirm from another angle why calls for health care reform began to gain widespread hearing during the 1990s: Americans were unhappy with their system of health

191

care. Compared to a decade earlier, fewer people felt satisfied with the health care they were able to obtain, and a majority believed that doctors were "unfair in the prices they charge." Americans, it turns out, were considerably less happy with their health care system than are citizens of countries such as Canada and Great Britain. As *Time* magazine concluded, public hostility toward physicians was on the rise and "doctor bashing has become a blood sport."[1] These findings suggest that the rising concern with professional ethics has other sources in addition to a possible upsurge in conscience among practitioners.

Compared to other industrial countries, medicine in the United States has long enjoyed an extraordinary degree of autonomy. The result, until very recently, has been physician-controlled health care. The record is one of impressive achievements in health care for many, and yet also a case of abused autonomy and failed public responsibility. It is noteworthy that, compared to Canada and the Western European countries, the United States has consistently lagged in the areas of public health, preventive medicine, and universal inclusion in health care benefits.[2] As recently as the 1960s, however, medicine appeared to be the model of a mature profession.

The professions once seemed to be embodiments of the American middle class aspiration to contribute something of value to the world while achieving a respectable status. As we have seen, the professional ideal gained legitimacy in the United States not just as a middle class notion but as having value for everyone. Not that everyone was expected to become a professional. Rather, the professions' espoused values of competence, dedication, and service concretized a vision of how technical expertise could be made socially useful, leading individual ambition to serve the larger good. The spirit of professionalism was invoked to leaven that heaviness which monetary self-interest often imparts to ordinary occupations.

The economic dynamism of commercial competition has typically gone together with considerable economic inequality, and nowhere more so than in the United States. This has recurrently posed problems for a nation committed to democracy. An increasingly complex, technological division of labor has increased the demand for specialization, with its concomitant diversification of social perspective. For reformers earlier in the century, professionalism seemed to provide a way to mitigate these tensions. The merchant might for the sake of personal gain provide whatever was asked for. By contrast, the professional, guided by an understanding of public responsibility, could be trusted to render what was needed. By combining learning, skill, and public service professionalism itself became an ethical ideal.

Since the high-water mark of confidence in professionalism during the first postwar decades, however, that ideal has come under increasing criticism and attack.[3] As we have seen in earlier chapters, conspicuous failures of public policies formulated by experts in the arenas of urban reform, social welfare, and education fueled skepticism about professional claims to superior knowledge. The abuse of privileged positions by greedy professionals without effective control by their peers or public oversight has weakened the public legitimacy of professional self-regulation. In a less stable, more interrelated yet highly competitive economic environment, bonds of reciprocal loyalty between organizations and their employees have been rudely severed during a period of "downsizing," or what was once known as laying off workers.

In response, many groups seem bent on creating laws, rules, or regulations to control the behavior of professionals and managers—but also elected representatives, police, teachers, airline pilots, clerical workers—all of whom no longer seem to respond to the norms of custom or conscience. We have witnessed a tremendous rise in anxiety and anger focused on controlling the performance of persons, and sometimes organizations, which perform public functions. That, of course, describes much of the modern workforce. At least as often as it has been constructive, the result has been an enormous expansion in litigation, an escalation of mistrust, and a sense of collective impotence, even demoralization.

Historically considered, this urge to monitor and control at first seems puzzling. It goes against one of the longest observable trends of American life: the expansion and legal legitimation of areas of individual discretion and freedom. In fact, this new anxiety, and the tone of repression and nastiness which it has engendered, points up a great historical conundrum. The problem is that the whole notion of the conscientious discharge of one's function, traditionally described as an ethic of vocation, seems to be breaking down. At the same time, the ever more Byzantine elaboration of rules has failed to satisfactorily replace it. The furor over professional integrity is an expression of the great need modern societies have for professionalism as a reliable social ethic.

A vocation has traditionally meant an inward calling to an ethically guided pattern of life. Through such a life, an individual's abilities acquire value for all by their systematic application to social tasks. The idea, as we have seen, is religious in derivation, as Max Weber showed in his famous study of the Protestant ethic of the calling.[4] In the Protestant tradition a vocation was thought to be the fruit of a "conversion," a socially structured yet personally experienced sense of having been given a special task and thereby having found one's place in life. The idea of a profession, while not identical to this ethic of vocation, still intersects it at many points. The idea of profession implies both a systematic cultivation of certain disciplines and a disinterested, public spirit in the application of these skills.

In modern society, according to the accepted sociological wisdom established by Max Weber, the internalized ethic of vocation is headed for extinction. Along with the old humanistic ideal of education as moral cultivation, Weber argued that the internal spirit of occupational callings was being rendered obsolete by the expansion of technocracy.[5] Weber has proved to be a good prophet, as something like this seems to have gradually occurred, though not as rapidly nor as universally as he believed. The problem about unlimited rationalization is that there are many problems which cannot be resolved simply by applying more external controls, ad infinitum. Short of succumbing to comforting but wildly utopian nineteenth-century beliefs in self-regulating social mechanisms (whether the class struggle or the market), there is a problem of infinite regress. Someone, or some group, must somehow act out of conviction to make any institution function. This is obvious at the level of intimate relationships in institutions like the family. Children, for example, need unfeigned love to develop as human beings. Oddly, the implication of this truism is still resisted when it is extended to larger, more public institutions: but they, too, only work when a large proportion of their participants believe in them and care for them. This is the disposition which is named by the traditional notions of vocation and profession.

In late modern society the conditions of skilled work have become more difficult than ever to routinize through the application of external rules and controls. Where creative, responsive thinking and sustained cooperation are required, a successful work process comes to depend increasingly on the inner dispositions of the workers. If the ethic of vocation did not exist, our society would need to invent it now. This is the positive significance of the calls for ethics in the professional fields and indeed throughout the society. People are beginning to grasp with new intensity the objective need for responsible engagement and self-regulation. They are searching for ways to insure professional integrity, aware that it is a public good on which the welfare of all depends, but which cannot be ordered into existence simply by the manipulation of sanctions or rewards. Professional integrity is the outgrowth and legacy of the ethic of vocation. It can only be nurtured, given favorable institutional contexts, among free human agents who come to find an important part of their identity and meaning in the work they undertake.

In order to nurture responsible professionals, the institutional professional order must itself be organized with integrity of purpose. When institutional conditions are good, the causality works both ways, as subjective responses help shape, and are shaped by, the shared forms of practice. However, when the institutional arrangements do not support the development of vocational

195

integrity, a negative, downward spiral results, ending in the promotion of an opportunism which undercuts vocational integrity, producing the cynicism and demoralization notable in troubled areas of the professional enterprise today.

In many areas of American life, arresting this downward cycle and supporting an upward spiral will require something akin to a gestalt switch. Like those drawings in which two different objects can be seen depending upon which lines are perceived as the background and which the foreground, the continuous foregrounding of individual opportunity opened up by economic and technical advance reveals only half the picture. Even instrumental activity ceases to be productive when it consumes its necessary background of loyalties and social bonds, the institutional contexts which limit and direct various means toward their ends.

THE TWO GESTALTS OF PROFESSIONAL ETHICS

Contemporary discussions of professional ethics are complicated today by an argument going on over how best to approach the subject. This argument surrounds two contending philosophical conceptions of the nature and subject matter of ethics: the ethics of principles or rules versus an ethic of virtue or character. These two ethical theories take their orientation from the two contending gestalts through which modern society is understood.

The first, culturally dominant gestalt is that of philosophic liberalism. Liberal ethics has strong affinities for the familiar view of society as a realm in which individuals pursue their purposes either alone or in concert with others through activities instrumental in nature. It understands society as a field of opportunities for inventing one's own life, guided and constrained by institutional mechanisms governed by rules, among which ethical norms hold a prominent place. Accordingly, liberal ethics center attention on the value of autonomous decision making. By contrast, the focus of the second approach to ethics is upon character and mores, those shared habits of character upon which individual responsibility and virtue

196

depend. According to the ethics of character, moral rules play at most a secondary role in ethical life; the real focus of ethics should be on the delineation and development of good patterns of judgment and action.

The analytic ethics of principles derives its substance from the philosophic liberalism of Immanuel Kant and John Stuart Mill. For both Kant and Mill ethics was properly based upon principles of reason which are universal in the sense that they apply to all moral agents. These principles were also universal in that they could be justified by each moral agent on the basis of independent reflection. Ethicists who follow Kant's "deontological" or duty-ethics emphasize the rightness or wrongness of particular actions, asking whether an action could be made the general rule for all in a similar situation. Those who espouse Mill's revised utilitarian principle of universal benevolence stress the importance of consequences for judging the moral validity of a particular rule: Will adherence to it advance the welfare of persons generally? From these procedures come the familiar ethical principles such as Do no harm, and Tell the truth.

Despite differences in the ways in which they seek to justify their principles, adherents of rule-ethics agree that the commanding focus of attention should be occupied by the autonomy of moral agents, the ability of moral agents to think and act for themselves. Choice, in the sense of autonomous decision, represents for both deontologists and utilitarians the crucial moral source. This liberal ethic, whose contemporary form is sometimes identified as analytic ethics because of its derivation from the mid-twentieth-century philosophy of linguistic analysis, stresses the notion that ethics is above all about planning one's life well, which means making the right choices.

Within the ethics of principles, the applied ethicist is often cast in the role of coach. The ethicist's task is to provide professionals with a grasp of the whole theory of ethical norms and their justification, in order to make professionals more competent in the application of these principles.[6] "Apply" is used in analytic ethics in a particular sense of "deduce." Analytic ethicists use ethical cases to develop students' abilities to describe actions and situations so that they can be fitted into the general principles elucidated by theory. Of particular importance for this approach to ethics is the use of cases, known as quandaries, in which several principles seem to conflict. For example, how should a doctor respond to a heart patient whose delicate situation makes it likely that knowing the gravity of her situation could precipitate heart failure: should avoiding harm take precedence over truth-telling, or not? By using cases of increasing complexity and difficulty, the ethicist hopes to elicit from students a greater facility in applying ethical norms.

In their treatments of professional ethics, ethicists writing in this tradition have emphasized the individual professional in relation to clients, with the communities of practice and the organization of professional work often reduced to a background. As, for example, physicians and their institutional contexts are undergoing the stresses of growing complexity and interdependence, it is not surprising that doctors would be unclear about who they are becoming and what they should do. It is just such situations which create the demand, as Robert Veatch has written, for "some ordering of that chaos we term a tradition, some systematic structuring of medical ethics."[7] The purpose of this ordering, according to Veatch, is that "physicians, other health professionals, government health planners, and consumers of medical care . . . can have some grasp of where they stand and why they may be in conflict with others with whom they interact."[8]

Veatch proceeds to argue the need for ethical theory in the special, technical sense. Such a theory aims to produce a set of universal principles "governing social relationships" in general. Only from the perspective of such a unified theory of ethical norms, which would be applicable to all social relationships, can we hope to deduce appropriate principles for the guidance of medical relationships. Medical ethics, in other words, would become a special case of the more general theory.[9]

Certainly part of the appeal of this conception of professional ethics derives from its use of a rhetoric borrowed from the natural sciences. A general theory is to provide the principles governing all phenomena within a specified domain, thus providing the basis from which to deduce the special theories applicable to particular domains, such as medical relationships. The analytic split between theory and application also has obvious affinities with the familiar positivist conception of the relation of theory to technological application. In this approach to ethics, particular cases, ranging from confidentiality to abortion to euthanasia, can—so the theory goes—be resolved once they have been subsumed under the appropriate rules and principles. It is a style of ethical thinking which resonates with the great concern in bureaucracies and organizational settings about rules of procedure. Like the scientist or the organizational theorist, the applied ethicist is wont to speak in terms of "universal" theory, thereby drawing a sharp contrast to the "chaos that we term a tradition."

The rival approach focuses not upon rules but on the notion of ethos, or character, understood as a cultivated disposition toward good values. Its starting point is the observation that all individual opportunities are always also situations of interdependence. The very existence of individual choices and rights depends upon the disposition of other persons to respect and facilitate individual projects. At the minimum, these dispositions to cooperate and reciprocate, to respect rights and adhere to rules, require cultivation and support. The virtue approach thereby emphasizes what the ethics of principles takes for granted: that the most precious of modern values, the sacredness of individual lives, requires conscious attention and collective support. That is, the liberal values of freedom and equality cannot be sustained without the cultivation of reciprocity, trust, loyalty, and public spiritedness, the bedrock of civic culture.

This virtue-ethics or the ethics of character is currently enjoying a revival, thanks in part to the problems and lacks within the ethics of principles. Deriving from the practical philosophy of Aristotle, whose conception of practical rationality we met in previous chapters, this tradition was a source upon which the pragmatists Dewey and Mead drew in developing their psychologies and moralities of engagement and responsibility. Here "theory" means something quite different from the set of formal principles prized by analytic ethics. Theory, for the virtue tradition, is not so much a body of general principles as a search for a connected view of things.

This kind of theory develops in close relation to concrete cases and experience. Its function is not primarily to deduce solutions to ethical problems or to prioritize rules in the event of a conflict among duties. Instead, theory should assist reflection and contribute to the development of moral judgment.[10] Applying principles and rules requires judgment and, as even Kant had noted, the act of judgment whereby "the practitioner decides whether or not something is an instance of the rule" cannot always be guided by a rule, for that would create a regress of rules "that could go on indefinitely."[11]

For the virtue approach, professional moral discernment is thought to be learned and practiced together with the skills of a particular professional practice. The highest ethical achievement is understood as "practical wisdom," the *phronesis* which Aristotle wrote about, meaning the ability to act well in context. Practical wisdom, as we have seen in the discussion of practical rationality, demands the ability to balance the complexity of situations while maintaining consistent moral aims. An ethics of character finds its natural medium in the narrative of cases and the analysis of the historical dynamics of institutional contexts. So, while the ethicist who works within this tradition is also likely to use cases to elicit ethical thinking, the aim is to develop habits of moral cultivation rather than to solve quandaries.[12] Thus, one is more likely to emphasize examples and the contextual variations of life-decisions than to seek the best single decision in terms of theoretical principles.[13]

Both of these approaches to ethics, the one foregrounding individual initiative, the other highlighting interdependence, hold up important aspects of social reality which correspond to two of the three key dimensions of professional life. The ethics of principles articulates the truth of liberalism, the ethical value of individual choice and dignity, which is crucial for professional life. The ethics of character, on the other hand, emphasizes the communitarian truth, that meaning arises through relationship, making individual liberty dependent upon responsibility defined through communal expectations.[14] This corresponds to the dependence of the professional's individual human capital upon the social capital of the professional community.

As in professional life, so in the broader society, the tendency toward individual differentiation often pulls against the requirements of membership or integration into a social enterprise. Yet, both tendencies need each other. They are parts of the complex whole of a viable society or meaningful human life. Finding the balance, however, and the institutional conditions which can sustain that balance, are not simple tasks. The necessity for the third, civic perspective is precisely the need for trustworthy contexts which allow individuals and groups to better understand each other by seeing their own situations in light of the others' perspectives. Over time, and if sustained through conflict by a common loyalty to living together, these public dialogues enable a democratic society to generate consensus about ways for integrating individuals into meaningful relationships which enhance rather than erode personal freedom and dignity.

The persistence of conflicts between principles and character ethics, like that between tendencies toward differentiation and integrating efforts—think of conflicts over language in the public schools—illustrates the tensions generated within modern society. The conflicts between opportunity and community, choice and commitment are painful and real. However, they are frequently consequences of social transactions either insufficiently coordinated or too skewed by unequal power to permit the sustained development of mutual responsiveness among participants that characterizes civic democracy. The resolution to the riddle of how to make interdependence work without subordinating individuals to the collective is in large part a practical rather than a theoretical matter. The challenge is to develop publics comprehensive enough to recognize and restructure the often divided processes of interaction so that individuals can recognize themselves and their relationships as matters for common action. Developing an ethic of responsiveness is an important step toward enabling citizens, including professionals, to better engage the actual conditions of their lives and to more fully engage one another in a common effort. Such an effort at ethical reflection, in which deliberation is already an aspect of public action, takes account of the social grounding of the values prized by liberal theorists of autonomy as well as the vocational engagement central to character ethics.

THE PSYCHOLOGY OF ENGAGEMENT AND THE ETHICS OF VOCATION

Certain trends in psychological research provide useful insight into the conditions which can sustain vocational excellence while enhancing individual initiative. There is powerful evidence that creative engagement in activities, relationships, and social purposes is the key source of human identity and happiness. This is because attention, or the investment of psychic energy, is the way in which human beings develop and structure their personalities. The self, that elusive Holy Grail of contemporary culture, is from this perspective a function of how human beings focus their energies. The self grows by cultivation, but self-cultivation demands, paradoxically, an outward focus. In taking care of our gardens, our relationships, or our communities, we are literally making ourselves. As Mihaly Csikszentmihaly illuminated in his book, *Flow*, learning to focus attention in action is the source of whatever purpose or harmony human beings achieve in life. It is the key to so-called "intrinsic motivation."[15] Engagement with the present moment in all its prosaic, unfinished character turns out to be the magic door to the richness of life.

Upon reflection this process of cultivating meaning by caring for the things, persons, and practices of our world becomes less mysterious, if no less amazing. "When a person invests all her energy into an interaction," writes Csikszentmihaly, "she in effect becomes part of a system of action greater than what the individual self had been before." This "system of action" is typically a structured social practice which is informed by implicit norms and values and contains a purpose which can be achieved poorly or well. Through learning to take part in the activities of the practice, the individual self "expands its boundaries and becomes more complex than it had been."[16] Indeed, Csikszentmihaly notes that persons so engaged typically report a series of experiences which he calls the "flow" response, the term they themselves frequently use and gave him the title of his book.

Engaged persons report that, provided their capacities are such as to be challenged but not overwhelmed by the intrinsic demands of the activity, and that the activity is sufficiently structured to provide clear clues to performance, their self-consciousness disappears, time seems to slow down, and "they realize that they are willing to do it for its own sake . . . even when difficult or dangerous."[17] The continued practice of any such patterned engagement does indeed cultivate certain dispositions. This can be readily observed among the practitioners of a sport, a craft, or a professional skill. Practice develops a disposition to engage in the activity for its own sake, indeed to want to continue the practice. The flow experienced in such engagement is the chief motivational force driving the development of expertise.

This psychological process has ethical dimensions as well. Particularly striking is the development of the "autotelic" or self-directed personality. This kind of person in effect internalizes as a settled disposition the qualities of the engaged flow experience. Chief among these is the "non-self-conscious individualism" of autotelic people who are "bent on doing their best in all circumstances, yet they are not concerned primarily with advancing their own interests." Or rather, we might say that they have identified their interests with those of the practice or community of practice with which they are engaged.

This makes possible a transcendence of the confines of one's self-image, allowing the person to grow into the larger dimensions of the art, skill, or form of life being engaged. Such self-forgetfulness is the premise of self-development. It is also the root of creativity, that capacity to respond resourcefully to the potentialities inherent in the task or situation at hand. Responsiveness, then, is the presupposition of that practical wisdom engendered in the expert practitioner by attending to "the properties of the system, so that she can find a better way to adapt to a problematic situation."[18]

The development of these psychic dispositions or virtues of engagement is the essential stuff of life. By determining the limits of our concentration, success or failure in developing responsive attention determines our ability to find meaning and fulfillment, not only in work, but life as a whole. But, while each person is ultimately responsible for whether this psychic cultivation takes place or not, humans are intrinsically social beings. The willingness of adults to admit children into their practices of cultivation, the relative harmony or disorder of the family's practices of attention, indeed the disorder or harmony of the surrounding social institutions, powerfully affect each person's chances, and to some extent even ability, to develop meaningful engagement with life. In this way, the psychology of attention must engage with ethical and social issues.

As we have seen, the self develops through the cultivation of attention, shaping it into intentional disposition. But as the pragmatist psychology of meaning insists, since intention is always socially formed, it reaches its proper development in the stance of intelligent responsiveness. Meaning arises not simply out of activity, but out of relationship with human others who already embody in their lives and characters the pattern of a meaningful life built up in community.[19] On this view, interdependence turns out once again to be basic to the human situation, even affecting the most intimate features of individual psychology. Character is therefore essentially a disposition to respond to the world in appropriate ways, determined by how the agent interprets the situations of life.

That interpretation always develops through an ongoing "conversation" with significant others. This is to say that the formation of personality and personal decisions have strongly conversational features. A person acts within a stream of interaction. That person's own actions are thus always responses to the actions of others. Because those actions are interpreted as meaningful, as parts of a significant pattern in which the agent is engaged, even self-initiated actions are shaped in anticipation of how others will respond.

It is obvious that ideally all parties to such interactions benefit in the long run from a willingness to cooperate. This observation provides a kind of basic rationale for an ethic of cooperation and mutual trust. However, whether this is understood by any given group of individuals is heavily dependent upon the actual social "conversation" of which they have become part. So, if the experiential context of life rewards cooperation and trust, the individual will come to accept these attitudes as normal and rational responses to reality. If, on the other hand, experience validates a social context of distrust and threat, defensive self-interest will come to seem to such persons the obviously reasonable stance toward life. Such cycles of trust or distrust, rooted as they are in social relations and not just individual psyches, tend to develop powerful momentum, making the development of a social ethic of mutual trust and reciprocal aid, the key ingredient in a successful and just society, always a precarious project.

In this expanded context, we can now state with greater clarity the principal issue of professional ethics. Because the self is so thoroughly social, the important questions of life, including our most intimate issues of identity, are questions of how best to respond to the larger ongoing conversations which make up our social world. Freedom means the capacity to grasp the dynamics of one's situation and respond fittingly and well. Discerning the right and fitting response, however, is the subject of ethics as such. From this viewpoint, professional ethics emerges in important part as a struggle for existential meaning in the public world of work.

This search for integrity, however, goes on among practices

and institutions that sustain purposes which make claims on us. The search for personal meaning inevitably draws us into dialogue and contention with others. It forces us to adopt a stance toward the possibilities offered to us and those others by the social world in which we find ourselves.[20] Professional ethics thus falls within the subject matter of a "politics" in the classical sense of an inquiry into the just and worthy forms of the common life. An adequate conception of professional ethics must therefore move from the questions of individual meaning and vocation through consideration of social and institutional contexts within which these arise and develop. It must include the rules which govern those contexts, seeking to make sense of the dynamics of these social situations so as to deliberate about how to respond to them.

Despite an institutional history which has made professionalism all too likely to take a purely technical bent, insulated as much as possible from the claims of larger purposes, American experience also provides striking examples of professionally trained civic leaders. Examples of this type, which have played major roles at the highest national levels, help illustrate the complex nature of civic judgment. They also reveal why the development of networks of positive interdependence must be a preeminent goal of civic politics. George Catlett Marshall was such a figure, a citizen-soldier in the line of Washington. Chief of staff for the entire Allied war effort during World War II, then secretary of state under Harry Truman, Marshall is most famous for his plan for the postwar reconstruction of Europe, a cooperative arrangement between the United States and Western European nations which laid the basis for the European Economic Community.

Marshall was a professional soldier, educated at the Virginia Military Institute, and a decorated combat officer of World War I. But through appointments as military attaché to diplomatic missions, Marshall gained an extraordinary understanding of the interplay between politics, commerce, and military force in world affairs. According to Dean Acheson, who succeeded Marshall as secretary of state, Marshall grasped the hard fact that relations among states pose problems which are "not susceptible to an answer" but only to "an action which is less disagreeable than some other action when probably no action is altogether good."[21] Marshall, according to Acheson, excelled in the prudence of the Aristotelian *phronimos*, or person of practical wisdom. Marshall could take his bearings in a complex situation, and engage with the dynamics of the situation through the medium of his specific knowledge, turning his province of expertise into a useful point of entry toward seeking a positive outcome to the larger processes in which he found himself engaged.

Those qualities came to the fore in Marshall's conception of the plan for postwar European reconstruction. In surveying the social and political problems confronting the Europeans after the war, Marshall had been struck by the deleterious effects of a decade during which interconnections of all kinds, cultural and intellectual as well as commercial, had been broken by the fascist drive for national self-sufficiency. As Marshall saw it, the only lasting road to economic prosperity lay through building connections across the frontiers of the traumatized continent, thereby sowing the seeds of new forms of interdependence which could generate a new, more pacific European civilization.

It is equally noteworthy that in the speeches in which he set out the idea for the reconstruction plan, to groups at Princeton and Harvard, Marshall proclaimed the need for Americans, especially American leaders, to "renew in their minds" the "period of the Peloponnesian Wars and the Fall of Athens," a fall which Marshall stressed was due largely to the arrogance of Athenian power. Marshall intended this as a warning against the hubris of taking one's own interests, personal, group, or national, as identical to the good of others.[22] While Marshall's warning went tragically unheeded at home, as the history of the cold war in general and Vietnam in particular would show, his aim of building the basis for a stable Atlantic peace succeeded. However, his efforts to bring these matters before the American public, as well as his counsel about how to consider them, stand as powerful reminders of the possibilities as well as the limitations of public judgment.

"MODERNIZED OLD AGE" AND THE QUESTION OF THE GOOD LIFE

Whether or not the public is ready for such complex deliberation, contemporary society is already facing challenges which call for the exercise of not only informed professional judgment but public judgment that is informed by professional expertise. To illustrate, consider the difficult case of health care in our increasingly aging society. Recently, Daniel Callahan has effectively shown the moral significance of health care for the most fundamental questions about our civilization, arguing that these are problems which require collective deliberation and a response which is not only ethical but political in its classic sense. Callahan questions whether the dominant liberal ethical and political understandings are adequate to guide American society as it confronts increasingly difficult choices concerning medicine and aging. We will follow Callahan's argument part of the way in order to suggest how such work may lead toward much-needed supplements for the inadequacies of the liberal model of professional ethics, and toward a wider understanding of ethics as integral to professionalism in a democracy.

In *Setting Limits* Daniel Callahan has described how the technological augmentation of the powers of medicine has encouraged an expansionary vision of life and health. This expansionary vision has strong affinities for the liberal vision of the good life. Its practical premise is the same set of institutional arrangements which has undergirded the growth of the consumer society, and like that form of life, the expansionary vision of life and health has met any notion of limit as a threat to autonomy.

In what Callahan calls the "modernization of old age," the later years of life have come to be looked to as a time for individual self-realization beyond responsibilities to the younger generations or society at large. Long life and health have become normal expectations, not the results of good fortune. "Modernized" old age, writes

Callahan, "is no longer a time of old-fashioned disengagement and preparation for death." Instead, it becomes a "continuingly active involvement in life and a persistent struggle against decay and demise."[23]

The consequences of this change have been profound. "Medicine becomes not just a way of curing or controlling disease, but no less a way of trying to cure or control the problems of life."[24] Life itself seems to shake off its traditional limits and open up to an ever greater, if not indefinite, expansion of possibilities for individual self-actualization. Accordingly, modern medicine's promise of escape from suffering and early death has become so important that it has implicitly become accepted, even demanded, as a right which all Americans should be able to enjoy.

Unfortunately, if Callahan is correct, this whole vision is running up against major obstacles, the most intractable of which are of technological medicine's own making. The first problem is that the high-technology, acute care medicine which has in many cases extended life is often also responsible for plunging the aged into years of prolonged suffering. Medicine has improved the situation of aging for many elderly people. This is one of its great achievements. On the other hand, medicine's single-minded concentration upon extending life at any cost often has, especially for those in the seventies and over, the debilitating effect of consigning the patient who becomes ill to a painful, dependent, and financially exhausting life which is a cruel caricature of the promise of "modern maturity."

The second problem Callahan identifies is economic, and ultimately, social. Demographically, America is becoming an aging society. Both as a proportion of the population and in absolute numbers, far more people are reaching the biblical "four-score and ten" and beyond. As the post–World War II baby boom ages, the nation's population will become progressively top-heavy as a larger and larger proportion of citizens reach old age. At the same time the cost of aggressively extending life at its upper limits has grown enormously. Increasingly, Callahan argues, the United States will face conflict which pits the old against the young. How will the nation justify the commitment of an increasing proportion of national resources to people in the last years of life when it means that fewer resources can go to education or child care, and that the future must be mortgaged to prolong the lives of the aged with chronic illness?

The third problem is less obvious, but in the long run it is the most unsettling. Callahan claims that our technology-driven medicine, together with the individualistic understanding characteristic of a "modernized" old age, undercuts its own premises. A just allocation of resources among the generations will require some widely accepted and reasonably durable notion of human needs, especially the particular needs of the aging. But the development of new medical technologies makes it clear the what counts as "need" is really a conception of the good. Needs are artifacts of public deliberation, a "reflection of what we think people require for an acceptable life."[25]

A modernized conception of life sees endlessly open choices as the self-evident good, one which justifies itself by the experience of increasing happiness. Driven by technological progress, a society so guided leaves it up to individuals to work out the practical meaning of "an acceptable life." This is something, however, which few persons, whatever their age or situation, have sufficient resources for doing by themselves. The liberal assumption that individuals are best left on their own in the realm of meaning, when acted upon, only adds to the difficulty of arriving at a consensus about what Callahan calls "the wellsprings of moral obligation toward the elderly in general and our elderly parents in particular." This poverty of articulable shared meaning hampers collective decision making and amounts to a serious "communal deficit."[26]

The lack of widely shared convictions about moral obligation afflicts the elderly in a special way. In a social climate suffused with the ethos of open choices uncomplicated by the complexities of solidarity, the point of their lives and their place and value in the world go unaffirmed. Often they are simply ignored. This, too, is exacerbated by the conjunction of technology-driven modernization with individualism. The elderly, particularly as their strength fails, must struggle to maintain their self-worth against a context which exalts only autonomy and expanding horizons.

As society approximates in some areas of practice the open horizons vision of liberal theory, then, the outcomes violate many of our considered moral convictions about mutual connection and responsibility. Modern economics and technology have produced real gains in longevity and opportunity which are essential to preserve. However, in order to be humanly meaningful, these gains must be connected to the sort of life-defining goods Callahan enumerates. Among these he places the opportunity to do meaningful work, share human love, participate in the full range of family life, live in community, and pursue moral ideals. These goods are indeed open choices, but they are also more. They represent possibilities for a person's participation in social practices from which the individual can draw the capacity to form a lasting character and sense of integrity. Only in this way, Callahan argues, is it possible to find life meaningful in itself.

The price of an unbalanced form of life in which the goods intrinsic to particular practical commitments are subordinated to continuing modernization is not borne only by the aged. Such a culture can make scant provision, Callahan notes, for coping with one of the consequences of the vast increase in the numbers of the dependent elderly: they are increasingly being returned to their children for care. The results are often oppressive and "our secular morality (though not perhaps our religious traditions) provides few resources for living lives of unchosen obligations."[27] The point is not to rationalize an enforced mobilization of the younger to sustain elders the collective provision cannot or will not support. Rather, it is to suggest how morally bankrupt our culture of "modernized old age" is when confronted with the problem of learning to live well in the face of limitation.

The conclusion Callahan draws is that if we are to deal in a just and humane way with the changing national needs for medical care, we must undertake a "major effort to reorient medicine away from its captivity by the modernizing, technology-driven, borderless 'medical need' model of care for the aged." Life-extending treatment must be given in light of a "natural life span," the borders of which will vary across individuals, so that the key policy goal becomes a fuller rather than a longer life span where the latter is bought at the price of chronic illness, suffering, and burdens on others. This effort will require a "parallel reorientation of the general public," who, like physicians, will be reluctant to give up their old "captivity" to the mirage of ever-expanding horizons promised by technological medicine.[28] For the sake of a life worth living, we must freely embrace limitation.

The really difficult conclusion is that such a massive policy change "can be morally acceptable only within a context that accords meaning and significance to the lives of the individual aged and recognizes the positive virtues of the passing of the generations."[29] That is to say that a morally tolerable system for providing health care can only take root if it functions within, and lives symbiotically with, a vital culture of civic values. Achieving this reorientation of policy, Callahan concedes, will require a long process of public debate and persuasion. We may note that it will also demand new emphases in the education of professionals to prepare them to sustain the sort of connections and continuous dialogue that this ongoing process requires.

That process, in turn, will require institutional arrangements which open up space for public discussion about the ends medicine should serve and its means. For such discussion to take place, neither technological necessity nor economic pressures can be allowed to work automatically. To make such dialogue fruitful, a medical ethic concerned with more than autonomy and open choices, valuable as these are, is clearly a necessity. Physicians must be especially attentive to restoring health and alleviating human suffering, yet also aware that these goods are part of a large fabric of meaning to which their work and institutions contribute. Medical problems, such as the continuation of life when the biological gains can only be small and the quality of life improved even less, are also moral problems and will have to be defined as such. The aim of cure at all costs must be reintegrated within the more encompassing goals of compassion and care for the aging person's life in its integrity.

The complicated situation of aging in American society is a microcosm of the many webs of interdependence which the developing technology and economy have woven, often over the heads of participants. This complexity, unless it is mastered cognitively and given moral meaning through reshaping our institutions, is likely to produce a host of unintended miseries, such as those ironically generated by increasing longevity when it is accompanied by chronic illness. Professionals are often those most strategically placed to begin focusing public attention on these issues. They are also often the groups first charged with dealing with them. The moral integrity and civic capacities of professional groups is accordingly a significant public concern.

The question becomes, can professionals in their individual and collective lives learn to think and act cooperatively with us, as both experts and citizens?[30] These are the defining questions for a professional ethics of responsibility appropriate to our times. Health care is exemplary of the larger tasks of the professional enterprise: the very economic and technological forces which induce self-seeking professional behavior are also generating problems which reveal more clearly than ever before the profoundly civic nature of the professional enterprise. The problems of health care have their analogies in education, the law, journalism, and other professional fields. Just as individual professionals must be in some degree moral philosophers, so professionals in their organizational lives must be active citizens, committed to working out a common good as new problems and possibilities arise.

RENEWING THE MORAL SOURCES OF CIVIC PROFESSIONALISM

Whether professionals play their civic roles well or badly has, as we have seen, a great influence on the welfare of all members of society. But, under contemporary conditions, the civic role of professionals increasingly means learning to bring their particular expertise into a larger, more complex deliberation about ends as well as means. The challenges confronting us around modern health care and old age exemplify a larger fact. Most of the really critical issues, from equality for women and minorities, equity and stability in the global economy, the viability of families and communities, to environmental protection cannot be addressed without drawing upon professional expertise. On the other hand, the ability of professional groups to contribute to resolving these problems are, as we have seen, very uneven. Like many of the health care providers and policy makers encountered by Callahan and Prothrow-Stith, or the educators described by Bok, other professionals also lack an understanding expansive enough to be useful in crucial public deliberations.

This is why the furtherance of civic orientations among professionals is becoming increasingly significant. The value of the current interest in professional ethics, then, is that it provides an opening on the agendas of professional reform and public discussion for the concerns of civic professionalism. In order to strengthen civic tendencies in the professions, it is important to work toward a civic public philosophy which can affirm professional concerns while giving them a larger mission. At the same time, it is necessary to press on with the construction of actual social contexts in which professional groups can learn and practice the attitudes of a responsible elite, of what Lester Thurow calls a "progressive establishment." This is a task which cannot succeed without effective enfranchisement of a more diverse and active public of citizens.

Fortunately, there are several moral sources in contemporary American culture which can contribute to an ethos of vocational responsibility. The liberal ideals of free choice and personal dignity remain central to any conceivable good society, but their proponents benefit along with everyone else once they recognize that these ideals can only be realized through the cultivation of social and personal virtues, as some liberal thinkers have come to accept.[31] But the adherents of virtue ethics can also benefit from a serious engagement with the importance to their own purposes of those very liberal values of self-direction and responsibility for oneself.

To these should be added the important contributions of religious ideas, especially of biblical covenant, which have been so important in American life. In covenantal morality, obligations arise for professionals from the relationships which have made their practice possible, connections with the past as well as to colleagues, clients, and institutions. In this view, these benefits demand in return a loyalty on the part of recipients to handing on these goods to others.[32]

Feminism and environmentalism, among other contemporary social movements, provide articulations of important professional values in ways which have become compelling to many. Several strands of feminist thinking emphasize the importance of struggling to balance the sometimes conflicting values of personal exploration and differentiation with the desire for connectedness and mutual loyalty.[33] Within the environmental movement, some thinkers are drawing on theories developed in modern biological research which see all ecosystems as dependent upon an evolving balance or synthesis between the two polar processes of differentiation and integration. The ecological perspective provides a powerful rationale for understanding the chief ethical imperative as devising patterns of living which can support increasingly individuated yet interrelated growth.

Articulating moral possibilities is vital for solving the problems of professional life. It is equally true, however, that the articulation of meaning is likely to remain confined to the realm of ideas unless it is accompanied by the development of the social

215

bases which render ethical ideals plausible and practicable. For civic professionalism those social bases are the educational system, including its linkages with the occupational domain, and also the networks of social capital among organizations which make a particular place or sector of society able to act in concert to address its needs.

At the level of professional groups and the major organizations which train or employ professionals, there is need for leaders who understand these frequently delicate patterns of relationship on which practical intelligence and civic cooperation depend. At the other end of society, among the large populations of alienated and marginalized citizens, there is also serious need for leaders who can weave networks of mutual recognition to enable the powerless to command respect and so take effective part in democratic life.

This neglected civic role has been taken up by one national organization, the Industrial Areas Foundation. The IAF is actually a kind of support organization of professional community organizers, founded in the 1940s by Saul Alinsky. Today's IAF works toward an explicitly civic vision of democratic empowerment which, starting with the congregations of local religious organizations, works to build larger relationships over time. The aim, in the words of one organizer, the Reverend Leo Penta, a Roman Catholic priest, is to establish "islands of political community, spaces of action and freedom in the sea of bureaucrats, political image-mongers, and atomized consumers."[34]

By concentrating on developing politically effective networks, rooted in local religious loyalties, the politics of the IAF complements the aims of civic professionals in other areas. Leo Penta is correct, even if overstating the case, that all such efforts, no matter how important for the persons involved, will remain mere "islands" of citizenship in a hostile or indifferent sea so long as they remain alone. Like the other examples of dedicated civic professionals encountered earlier, however, the islands of public life created by these efforts provide the basis for a larger archipelago of great potential value.

For all who come to take part in their life, these contexts provide a practical experience and training in the ethical capacities necessary for resolving the harmful exclusions and painful dichotomies which beset contemporary society. Where it successfully takes hold, civic professionalism begins to make integrity a practical rather than a utopian possibility for living.

8

EXPERTS AND CITIZENS:

The Promise of Professional Life

INTEGRITY AND PROFESSIONAL LIFE

In American imagination, integrity is closely associated with the world of professional life. The heroic physician, the fighting lawyer, the dedicated teacher are staples of popular culture, along with the wise judge, the healing nurse, and the crusading journalist. These figures are typically portrayed as moral exemplars whose personal dedication visibly strengthens the larger fabric of the community. Yet, today there is also a widespread perception that professional integrity is breaking down or is seriously at risk of doing so. This anxiety suggests that many people feel socially vulnerable, personally threatened by loss of professional integrity. It testifies to the importance of professional functions in modern society, even when professionals hold little power over others.

Earlier chapters have unraveled this apparent contradiction by developing a critique of professionalism which has linked its moral dimensions to its history and social situation. By viewing professionalism as an evolving social enterprise, that critique was able to highlight the complex interconnection that needs to exist between personal integrity and vocational performance in modern society, for integrity is a particularly modern concern. Modern societies hold out to individuals many vocational choices and opportunities for personal satisfaction. Traditional ties and moral constraints have loosened, yet individual lives have become ever more intricately tied into unseen networks of interdependence, increasing the need for forethought and large-scale cooperation. This conjunction of developments provides both the exhilaration of personal freedom and an increasing burden of individual responsibility. Coherence and significance in modern life are of necessity highly personal achievements and yet deeply dependent upon social relationships.

Integrity mediates these tensions. It implies that one is honest and fair, that one is at home with oneself in one's desires and decisions. Integrity thus strengthens individuality by raising the quality of the individual's life beyond the mere pursuit of satisfaction, giving a distinctive style to one's words and acts. But integrity also has a social dimension. It only acquires content through relationships, by caring for persons and purposes and sustaining commitments. This is why integrity is so naturally bound up with the commitments and relationships involved in work and calling.

Integrity is never a given, but always a quest that must be renewed and reshaped over time. It demands considerable individual self-awareness and self-command. Yet, it also depends for its realization upon the availability of actual social possibilities, since some situations clearly make it more likely that an individual can achieve integrity than others. It is therefore significant that the moral imagination so readily reaches toward professionals to exemplify integrity. In fact, the qualities of integrity and the demands of professional life are in this way remarkably congruent. Integrity of vocation demands the balanced combination of individual autonomy with integration into shared purposes. Individual talent needs to blend with the best common standards of performance, while the individual must exercise personal judgment as to the proper application of these communal standards in a responsible way.

The complex requirements of integrity define two of the basic dimensions of professional life. Professional occupations provide recognized opportunities for individuals to make something of their talents and capacities. On the other hand, this is possible only through personal commitment to the disciplines of a community of practice. At its best, professional life enables individual freedom to find fulfillment as it advances the well-being of the larger society. The person who succeeds in mastering the standards and aims of a professional discipline achieves a substantial focus for living, a purpose which relates the individual to others and the world in a significant way. As the novice learns the practices and values of a professional community through learning to trust mentor figures, the developing professional is also coming to view self and world as that community does.

Institutions count on this by supporting and stabilizing these achievements. Organized professional communities uphold the integrity of particular purposes, as with the values of care for health or education or technical efficiency. At the same time, however, professional organizations are interests among other interests in civil society. The way they see themselves and the world is influenced not only by their internal concerns but by the kind of interaction they have with the other members of society. The quality of this interaction in turn depends heavily upon the extent to which qualities of civic cooperation prevail in the larger social environment.

This represents the third, or civic dimension of professional life. Where the levels of trust, self-restraint, and degree of cooperation are high, where social interactions include most parts of that environment on an equitable footing and are perceived as mutually beneficial, professional organizations are more likely to behave as "good citizens," taking responsible, often leadership roles in the society's life. In return the professions maintain good will, public support, and often prestige. In such circumstances, individual professionals are likewise likely to find their efforts at integrity recognized and rewarded. These are the conditions of positive interde-

221

pendence. Conversely, however, where civic cooperation is weak or sporadic, mediation between individual goals and social need is likely to break down, releasing aggressive efforts to escape social responsibility, with all their corrosive effects upon democratic life. A direct consequence is the worsening of possibilities for integrity in professional life. Many of the disagreeable aspects of contemporary professional activity have their root causes in this experience of negative interdependence.

From this perspective, then, the professional enterprise is an important modern civic institution. The professions have pioneered and continue to model a socially attuned way to organize work, thereby providing a potential democratic resource through bringing the concerns of citizenship into a wide variety of specialized occupations. The integrity of professional life, indeed its whole future, is bound up in the health of civic culture in the United States. This is why discussions of professionalism are necessarily not only ethical but political. They concern the shape of the civil society which lies at the basis of democracy.

In modern civil society no group or institution enjoys permanently guaranteed status. Social relations remain open and fluid. Professions complete with other professions and other organizations, often to the benefit of society.[1] But what matters decisively is the prevailing climate of social interaction as a whole. In this important sense, the whole is always more than the sum of its parts. The peculiar strengths of strong civic cultures in the economic as well as social dimension derive from just this holistic effect of widespread and pervasive patterns of public cooperation.[2]

By most accounts, the United States has been suffering from a pervasive decline of social trust and a fraying of civic bonds, weakening the capacities for cooperative organization on which a vital democracy depends. It is this situation which gives urgency and value to the renewal of the civic orientation of professionalism and its effective institutionalization. The reforms and experiments discussed in previous chapters suggest the directions in which such an approach would lead. It is now time to test the comprehensiveness of this understanding of the professional crisis by revisiting the critics of professionalism already surveyed.

CONTEMPORARY CRITICISMS OF PROFESSIONAL INTEGRITY

The major critics of professionalism we have encountered have written from a variety of points of view. James Fallows wrote as a concerned journalist with extensive experience in East Asia who criticized professionalization as the opening wedge for a mandarin culture which would snuff out the admirable openness and flexibility of American society in favor of a morally dubious model of social hierarchy. Barbara Ehrenreich, by contrast, took a reformist approach, seeking to defend—and even extend—the positive qualities of professional work, especially what she called its "secret pleasure principle" of engaged expertise, while criticizing the corruption of professional purposes through collusion with the spurious rewards offered by the corporate consumer economy.

Robert Reich assumed the critical distance of the social scientist, showing how technological and economic innovation has been the motor inexorably driving massive changes in the U.S. and world economy, with the consequence that highly skilled symbolic analysts were gaining power and wealth even as they freed themselves from their earlier ties to place and society. This "dark side of cosmopolitanism" was the principal theme of Christopher Lasch's indictment of the "culture of critical discourse," the professional lingua franca, which has made the expansion of the professional enterprise a destructive force, eclipsing and denigrating the morally healthier traditions of local cultures. Lasch's stance is that of an even more distanced critic, more of an outsider radically at odds with the direction of current events, yet a critic with deep commitment to democratic ideals and civic values. Despite its apparent extremism, this line of criticism has, as we have seen, been mounted from the both the right and the left of the political spectrum in America and continues to be voiced by thoughtful observers.[3]

Taken together, these criticisms add up to a massive assault on the viability of the professional enterprise. Taken one at a time, however, most of the criticisms are less convincing than they seem at first glance. Taken without further qualification, many of the criticisms turn out to be one-sided and simplistic, providing few leads as to how to cope with the problems they so sensationalistically elaborate.

For example, the argument put forward by Fallows in *More Like Us* gives some structure to a widespread perception of professionalism. And so, while it is seriously flawed, it is worth attending to with some care. Fallows proposes two ideal types of modern society.[4] One is the East Asian model of a highly stratified, mandarin capitalism organized by a powerful and pervasive state for winning the international trade competition. In this model, individuals count for little except to be slotted into specialized tasks for life, and social order is a means toward national economic effectiveness. Fallows's other model, which he takes to be true to the American case, is a loose, laissez-faire society focused upon economic growth for the sake of individual satisfaction. Here, individuals are free and flexible, while social order results largely from spontaneous generation.

Fallows attacks professionalization, the spread of credentialing through schooling, and other manifestations of creeping mandarinism. While there is much validity in his criticism of these tendencies as antidemocratic, it is important to note that what he is describing are all long-standing features of the organizational professions and therefore of the industrial order which America—not East Asia—pioneered. That system, as we have seen, developed not through state imposition but from the decisions of the winners at laissez-faire competition, the financiers and industrialists who brought the anarchy of Gilded Age market-driven capitalism to heel by developing the corporation structure to organize, regulate, and control from above.

That order was much "more like us" than Fallows allows. That is, its appearance and long-term success, particularly during the postwar period, became plausible as the result of the American reliance upon markets, hierarchical corporations, and government to regulate the national economy, with little encouragement of public cooperation among social and economic groups. This contrast would have appeared quickly had Fallows noted the ways in which many postwar European nations, especially Scandinavia, the Benelux countries, and West Germany achieved economic prosperity through a strategy of public cooperation among social interests. Fallows's blindness to this third, civic alternative leads him to imagine that professionalism can only mean the organizational professions at their most irresponsible.

On the other hand, in *Fear of Falling*, Barbara Ehrenreich comes much closer to seeing the professional enterprise as a multi-sided phenomenon with promise for the future of democratic society.[5] However, while Ehrenreich documents both the positive potentials of professionalism for humanizing work and the destructive effects of the unrestrained social competition set off by the breakdown of the postwar social compromise in America, she seems to notice only the effects of the corporation system on professional life. The larger, more complex field of civic interaction is thus not part of the purview of her critique, either. The consequence is a conclusion which presents the admirable utopian goal of somehow enabling professional values to flourish in their integrity throughout the occupational world, but no sense of what kind of social processes might help advance that goal, aside from the reining-in of corporate capitalism.

The critique by Robert Reich in *The Work of Nations* presents the widest canvas on which to view the problems of professional life.[6] Because of his commitment to a theory of social change in which technology and the economy direct events, Reich is strong on analysis but short on suggestions for response. His story line is one of the breakdown of a technological and economic order and the resulting uncertainties and confusion. Like Fallows, Reich views the professional enterprise wholly in terms of the organizational model. Unlike Fallows, Reich understands that American society has never in this century been simply a realm of spontaneous order and national efforts to induce social cooperation have played an important role.

Reich makes an important contribution by stressing the opening of the national economy to global competition as a primary destabilizing force. But Reich, too, seems to see the possibilities of societal action as essentially divided between the market and corporation or government control and regulation as organizers of interaction. One might argue that he sees both the liberal truth of enterprise as opening possibilities and the complementary communitarian truth that meaning comes through ethical relationship, but cannot conceive a structure of public cooperation which could mediate and direct the two. When he does think of social cooperation, either in the American case of World War II or the European social democracies, it is the national state which dominates the stage, giving a virtual soliloquy. Unsurprisingly, he makes little of the forms of civic cooperation which do appear in his analysis, including that among denizens of the "symbolic analysis zones."

The critique of professionalism presented by Christopher Lasch in *The True and Only Heaven* focuses upon the cultural style and effects of professionalism.[7] This focus upon ideas and modes of thought, however, while acute and illuminating, proves one-sided. Lasch is well aware that the characteristic mentality of any group is tied to much more than the cognitive dimension of life, especially the social experiences of those who espouse the mentality. He performs a valuable function by pointing up the ways in which the "critical discourse" culture of the American professional middle class developed in opposition to the themes of agrarian and working-class populism which he prefers on moral grounds. But Lasch

226

tends to blame middle class professionals for an undemocratic contempt for the people rather than to account for why those attitudes seemed so reasonable to the metropolitan mind. This leaves no foothold for any contemporary strategy for reconsideration or reconciliation.

Lasch also minimizes the genuine positive values of professional attitudes such as the embrace of rational proof and critical standards of evidence, even of the integrity of technique and performance. Yet, there is good evidence that these attitudes, which are essential to sustaining complex interdependence, are alive and well among professionals despite powerful contrary pressures. In business contexts, for example, professionals frequently serve to "mobilize ethical consciousness" within firms. According to some research, professionals are "characteristically more interested in doing things right than in doing them expediently."[8]

By training and "instinct," that is, professionals turn out to be inclined to guard the integrity and quality of products and services. "Thus a design engineer is likely to resist price-fixing on heavy equipment, since the purchase criteria in this instance would not necessarily include quality and contribution." Professional standing can play a similar ethical role: "A corporate auditor would find it difficult to face peers . . . if evidence of fraud in the firm's financial dealings were revealed."[9] While individuals may be better or worse at practicing responsibility, professional education and conditions of work seem to foster this virtue more than the average occupation. Whatever its consolations for the conscience, the stance an outside critic such as Lasch adopted is not always useful if one wants to understand the whole phenomenon under scrutiny. A more engaged method of critique, like that of pragmatist reconstruction adopted in Chapter 5, at least sometimes can provide a fuller picture, and therefore a more accurate basis for reflection.

The sense of professional responsibility may, however, be narrowly circumscribed. It may never go beyond the circle of respected peers to include civic interaction. Much recent criticism of law and medicine, for example, makes just this point. And certainly it is a criticism which can rightly be extended to many fields. But if both expertise and public cooperation are crucial to the life of modern societies, then the question becomes how to enhance and expand the practical parameters of professional responsibility— and to bring it within the discipline of a more representative public conversation. While the stance of practical critique does not in itself provide a detailed program for how to do this, it does suggest the outlines of what must be done.

CIVIC PROFESSIONALISM AND THE DEMOCRATIC PUBLIC

The strongest contribution the professions have made to the development of civic culture has stemmed from their role as mediating institutions. Professional organizations have mediated the concerns of social responsibility and individual integrity with economic and technical achievement. To mediate is to bring conflicting aims into a viable symbiosis, to turn an either-or choice into a both-and possibility. Within a culture heavily focused upon wealth and profit, professionalism has been able to assert, if not to embody fully, the superior claims of intrinsic quality and service. The issue of civic professionalism thus describes one condensed form of the central problems facing advanced technological societies: how to reconstruct the either-or of economic growth versus social and cultural solidarity into a both-and of technical progress in the service of a sustainable common good; how to develop leadership groups which will serve rather than undermine solidarity and collective self-development.[10]

In practice, professionals must mediate between sometimes sharply conflicting standards of practice, often within the same institutional venue. We have seen several examples of these conflicts in some detail in previous chapters, as well as cases of new initiatives toward building the social partnerships which can effectively mediate those conflicts. To coalesce from those hints at resolution a general logic of effective mediation, a case from the emerging field of environmental planning will serve as an extended example of the

228

potentials inherent in a professionalism that understands itself as part of a democratic civic order.

This is the hope held out by Tony Hiss in *The Experience of Place.*[11] The central thesis of Hiss's book might be stated as "awareness matters—and awareness of place perhaps most of all." How we perceive our surrounding environments, particularly as those environments undergo stressful, human-induced change, matters urgently for our well-being and that of our heirs. Hiss stresses that our connections with the places we inhabit form a close, enveloping bond, "almost a continuum with all we are and think," which molds our understanding and is "now necessary for us to survive." Thus, "overdevelopment and urban sprawl can damage our own lives as much as they damage our cities and countryside."[12] Hiss's thesis, in fine, is that disconnection breeds apathy and a diminished life, but connectedness empowers.

The project Hiss calls us to is twofold: to better recognize the defining importance of our complex connectedness to our world, and then to cultivate this sense of connectedness into a loyalty to place that can inform our lives as active citizens. In this call Hiss is going against the basic assumptions of the dominant economic view, but he is in the company of those who see a focus upon locality as integral to economic and social, as well as ecological well-being, in time to come.[13]

In Tony Hiss's view, we have to start doing three things at once. We have to "make sure that when we change a place, the change agreed upon nurtures our growth as capable and responsible people while also protecting the natural environment and developing jobs and homes enough for all."[14] The key to combining these heretofore antagonistic purposes of economic development and environmental enhancement, according to Hiss, is recognizing that human beings have a powerful capacity to perceive, respond to, and nurture these complex interconnections. In his revisionist account, it is the purpose of design and planning to overcome the fragmentation of much contemporary life by putting us perceptually as well as cognitively into connection with the social and natural processes through which we all too unknowingly live our lives. By so defining the end of the design and planning professions, Hiss has opened unsuspected democratic possibilities in fields often criticized for their high-handed elitism.

Hiss invokes the landscape architect Frederick Law Olmsted and the regional planner Benton Mac Kaye as the path-breaking heroes whose sense of things we need to recover. One of the contemporaries to whom Hiss gives considerable attention is Robert D. Yaro, a former public servant, a professor of planning, and an author with hands-on experience in municipal and state planning agencies who is now a planner for the nonprofit Regional Plan Association of New York. Yaro has spurred new public experiments in land-use planning in New England which have major potential for replication elsewhere.

At the root of Yaro's thinking stands Benton Mac Kaye, a regional planning pioneer of the 1920s and 1930s, and associate of Lewis Mumford in the Regional Planning Association of America which inspired new departures during the New Deal. Mac Kaye is today best known for his vision of the Appalachian Trail. The point of the Trail was more than simple recreation or nature-romanticism, and even more than a device to contain urban sprawl. It was also conceived as educational, a way to provide an awareness of the limits and the connections between natural landscapes, productive landscapes, and cities. As Mac Kaye saw it "you changed people's mental maps by first altering their physical maps."[15]

Yaro has developed practical strategies for continuing Mac Kaye's insights into the twenty-first century. Central to this approach is the notion that "landscape connectedness" can reinvolve modern "ex-urban" Americans in the patterns of interconnection to which they are typically oblivious. The result, in Yaro's experience, can be a new kind of empowerment. Once citizens come to appreciate the larger pattern of their lives, he has found, they often become active stewards of the land they inhabit and love. As Yaro sees it, since the industrial revolution, we have accepted the either-or of economic growth versus a healthful, attractive, and sustainable environment. His discovery has been that today these goals can become both-and. Yaro's approach has been creative of both ideas and institutional practice. The new state planning agencies he helped develop have produced, in partnership with various interested citizens' organizations, a visual survey of the landscape on Mac Kaye-like principles: dividing regions into their visual components of natural landscapes, working landscapes such as farms, and urbanized zones. Through a variety of means, especially public meetings in the several regions surveyed, citizens were presented with the results of the survey. This is Mac Kaye's principle of changing (or creating) visual maps in order to change mental maps.

Yaro and his associates' second innovation, which goes beyond Mac Kaye, has been the discovery that it is possible to develop a region to the same population density typical of sprawling suburban tracts without violating the visual configurations of working and natural landscapes. The key turns out to be clustered development in towns, thereby permitting the working landscape to continue to function. In Hiss's summary, Yaro discovered that "areas can conceal density only by working with connectedness; and the process of working with connectedness is politically acceptable, because it's basically a democratic procedure rather than something outsiders can control or impose—all they can do is tap into local people's hidden expertise about connectedness ('The job is not to "plan" but to *reveal*.')."[16]

The outcomes have been striking: innovation at the levels of institutional design and in the practice of planning. Yaro's approach as a state official has been to create regional public land-use planning agencies organized as social-governmental partnerships. These agencies engage citizens along with developers, farmers, bankers, and other interested parties in a complex planning and decision process. As part of these new arrangements, governmental and private-sector professionals function as parts of a larger process in which decisions have to be genuinely collaborative. Besides the survey, planners and other experts provide economic, demographic, and ecological analyses to help participants grasp and think about the whole, including the trade-offs and compromises which a both-and approach demands.

As Yaro sees it, "a new approach to community development is in the making—one that asks people to think about the long-term needs of a place and of all its residents." He describes the process as one of "building local institutions that take over the job of looking after public value on a volunteer basis, and we're learning how to reinvest in areas so that they'll be more valuable to the next generation than they are to ours."[17] All this recalls and seems to verify John Dewey's faith in the power of democratic participation to foment genuine learning and collective development. In addition the routine functions of architectural and planning professionals have undergone a metamorphosis.

Professionals have here worked to stimulate rather than to supplant popular involvement. The result has been that traditionally professional concerns with the integrity of the process as well as good outcomes have become shared among a much wider community of interested citizens rather than jealously restricted. "I think we can now show that stewardship springs from connectedness," Yaro says, that "it gives people back a sense of thinking responsibly on behalf of the whole community, and it sends a shiver up the spines of the gatekeepers, by reminding them that someone can take away their keys."[18] The new role of the planning professionals here is to educate, to encourage, and to exemplify ecological responsibility as well as facilitate public debate. It is to hold up for all the high standard of minds capable of appreciating connectedness joined with hearts willing to respond.

It is important to notice how in this case professional leadership, as exercised by Robert Yaro, was spurred and complemented by democratic participation. The generation of ecologically responsible, economically and socially dynamic, yet really shared development plans was the joint outcome of long-term debate and deliberation among all the concerned parties. This whole process was supported by the public sector, sustained by intense private-sector involvement and citizen organization, and catalyzed by professionals acting as institutional citizens. Both in process and outcome, it raises hopes. But can the point be generalized beyond the sphere of land-use planning? Is the connection, which Yaro and Hiss, following Mumford and Mac Kaye, find between natural and human social ecologies compelling enough to redirect the narrow and rigid outlooks of so much contemporary professional practice? From another unexpected quarter appear some grounds for a possible affirmative answer.

Rebuilding and enhancing connectedness may be the theme around which to fashion a civic professionalism for our time. This rediscovery of the public or civic dimension of professional work promises new forms of professional citizenship. It also reveals the limits of the technical orientation which prevails in much of contemporary professional culture. The parallels between the new planning practices and the renewed concern with prevention in health care that we encountered in Deborah Prothrow-Stith are arresting. Innovative planning practices which illuminate connectedness activate attentive publics and build new regional planning institutions. Similarly, the discovery that the lives of the least advantaged Americans can be markedly improved by regenerating fraying social bonds promises ways to address some of the nation's most daunting ills. In the case of planning, the impetus moves from place and perception toward concern and responsibility for the quality of life in cities and regions. In public health or social medicine, widespread youth violence is understood as tied to a failure of the moral ecology. Treatment requires that distraction, despair, and aggression must be grasped as results of a breakdown of connection and trust in order to focus on building the social bonds which can support attention and responsibility, both among the underclass poor and between them and the mainstream institutions of the society.

The tentative result, in both cases, has been to arrest a downward spiral of entropic loss, of environmental value in the one case, of social capital in the other. At root the problems and the solutions are analogous. The role of professional expertise, in both cases, is being redefined away from providing discrete technical interventions. Instead, professionals are giving continuing attention to the institutional and cultural infrastructure needed to sustain a viable modern society.

But the two cases are even more closely joined. Without the generation of a kind of social "public space," meaning those patterns of mutual accountability and cooperation which generate social capital and through which alone a democratic public can develop, there can be no viable public space in the physical sense. The former provides the invisible support and moral endowment which sustains the latter. As contemporary experience shows quite clearly, in the absence of generous endowments of social capital, physical public spaces will be abandoned in fear as citizens retreat behind private techniques of isolation. Both physical and social public space are necessary for a full democratic life. But while physical public space can by definition be the concern of only some professionals, all professional work bears directly on, and finds its meaning in, the enhancement of connectedness in social "space."

THE HISTORICAL SIGNIFICANCE OF CIVIC PROFESSIONALISM

We can imagine these developments as the promise of a new phase of professionalism. This new phase would extend into the coming global era which Harold Perkin has called the "historic task" of professionalism. That task has been "to moralize a potentially amoral competition and to set limits to the exploitation of workers, victims of adulteration and pollution in all classes, and of society at large by fraud, embezzlement, and tax evasion."[19] While Perkin is describing Britain, the attitude he presents fits well the civic purposes we have identified at the core of the professional enterprise in the United States.

In Britain today, as Perkin portrays his society, competing groups of professionals, differently linked to the corporations, government, or independent sector organizations, wrangle over the utility of economic regulation and the welfare state versus a resurrected faith in laissez-faire. But, as Perkin points out, these ideological battles presuppose the outmoded dichotomy, common to the nineteenth-century economics of both Ricardo and Marx, that industry is productive, while services are parasitic. The arrival of high-technology industry and the belated discovery of human capital has made that whole argument—which since the '70s has come once again to dominate political debate—hopelessly obsolete. Or, as Perkin tellingly comments about the facile claim that public sector services are parasitic upon private sector productivity: "It is just as valid to claim that the public sector produces and maintains, through the education and health services, most of the skills on which the private sector depends." Thus, commenting on British (or American) political debate Perkin concludes, "in a complex interdependent society such claims and counterclaims are as naive and unhelpful as the pot calling the kettle black."[20] In passing, Perkin notes that the currently most successful national economies, Germany and Japan, have for some time extended far more of the features of professional work to factory and service workers than have Britain or the United States.[21]

It was the economic historian and theorist of the British Labor Party, R. H. Tawney, who classically linked professionalism with social function and the common good. By doing so Tawney provided a vision of how to humanize and more fully democratize the twentieth-century society of large-scale industry. Tawney defined a profession as "a trade which is organized, incompletely, no doubt, but genuinely, for the performance of function . . . an activity which embodies and expresses the idea of social purpose."[22] Not abstract credentials, but demonstrated expertise and effective collective responsibility were his criteria for a profession. But these hung on the practical embodiment of recognized social purposes. Tawney thought the idea sounded strange because, during the era of laissez-faire enterprise in Britain, the notion of social purpose had receded into a vestigial existence in certain realms of state and church.

Tawney argued that a more interdependent and complex society cannot do without the recognition of common purposes and the professional solidarities which derive from that recognition. "A wise system of administration," he wrote in implicit refutation of the disciples of Taylor, "would recognize that professional solidarity can do much of its work for it more effectively than it can do for itself, because the spirit of his profession is part of the individual and not a force outside him." Indeed, continued Tawney, it is only by fully developing professionalism in all occupations that "what is mechanical and obstructive in bureaucracy can be averted."[23]

In the contemporary context, Fred Block has emphasized the economic importance of this "spirit of professionalism." Block points out that if accountants simply "cooked the books" in the way their clients told them to, "the basic data necessary for the investment process would be unreliable." If bankers were free to maximize their returns, "not at all constrained by a professional commitment to prudence," there would be little financial stability. That is, no modern economy—let alone a decent society—could survive a regime of purely unregulated, "rational" instrumental behavior.[24] If Tawney's observation proved prescient for industrial bureaucracies, though largely unheeded, how much more apt is it for building the flexible, service-intensive and publicly responsive organizations needed for the next phase of modern civilization?

Writing at the same period in the United States, Alfred North Whitehead provided what has become a kind of leitmotif for the future now upon us. "The fixed person for fixed duties," wrote Whitehead, "who in older societies was such a godsend, in the future will be a public danger."[25] But it is not often noticed that Whitehead went on to point out that one of modern philosophy's weaknesses was its failure to grasp that the great expansion of possibilities enjoyed by the fortunate modern individual was not the cause but the emergent effect of a more interdependent and cooperative social order. That is, a good life under the more flexible conditions of the emerging economy, will require a deeper, and more conscious, mutual commitment between individuals and social institutions. The solidarity this will demand cannot be expected to spring from the spark of natural sympathy alone. It must be cultivated and regularly replenished through the connectedness displayed and strengthened in social cooperation. Few kinds of work would seem better fitted to these needs of the new era than professions with a civic orientation.

By its inherent logic, civic professionalism proposes an ideal of self which complements the social imperative to achieve a positive outcome to interdependence. That ideal corresponds in one important way to the aspirations of the pervasive contemporary search for self-actualization and takes it beyond itself. Positive interdependence, that is, demands of the individual a high degree of self-awareness and a major effort to development one's powers. But it then demands more. The goal of self-actualization itself must be transcended, or perhaps better, reoriented by integrating individual goals with those of the larger community. The logical fulfillment of this process is a kind of character for whom what happens to these larger commitments is as important as what happens to the self, or more so.

This, of course, is the outline of integrity in professional life. According to some psychologists, it is also a description of a meaningful and happy life.[26] This is only to repeat in contemporary idiom a much more ancient view: that what makes one free and renders life worth living is finally neither satisfying one's desires nor accomplishing one's purposes, valuable as these are, but learning to act with the good of the whole in view, building life act by act, happy if each deed, as far as circumstances allow, fulfills its proper end.[27] Anyone who has been stirred and inspired by a committed teacher, an attentive health care provider, a dedicated pastor or rabbi, anyone who has experienced a well-functioning business firm or public agency, school or cultural institution, has glimpsed the enlivening possibilities inherent in communities of professional purpose. There, already manifest, is the promise of professional life.

ENDNOTES

INTRODUCTION

1. See Francis Fukuyama, *The End of History and the Last Man* (New York: Free Press, 1992), p. 200.

2. Daniel Cohn-Bendit, "Heimat Babylon: The Challenge of Multi-cultural Democracy," *New Perspectives Quarterly* (Winter, 1993), pp. 4–7; p. 7.

3. Samuel P. Huntington, "The Clash of Civilizations?" *Foreign Affairs*, 72, no. 3 (Summer 1993), pp. 22–49.

4. For the case of Great Britain, see Harold Perkin, *The Rise of Professional Society: England Since 1880* (London and New York: Routledge, 1989). The American case, while importantly different, benefits from comparison with the story set forth by Perkin.

5. Lawrence Haworth has provided the most suggestive and far-ranging effort to conceive professionalism as a social ethic of responsibility within modern society. See *Decadence and Objectivity* (Toronto: University of Toronto Press, 1977); also *The Good City* (Bloomington, IN: Indiana University Press, 1963).

6. The tendency toward reductionism has been widespread in the sociological literature. Even very good studies of the professional phenomenon have not entirely escaped the tendency, as will be noted in subsequent chapters.

7. See Robert A. Putnam, *Making Democracy Work: Civic Traditions in Modern Italy* (Princeton, NJ: Princeton University Press, 1993).

CHAPTER ONE

1. For example, see Peter M. Blau and Otis Dudley Duncan, *The American Occupational Structure* (New York: Wiley and Sons, 1976).

2. See Harold Perkin, *The Rise of Professional Society: England Since 1880* (New York: Routledge, 1989).

3. The importance of professionals and professionalism in modern society, especially the United States, was a major theme in the sociology of Talcott Parsons, so influential at mid-century. See Talcott Parsons, *Essays in Sociological Theory* (New York: Free Press, 1954). For a sense of the scope of the issue and its complexities, see Daniel Bell, *The Coming of Post-Industrial Society* (New York: Basic Books, 1976), an analysis Bell has updated in "The World and the United States in 2013," *Daedalus*, 116, no. 3 (Summer 1987). See also Magali Sarfatti Larson, *The Rise of Professionalism: A Sociological Analysis* (Berkeley and Los Angeles: University of California Press, 1977) and the discussion by Eliot Freidson, *Professional Powers: A Study in the Institutionalization of Formal Knowledge* (Chicago: University of Chicago Press, 1986), esp. pp. 48–58.

4. "The Quest for Doctors: Hospitals in a Quandary," *New York Times*, December 16, 1991.

5. In this sense professionalism functions as an important moral ideal in contemporary America, a "moral source" following the usage of Charles Taylor. See *Sources of the Self: The Making of Modern Identity* (Cambridge, MA: Harvard University Press, 1989), esp. pp. 91–110.

6. Quoted in Belinda Hulin-Salkin, "On the Front Lines," *Applause* 15, no. 5 (April, 1989), pp. 22ff.

7. Ibid.

8. "50 Hours for the Poor," *American Bar Association Journal*, December 1, 1987, p. 55.

9. Richard Bono, "Demands on Rabbis Are Increasing," *Jewish Exponent*, May 5, 1989, p. 3.

10. James Fallows, *More Like Us: Making America Great Again* (Boston: Houghton Mifflin, 1989), pp. 131–41.

11. Ibid., p. 139.

12. Among the works Fallows summarizes and relies upon are the following: Milton Friedman, *Capitalism and Freedom* (Chicago: University of

Chicago Press, 1962); Mancur Olson, *The Rise and Decline of Nations: Economic Growth, Stagflation, and Social Rigidities* (New Haven, CT: Yale University Press, 1982); Randall Collins, *The Credential Society: An Historical Sociology of Education and Stratification* (New York: Academic Press, 1979); S. David Young, *The Rule of Experts: Occupational Licensing in America*, (Washington, DC: Cato Institute, 1987). Fallows thus draws upon parallel strands of thought in economics, political science, sociology, and a current brand of political conservatism which is profoundly enamored of old-time laissez-faire economics.

13. The utilitarian conception of society, and the problems it poses for democratic politics, has been a major theme in political philosophy. For example, see Thomas A. Spragens, Jr., *The Irony of Liberal Reason* (Chicago: University of Chicago Press, 1981), esp. pp. 86–90; and William M. Sullivan, *Reconstructing Public Philosophy* (Berkeley and Los Angeles: University of California Press, 1982), esp. pp. 74–82.

14. Lester Thurow, *Going Head to Head: The Upcoming Economic Competition Among Europe, Japan, and the United States* (New York: William Morrow, 1992), p. 298.

15. For example, see the discussion of these systems in Ray Marshall and Marc Tucker, *Thinking for a Living: Education and the Wealth of Nations* (New York: Basic Books, 1992), pp. 43–62.

16. James Fallows, "Wake Up, America!" *New York Review of Books*, 37, no. 3 (March 1, 1990).

17. Barbara Ehrenreich, *Fear of Falling: The Inner Life of the Middle Class* (New York: Pantheon Books, 1989).

18. Ibid., pp. 13–15.

19. Ibid., p. 15.

20. Ibid., p. 248.

21. Christopher Lasch, *The True and Only Heaven: Progress and Its Critics* (New York: W. W. Norton, 1991), p. 531.

22. Ibid., p. 531.

23. Ibid., p. 530.

24. Ibid., p. 531.

25. Ibid., p. 534.

26. It is perhaps worth noting that in this attack Lasch uses the same language as Vaclav Havel, who mounted a similar critique of the Communist system in Czechoslovakia during the '70s and '80s—noting, however, that the problems were not confined to Marxism but endemic in modern ideologies as a whole. See Vaclav Havel, *Living in Truth*, ed. Jan Vladislav (London and Boston: Faber and Faber, 1986), esp. "The Power of the Powerless," pp. 36–122.

CHAPTER TWO

1. This point is made by Eliot Freidson, *Professional Powers: A Study in the Institutionalization of Formal Knowledge* (Chicago: University of Chicago Press, 1986), pp. 32–35.

2. See, for example, E. Digby Baltzell, *Puritan Boston and Quaker Philadelphia: Two Protestant Ethics and the Spirit of Class Authority and Leadership* (New York: Free Press, 1979), esp. pp. 57–106.

3. Donald Scott, *From Office to Profession: The New England Ministry, 1750–1850* (Philadelphia: University of Pennsylvania Press, 1978), p. 148.

4. The picture of American development presented in this chapter is indebted to the work of Robert H. Wiebe. See *The Segmented Society: An Introduction to the Meaning of America* (New York: Oxford University Press, 1975), and *The Opening of American Society: From the Adoption of the Constitution to the Eve of Disunion* (New York: Alfred Knopf, 1984).

5. See the discussion of these developments in Gordon S. Wood, *The Radicalism of the American Revolution* (New York: Alfred Knopf, 1992), esp. pp. 189–225.

6. Thomas Bender has called these free professionals of the early republic "civic professionals" to contrast them with the specialized "disciplinary professional" of the twentieth century. See his "The Cultures of Intellectual Life: The City and the Professions," in John Higham and Paul K. Conkin, eds., *New Directions in American Intellectual History* (Baltimore: Johns Hopkins University Press, 1979), pp. 181–95; also "The Erosion of Public Culture: Cities, Discourses, and Professional Disciplines," in Thomas L. Haskell, ed., *The Authority of Experts: Issues in History and Theory* (Bloomington, IN: University of Indiana Press, 1984), pp. 84–106. See also Peter Dobkin Hall, *The Organization of American Culture, 1700–1900: Private Institutions, Elites, and the Origins of National Identity* (New York: New York University Press, 1982).

7. See Alexis de Tocqueville, *Democracy in America*, ed. J. P. Meyer (Garden City, NY: Doubleday, 1969), pp. 264–67.

8. Quoted in William G. McLoughlin, *Revivals, Awakenings, and Reform: An Essay on Religion and Social Change in America, 1607–1977* (Chicago: University of Chicago Press, 1978), p. 139.

9. Quoted in Marvin Meyer, *The Jacksonian Persuasion: Politics and Belief* (Palo Alto, CA: Stanford University Press, 1957), p. 21. See also Robert H. Wiebe, *The Opening of American Society: From the Adoption of the Constitution to the Eve of Disunion* (New York: Alfred A. Knopf, 1984), esp. pp. 234–52.

10. The independent citizen as character ideal is discussed in Robert N. Bellah, Richard Madsen, William M. Sullivan, Ann Swidler, and Steven M. Tipton, *Habits of the Heart: Individualism and Commitment in American Life* (Berkeley: University of California Press, 1985), pp. 35–41.

11. Quoted in Meyer, *Jacksonian Persuasion*, pp. 281–82.

12. See "Author's Introduction," Tocqueville, *Democracy*, pp. 9–20.

13. Ibid., II, Part 2, Chapter 5, pp. 525–27.

14. Ibid., II, Part 1, Chapter 11, p. 465.

15. Ibid., p. 465.

16. Ibid., pp. 466 and 468.

17. William Appleman Williams, *The Contours of American History* (New York: W. W. Norton, 1966), p. 351.

18. See also Louis Galambos and Joseph Pratt, *The Rise of the Corporate Commonwealth: United States Business and Public Policy in the 20th Century* (New York: Basic Books, 1988). The notion of "market shelter" is a major organizing concept in Magali Sarfatti Larson's *The Rise of Professionalism: A Sociological Analysis* (Berkeley and Los Angeles: University of California Press, 1977).

19. Burton Bledstein has traced the development of these possibilities in post–Civil War America in *The Culture of Professionalism: The Middle Class and the Development of Higher Education in America* (New York: W. W. Norton, 1976).

20. Robert H. Wiebe, *The Search for Order: 1870–1920* (New York: Hill and Wang, 1967), pp. 111–12. For a critique of Wiebe's assumption that professionals and professionalism were the moving forces in the undeniable social

transformation which brought the professions new importance, see Walter P. Metzger, "A Spectre Is Haunting American Scholars: The Spectre of 'Professionalism'" *Educational Researcher* (August-September 1987), pp. 71–79.

21. This is a major theme of Richard Hofstadter's *The Age of Reform, From Bryan to FDR* (New York: Alfred Knopf, 1955), esp. pp. 148ff.

22. Karl Polanyi, *The Great Transformation: The Political and Economic Origins of Our Own Time* (Boston: Beacon Press, 1957), p. 152.

23. For example, see George W. Corner, *A History of the Rockefeller Institute* (New York: Rockefeller Institute Press, 1964).

24. See the discussion by Leonard Silk and Mark Silk, *The American Establishment* (New York: Basic Books, 1980).

25. On Frederick W. Taylor there is a considerable literature and considerable disagreement. See Monte Calvert, *The Mechanical Engineer in America: Structure and Aspirations, 1830–1910: Professional Cultures in Conflict* (Baltimore: Johns Hopkins University Press, 1967), and Samuel Haber, *Efficiency and Uplift* (Chicago: University of Chicago Press, 1964). For a skeptical view, see David Noble, *The Forces of Production: A Social History of Industrial Automation* (New York: Alfred Knopf, 1984).

26. Frederick Winslow Taylor, *The Principles of Scientific Management* (New York: Harper and Brothers, 1911), pp. 20–28.

27. See Sean Wilentz, *Chants Democratic: New York City and the Rise of the American Working Class* (New York: Oxford University Press, 1984); David Nobel, *Forces of Production*. Also see David Montgomery, *The Fall of the House of Labor: The Workplace, the State, and American Labor Activism, 1865–1925* (Cambridge, MA: Cambridge University Press, 1987); also Alan Trachtenberg, *The Incorporation of America: American Culture in the Gilded Age* (New York: Hill and Wang, 1982), pp. 64–69.

28. See Harold Perkin, "The Historical Perspective," in Burton R. Clark, ed., *Perspectives on Higher Education: Eight Disciplinary Perspectives* (Berkeley and Los Angeles: University of California Press, 1984), pp. 17–55.

29. This process is described in detail by Lawrence Veysey, *The Emergence of the American University* (Chicago: University of Chicago Press, 1965). See also Bledstein, *Professionalism*, as noted above.

30. See the story of the efforts to establish social scientific knowledge as the basis for institutional autonomy in Thomas Haskell, *The Emergence of Profes-*

sional Science and the Nineteenth-Century Crisis of Authority (Urbana: University of Illinois Press, 1977).

31. These developments are chronicled in Paul Starr, *The Social Transformation of American Medicine* (New York: Basic Books, 1982), esp. ch. 3–6.

32. Quoted in Veysey, *University*, p. 346.

33. W. E. B. Du Bois, *The Souls of Black Folk*, in John Hope Franklin, ed., *Three Negro Classics* (New York: Avon, 1962), esp. ch. 9.

34. Douglas Sloan, "The Teaching of Ethics in the American Undergraduate Curriculum, 1876–1976," in Daniel Callahan and Sissela Bok, eds., *Ethics Teaching in Higher Education* (New York: Plenum Press, 1980), p. 4.

35. This characterization relies on Veysey, *University*, noted above.

36. Max Weber, "Bureaucracy," in Hans Gerth and C. Wright Mills, *From Max Weber: Essays in Sociology* (New York: Oxford University Press, 1946), p. 243.

37. Wiebe, *Segmented Society*, p. 25.

CHAPTER THREE

1. James T. Kloppenberg, *Uncertain Victory: Social Democracy and Progressivism in European and American Thought, 1870–1920* (New York: Oxford University Press, 1986), p. 6.

2. For an overview of the issues surrounding the legal realist movement and sociological jurisprudence, see Robert Samuel Summers, *Instrumentalism and American Legal Theory* (Ithaca, NY: Cornell University Press, 1982); also William Rumble, *American Legal Realism* (Ithaca, NY: Cornell University Press, 1968).

3. See Samuel Haber, *Efficiency and Uplift: Scientific Management in the Progressive Era, 1890–1920* (Chicago: University of Chicago Press, 1964), pp. 52–59; and pp. 77–80.

4. Quoted in Alpheus Thomas Mason, *Brandeis: A Free Man's Life* (New York: Viking Press, 1946), p. 389.

5. See Robert L. Nelson, "Ideology, Practice and Professional Autonomy: Social Values and Client Relationships in the Large Law Firm," *Stanford Law Review* 37 (1985), pp. 533ff.

6. Louis D. Brandeis, "The Opportunity in the Law," in *Business—A Profession* (Boston: Small, Maynard and Co., 1914), pp. 315–16. This discussion of Brandeis follows David Luban, "The Noblesse Oblige Tradition in the Practice of Law" (Unpublished manuscript, University of Maryland Law School, 1987).

7. Ibid., p. 317.

8. See John P. Frank, "The Legal Ethics of Louis D. Brandeis," *Stanford Law Review* 17 (1965), pp. 683ff.

9. Aristotle, *Nicomachean Ethics*, trans. Martin Ostwald (Indianapolis: Bobbs-Merrill, 1965), 1141b; p. 157.

10. Harold Perkin, *The Rise of Professional Society: England Since 1880* (New York: Routledge, 1987), pp. 83–128.

11. Ibid., pp. 138–39.

12. Croly, *Promise*, p. 434.

13. John Dewey, *Democracy and Education* [1916], in *John Dewey: The Middle Works*, IX, 93, p. 105.

14. Lawrence A. Cremin, *Traditions of American Education* (New York: Basic Books, 1977), p. 94.

15. John Dewey, *Individualism Old and New* (New York: Capricorn Books, 1962, [1929]), pp. 51 and 55.

16. Jane Addams, *Twenty Years at Hull House* (New York: New American Library, 1961), p. 297.

17. Ibid., p. 95.

18. Ibid., p. 297.

19. Ibid., p. 300.

20. Herbert Croly, *The Promise of American Life*, ed. Arthur M. Schlesinger, Jr. (Cambridge, MA: Belknap Press of Harvard University Press, 1965), pp. 431 and 439.

21. Quotation in Charles Forcey, *Crossroads of Liberalism: Croly, Weyl, Lippmann and the Progressive Era, 1900–1925* (New York: Oxford University Press, 1961), pp. 22–23.

22. Ibid., p. 23.

23. Vincent Scully, Jr., *Modern Architecture: The Architecture of Democracy* Revised Edition (New York: George Braziller, 1974), pp. 11–12.

24. Susanne K. Langer, *Feeling and Form: A Theory of Art* (New York: Scribner and Sons, 1953) quoted in Kevin Lynch, *The Image of the City* (Cambridge, MA: MIT Press, 1960), p. 13.

25. See John Rykwert, *The Idea of a Town* (Princeton, NJ: Princeton University Press, 1976).

26. Scully, *Modern Architecture*, p. 12.

27. Kenneth Frampton, *Modern Architecture: A Critical History*, rev. ed. (London: Thames and Hudson Ltd., 1985), pp. 23–25.

28. This is a major theme in John R. Stillgoe's study, *The Common Landscape of America: 1580–1845* (New Haven, CT: Yale University Press, 1982). The long-term effects of this pattern are discussed in Richard M. Merelman, *Making Something of Ourselves: On Culture and Politics in the United States* (Berkeley: University of California Press, 1984), esp. pp. 53ff.

29. On Olmsted, see Thomas Bender, *Toward An Urban Vision* (Baltimore: Johns Hopkins University Press, 1982) ch. 7.

30. See the discussion by Bernard Michael Boyle, "Architectural Practice in America, 1865–1965—Idea and Reality," in Spiro Kostoff, ed., *The Architect: Chapters in the History of the Profession* (New York: Oxford University Press, 1977), pp. 309–44.

31. Sullivan quoted in Lewis Mumford, *The Brown Decades: A Study of the Arts in America: 1865–1895* (New York: Dover Books, 1971 [1931]), pp. 63 and 73.

32. Paul Boyer, *Urban Masses and Moral Order in America* (Cambridge, MA: Harvard University Press, 1978), p. 272.

33. Quoted in Thomas S. Hines, *Burnham of Chicago: Architect and Planner* (Chicago: University of Chicago Press, 1974), p. 174.

34. Quoted in Hines, *Burnham*, pp. 328–29.

35. Ibid., p. xvii.

36. For an overview of these contrasting developments, see John Friedmann and Clyde Weaver, *Territory and Function: The Evolution of Urban Planning* (Berkeley and Los Angeles: University of California Press, 1979), pp. 19–86.

37. Lewis Mumford, *The Culture of Cities* (New York: Harcourt, Brace and World, 1966 [1938]), pp. 484–85.

38. Lewis Mumford, *Sticks and Stones: A Study of American Architecture and Civilization*, 2nd rev. ed. (New York: Dover Publications, 1954 [1924]), p. 60.

39. Ibid., p. 113.

40. Ibid., pp. 110 and 106.

41. Hannah Arendt, *The Human Condition* (Chicago: University of Chicago Press, 1958), p. 153.

42. Ibid., p. 153.

43. See, for instance, Thorstein Veblen, *Engineers and the Price System* (New York: Huebisch Publishers, 1921).

44. See the treatment of Mumford by Casey Nelson Blake, *Beloved Community: The Cultural Criticism of Randolph Bourne, Van Wyck Brooks, Waldo Frank, and Lewis Mumford* (Chapel Hill: University of North Carolina Press, 1990), esp. pp. 290–91.

45. Walter Lippmann, *Preface to Morals* (New York: Time-Life Books, 1964 [1929]), pp. 106–7.

CHAPTER FOUR

1. John Locke, *Second Treatise of Government*, ed. C. B. Macpherson (Indianapolis: Hackett Publishing, 1980), V, 49, p. 29.

2. National Resources Planning Board, Pacific Southwest Regional Office, *After the War—New Jobs in the Pacific Southwest*, quoted by Mel Scott, *The San Francisco Bay Area: A Metropolis in Perspective*, 2nd ed. (Berkeley and Los Angeles: University of California Press, 1985), p. 258.

3. See Henry R. Luce, "The American Century," *Life*, February 11, 1941, pp. 61–65.

4. See, for example, the description of the formation of American foreign policy in the early postwar era provided by Walter Isaacson and Evan Thomas, *The Wise Men: Six Friends and the World They Made* (New York: Simon and Schuster, 1986).

5. Daniel Bell, *The Coming of Post-Industrial Society: A Venture in Social Forecasting* (New York: Basic Books, 1976), pp. xii and 126–27.

6. Bell, "Labor in Post-Industrial Society," *Dissent*, 19 (Winter, 1972), pp. 70–78. See also the corroborating estimate by sociologist Eli Ginzberg, "The Professionalization of the U.S. Labor Force," *Scientific American*, 240, no. 3 (March, 1979).

7. Bell, *Post-Industrial Society*, pp. 373ff.

8. Ibid., p. 377.

9. Harold Perkin, *The Rise of Professional Society: England Since 1880* (London and New York: Routledge, 1989), pp. 3–4.

10. Ibid., pp. 331ff. T. H. Marshall's notion of "social citizenship" has found new expression the United States in the work of Michael Walzer. See his *Spheres of Justice: A Defense of Pluralism and Equality* (New York: Basic Books, 1983).

11. John Kenneth Galbraith, *The New Industrial State* (Boston: Little, Brown, 1967), pp. 58–59.

12. Talcott Parsons, "Professions," vol. 12 of *International Encyclopedia of the Social Sciences*, ed. David L. Sills (New York: Macmillan-Free Press, 1968), p. 545.

13. Ibid., p. 536.

14. Ibid., p. 542.

15. Ibid., p. 543.

16. Ibid., p. 536.

17. Cited in David Halberstam, *The Best and the Brightest* (Greenwich, CT: Fawcett Publications, 1969), p. 272.

18. The reference is to Marshall's speech at Princeton in the Spring of 1947 in which he exhorted his audience to take to heart the lesson of Athens' over-extension during the Peloponnesian Wars, quoted in Forrest C. Pogue, *George C. Marshall: Statesman, 1945–1959* (New York: Viking Press, 1987), p. 524.

19. See Peter Seinfels's knowledgeable tour through the neoconservative movement in its heyday: *The Neo-Conservatives: The Men Who Are Changing America's Politics* (New York: Simon and Schuster, 1979).

20. See William H. Whyte, Jr., *The Organization Man* (New York: Simon and Schuster, 1956).

21. Clark Kerr, *The Uses of the University* (Cambridge, MA: Harvard University Press, 1972), pp. 87–88.

22. Ivan Illich, *Tools for Conviviality* (New York: Harper & Row: 1973), pp. 11–13. See also Illich, *Celebration of Awareness: A Call for Institutional Revolution* (Garden City, NY: Doubleday and Co., 1970).

23. See in this connection the work of Ronald Inglehart, *Culture Shift in Advanced Industrial Society* (Princeton, NJ: Princeton University Press, 1990).

24. See James Davison Hunter, *Culture Wars: The Struggle to Define America* (New York: Basic Books, 1991).

25. See Lester Thurow, *The Zero-Sum Society: Distribution and the Possibilities for Economic Change* (New York: Basic Books, 1980).

26. Quoted phrase is the title of John Kenneth Galbraith's book: *The Culture of Contentment* (Boston: Houghton Mifflin, 1992). On the effects of recent economic changes upon the distribution of income and its social consequences, see Kevin Phillips, *The Politics of Rich and Poor: Wealth and the American Electorate in the Reagan Aftermath* (New York: Random House, 1990). At the same time, other observers have documented the tendency for increasing pressures in professional and managerial occupations to crowd out all other aspects of life. See Juliet B. Schor, *The Overworked American: The Unexpected Decline of Leisure* (New York: Basic Books, 1992); also Amy Saltzman, *Downshifting: Revisiting Success on a Slower Track* (New York: Harper-Collins, 1991).

27. Barbara Ehrenreich, *Fear of Falling: The Inner Life of the Middle Class* (New York: Pantheon Books, 1989), p. 198.

28. See the discussion in Chapter 2.

CHAPTER FIVE

1. As in Thomas J. Kuhn, *The Structure of Scientific Revolutions* (Chicago: University of Chicago Press, 1962).

2. On this theme, see Jürgen Habermas, *The Structural Transformation of the Public Sphere: An Inquiry Into a Category of Bourgeois Society* (Cambridge, MA: MIT Press, 1989). Habermas's perspective intersects directly with that of the pragmatist Progressives, and his later work has come to take conscious direction from Dewey in particular.

3. Croly's vision for a renewed American nation is discussed in Chapter 3. See also Herbert Croly, *The Promise of American Life* (Cambridge, MA: Belknap Press of Harvard University Press, 1965 [1909]).

4. Daniel Bell, *The Cultural Contradictions of Capitalism* (New York: Basic Books, 1976). See also the argument of Colin Campbell that modern hedonism, no less than the modern ethic of achievement, is the secularized outcome of a Protestant culture which trained individuals to attend to and control inner states, including feeling, thereby creating a technology of emotional self-manipulation that could be turned to self-gratification as well as to the service of God. Colin Campbell, *The Romantic Ethic and the Spirit of Modern Consumerism* (Oxford and New York: Basil Blackwell, 1987).

5. These parallel, though contrasting, logics define the "utilitarian" and "expressive" strands of American individualism. For a description and critique, see Robert N. Bellah, Richard Madsen, William M. Sullivan, Ann Swidler, and Steven M. Tipton, *Habits of the Heart: Individualism and Commitment in American Life* (Berkeley and Los Angeles: University of California Press, 1985). See also Alasdair MacIntyre's contrast of "manager" and "therapist" in *After Virtue: A Study in Moral Theory*, 2nd ed. (Notre Dame, IN: Notre Dame University Press, 1984), pp. 22–29.

6. Louis Auchincloss, *Diary of a Yuppie* (Boston: Houghton Mifflin, 1986), p. 26.

7. For a remarkable exploration of these issues through psychological case histories, see David Levinson, *Seasons of a Man's Life* (New York: Ballantine Books, 1978). These findings were given a more up-beat packaging by one of Levinson's collaborators, Gail Sheehy, in *Passages: Predictable Phases of Adult Life* (New York: Bantam Books, 1977).

8. The first strategy corresponds to what theorists of collective action call the "free rider" problem. The second is a version of the "prisoner's dilemma." In both cases, only cooperative activity provides an enduring solution to the problem of individual security and well-being. For an overview of these concepts and their applications, see Elinor Ostrom, *Governing the Commons: The Evolution of Institutions for Collective Action* (New York: Cambridge University Press, 1990).

9. See Cornel West, "Nihilism in Black America," *Dissent* (Spring, 1991), pp. 221–26.

10. Robert B. Reich, *The Work of Nations: Preparing Ourselves for 21st-Century Capitalism* (New York: Alfred Knopf, 1991).

11. Ibid., p. 81.

12. Ibid., p. 87.

13. Ibid., p. 178. Compare Reich's figure with the demographic study done in the late '70s by sociologist Eli Ginzberg, who described about one quarter of the workforce as "professional and managerial." See Eli Ginzberg, "The Professionalization of the U.S. Labor Force," *Scientific American* 240, no. 3 (March 1979).

14. Reich, *Work of Nations*, p. 230.

15. Ibid., p. 309.

16. Ibid., pp. 234–35.

17. Lester Thurow, *Going Head to Head: The Upcoming Economic Competition Among Europe, Japan, and the United States* (New York: William Morrow, 1992).

18. Ibid., p. 244.

19. Ibid., p. 242.

20. See John Dewey, *Reconstruction in Philosophy*, enlarged edition, (Boston: Beacon Press, 1957), esp. pp. 26–27 and 51ff. See also Richard J. Bernstein, *Praxis and Action* (Philadelphia: University of Pennsylvania Press, 1971), pp. 200–29; Robert C. Neville, *Reconstruction of Thinking* (Albany: State University of New York Press, 1981); Richard Rorty, *Consequences of Pragmatism* (Minneapolis, MN: University of Minnesota Press, 1982); Cornel West, *The American Evasion of Philosophy: The Genealogy of Pragmatism* (Madison, WI: University of Wisconsin Press, 1989); and Robert B. Westbrook, *John Dewey and American Democracy* (Ithaca, NY: Cornell University Press, 1991). The following discussion also draws upon the contemporary development of Deweyan practical reasoning by Charles W. Anderson, *Pragmatic Liberalism* (Chicago: University of Chicago Press, 1989), and *Prescribing the Life of the Mind: An Essay on the Purpose of the University and the Cultivation of Practical Reason* (Madison, WI: University of Wisconsin Press, 1993), esp. pp. 11–23.

21. The notion of "human capital" has come to play an important role in contemporary social research in highlighting the practical significance of shared expectations and moral ties. For an explication of the concept, see James S. Coleman, *Foundations of Social Theory* (Cambridge, MA: Harvard University Press, 1990), pp. 300–21.

22. For an elaboration of this "pedagogical" dimension of institutions, see Robert N. Bellah, Richard Madsen, William M. Sullivan, Ann Swidler, and Steven M. Tipton, *The Good Society* (New York: Alfred Knopf, 1991), pp. 1–18 and 287–304.

23. Philip Selznick speaks of "institutional integrity" as a quality of organizational behavior when the members of an organization have come to understand themselves as having responsibilities toward the larger interdependent processes in which they take part. See Philip Selznick, *The Moral Commonwealth: Social Theory and the Promise of Community* (Berkeley and Los Angeles: University of California Press, 1992), pp. 357ff.

24. The use of the term public philosophy here draws on earlier work. See my *Reconstructing Public Philosophy* (Berkeley and Los Angeles: University of California Press, 1982), esp. pp. 9–10.

25. Deborah Prothrow-Stith, *Deadly Consequences: How Violence Is Destroying Our Teenage Population and a Plan to Begin Solving the Problem* (New York: HarperCollins, 1991).

26. A number of scholars have recently taken up the issue of causes, remedies, and responsibilities for these massive problems, thereby giving rise to a new debate which forms part of the larger context for Prothrow-Stith's work. See William Julius Wilson, *The Truly Disadvantaged: The Inner City, the Underclass, and Public Policy* (Chicago: University of Chicago Press, 1987); Roger Lane, *William Dorsey's Philadelphia and Ours: On the Past and Future of the Black City in America* (New York: Oxford University Press, 1991); see also Cornel West, "Nihilism in Black America," *Dissent*, Spring 1991, pp. 221–26.

27. These and subsequent quotations are taken from an interview conducted by the author with Deborah Prothrow-Stith in Boston, October 25, 1991.

28. The reference is to Lasch's critique of historical optimism as an ingredient in the professional "culture of critical discourse," which he attacks in *The True and Only Heaven: Progress and Its Critics* (New York: W. W. Norton, 1991). This critique is discussed in Chapters 1 and 8.

29. Thurow, *Head to Head*, p. 268.

CHAPTER SIX

1. Derek Bok, "Reclaiming the Public Trust," *Change*, July/August 1992, p. 18.

2. See, for example, James Hershberg, *James B. Conant: From Harvard to Hiroshima and the Making of the Nuclear Age* (New York: Alfred Knopf, 1993).

3. See Nicholas Lehmann, "The Smart Club Comes to the White House," *New York Times*, Sunday, November 29, 1992.

4. See Randall Collins, *The Credential Society* (New York: Academic Press, 1979); and James Fallows's attack on credentialism discussed in Chapter 1.

5. Derek Bok, *The Cost of Talent: How Executives and Professionals Are Paid and How It Affects America* (New York: Free Press, 1993).

6. Ibid., pp. 223–48.

7. Sam Bass Warner, Jr., provides a critical sketch of James Bryant Conant as the architect of a national system of elite talent selection in *Province of Reason* (Cambridge, MA: Belknap Press of Harvard University Press, 1984), pp. 213–47.

8. See, for example, the disturbing study, drawing upon opinion polling data, of the disjunction between the informational orientation of American elites and the public hunger for informed value judgments by Daniel Yankelovich, *Coming to Public Judgment: Making Democracy Work in a Complex World* (Syracuse, NY: Syracuse University Press, 1991).

9. Auguste Comte set out this program in *The Positive Philosophy*, trans. Harriet Martineau, 2 vols. (London: 1853). See also Auguste Comte, *Introduction to Positive Philosophy*, ed. Frederick Ferre (Indianapolis, IN: Hackett Publ., 1988); and Frank E. Manuel, *The Prophets of Paris* (Cambridge, MA: Harvard University Press, 1962); also William M. Simon, *European Positivism in the Nineteenth Century: An Essay in Intellectual History* (Ithaca, NY: Cornell University Press, 1963).

10. See August Comte, *The System of Positive Polity*, trans. J. H. Bridges et al. (London: 1875–1877). Also Auguste Comte, *The Catechism of Positive Religion*, trans. Richard Congreve (London: Kegan Paul & Co., 1958).

11. It is interesting that Herbert Croly's lifelong moral commitment to improving the human lot may also be a legacy of a positivist upbringing, however much Croly was later to criticize and repudiate features of positivism. Croly was "baptized" by his parents in the Comtean Religion of Humanity, of which his father was a leading exponent in the late nineteenth century. See David W. Levy, *Herbert Croly of the New Republic: The Life and Thought of an American Progressive* (Princeton, NJ: Princeton University Press, 1985).

12. Ernest Gellner, *Plough, Sword, and Book: The Structure of Human History* (Chicago: University of Chicago Press, 1988), p. 262.

13. Ibid., p. 262.

14. In *Cosmopolis*, Stephen Toulmin argues that there were two founding traditions of modernity rather than one. Before the chaos of the Wars of Religion had terrified and rigidified European attitudes, the humanists of the sixteenth century announced a vision of life based upon dialogue, tentativeness, and contextual prudence, a vision almost covered over by the aggressive scientific rationalism initiated by René Descartes and Thomas Hobbes. See Stephen Toulmin, *Cosmopolis: The Hidden Agenda of Modernity* (New York: Free Press, 1990).

15. See especially Thomas S. Kuhn, *The Structure of Scientific Revolutions*, 2nd ed. (Chicago: University of Chicago Press, 1962). Also Toulmin, *Cosmopolis*.

16. Donald A. Shon, *The Reflective Practitioner: How Professionals Think in Action* (New York: Basic Books, 1983), p. 33.

17. Ibid., p. 34.

18. Ibid., p. 40.

19. Ibid., p. 50.

20. Ibid., p. 68.

21. Ibid., pp. 236–66.

22. Schon has suggestively developed some of these implications in his *Educating the Reflective Practitioner: Toward a New Design for Teaching and Learning in the Professions* (San Francisco: Jossey-Bass Publishers, 1987), esp. pp. 305–16.

23. For examples of the first, pessimistic assessments, see Robert Howard, *Brave New Workplace* (New York: Viking, 1985); David F. Noble, *Forces of Production: A Social History of Industrial Automation* (New York: Oxford University Press, 1986); Harley Shaiken, *Work Transformed: Automation and Labor in the Computer Age* (New York: Holt, Rinehart and Winston, 1985). For the second, more optimistic view, see Michael J. Piore and Charles F. Sabel, *The Second Industrial Divide: Possibilities for Prosperity* (New York: Basic Books, 1984).

24. Shoshana Zuboff, *In the Age of the Smart Machine: The Future of Work and Power* (New York: Basic Books, 1988).

25. Ibid., p. 9.

26. Zuboff draws on many of the same studies of executive work upon which Schon also partly relies, especially those of Henry Mintzberg, *The*

Nature of Managerial Work (New York: Harper & Row, 1973). See Zuboff, *Smart Machine*, pp. 97–123.

27. Both these characterizations are discussed in earlier chapters. See Robert B. Reich, op. cit., and Christopher Lasch, *The True and Only Heaven: Progress and Its Discontents* (New York: W. W. Norton, 1991).

28. Hubert L. Dreyfus and Stuart E. Dreyfus, *Mind over Machine: The Power of Human Intuition and Expertise in the Era of the Computer* (New York: Free Press, 1986).

29. Ibid., pp. 16–51, which provides a summary of the theory.

30. Ibid., p. 31.

31. Ibid., p. 35.

32. Ibid., p. 121.

33. See James S. Coleman and Thomas Huffer, *Public and Private High Schools: The Impact of Community* (New York: Basic Books, 1987). See also James S. Coleman, "Social Capital in the Creation of Human Capital," *American Journal of Sociology*, 94 (February 1993), Supplement, pp. S95–S120.

34. Robert C. Putnam, "The Prosperous Community: Social Capital and Public Life," *The American Prospect* no. 13 (Spring, 1993), pp. 35–42, p. 57.

35. This, in highly condensed form, is the provocative and helpful argument of Albert Borgmann. See his *Technology and the Character of Everyday Life: A Philosophical Inquiry* (Chicago: University of Chicago Press, 1984), and *Crossing the Postmodern Divide* (Chicago: University of Chicago Press, 1992).

36. See Patricia Benner, *From Novice to Expert: Excellence and Power in Clinical Nursing Practice* (New York: Addison-Wesley, 1984). Benner points out that the denigration of nursing as a profession reflects not only the low public status accorded women but also the devaluing of personal care as contrasted with the technological interventions provided by medicine.

37. Ray Marshall and Marx Tucker, *Thinking for a Living: Education and the Wealth of Nations* (New York: Basic Books, 1992), pp. 44–48.

38. Jonathan Boswell has amassed strong evidence for the idea that long-term social success in modern societies requires the development of institutionalized patterns of what he calls "public cooperation" of which the European educational systems are examples. See Jonathan Boswell, *Community and*

the Economy: The Theory of Public Cooperation (London and New York: Routledge, 1990), pp. 56–76.

39. W. E. B. Du Bois, *The Souls of Black Folk* (New York: Vintage Library of America, 1990), pp. 8 and 9.

CHAPTER SEVEN

1. Quoted in *Health Letter*, Public Citizen Health Research Group, 5, no. 12 (December 1989), pp. 2–3. The *Time* data which this article cites is confirmed by a recent Harris/Harvard School of Public Health Survey reported in the same article.

2. One explanation locates the problem in the differing professional and ethical bases of public health versus acute care approaches in the development of medicine; see Paul Starr, *The Social Transformation of American Medicine* (New York: Basic Books, 1982); and Larry R. Churchill, *Rationing Health Care in America: Perceptions and Principles of Justice* (Notre Dame, IN: Notre Dame University Press, 1987).

3. See Barbara Ehrenreich, *Fear of Falling: The Inner Life of the Middle Class* (New York: Pantheon, 1989).

4. Max Weber, *The Protestant Ethic and the Spirit of Capitalism*, trans. Talcott Parsons (New York: Charles Scribner's Sons, 1958). See also Hans Gerth and C. Wright Mills, *From Max Weber: Essays in Sociology* (New York: Oxford University Press, 1946).

5. Weber's general conception of rationalization, of which this is one aspect, has had an enormous impact on twentieth-century social thought. David Riesman's famous analysis of the loss of "inner-directedness" in modern organizations could be taken as one application, as is Alasdair MacIntyre's analysis of "bureaucratic individualism." See David Riesman, with Nathan Glazer and Reuel Denney, *The Lonely Crowd: A Study of the Changing American Character* (New Haven, CT: Yale University Press, 1950); also Alasdair MacIntyre, *After Virtue: A Study in Moral Theory*, 2nd ed. (Notre Dame, IN: Notre Dame University Press, 1984).

6. The literature on professional ethics within this "applied ethics" approach is considerable and contains a wide variety of points of view as to how ethical principles are to be rationally grounded. The common theme

among what can be characterized as deductive theories, however, is that principles can be grounded independently of the practices and contexts for which they serve as norms. Because of this independent and foundational position of ethical theory, ethical reasoning can be analyzed for its logical validity quite independently of the question of whether the principles or norms involved are judged ethically valid. Empirical facts about situations are highly relevant to ethical decision making, however, as these help identify those aspects of situations which are ethically relevant, i.e., those which can be subsumed under general principles and rules. For some representative samples of this approach, see Michael D. Bayles, *Professional Ethics* (New York: Wadsworth Publishing, 1981); Alan H. Goldman, *The Moral Foundations of Professional Ethics* (Totowa, NJ: Rowan and Littlefield, 1980); Robert M. Veatch, *A Theory of Medical Ethics* (New York: Basic Books, 1981). The major progenitor of contemporary applied ethics is John Rawls, *A Theory of Justice* (Cambridge, MA: Harvard University Press, 1971).

7. Veatch, *Theory*, p. 5.

8. Ibid., p. 5.

9. Ibid., pp. 113ff.

10. The reference is to Aristotle's opening discussion in Book One of *Nicomachean Ethics*.

11. Immanuel Kant, "On the Proverb: That May Be True in Theory, but Is of No Practical Use," in *Perpetual Peace and Other Essays*, trans. Ted Humphrey (Indianapolis, IN: Hackett Publishing Co., 1983), p. 61.

12. Attention to ethos is usually linked to the Aristotelian tradition in moral philosophy. This tradition has received important restatement by a number of recent thinkers. See Alasdair MacIntyre, *After Virtue: A Study of Moral Theory*, 2nd ed. (Notre Dame, IN: University of Notre Dame Press, 1984 [1981]). For an application of these ideas in religious ethics see Stanley Hauerwas, *A Community of Character: Toward a Constructive Christian Social Ethic* (Notre Dame, IN: University of Notre Dame Press, 1982). For this approach in the realm of professional ethics, see William F. May, "Professional Ethics: Setting, Terrain, and Teacher," in Daniel Callahan and Sissela Bok, *Ethics Teaching in Higher Education* (New York: Plenum Press, 1980), pp. 204–44. For the importance of ethos in the empirical study of professional life, see Eliot Freidson, *The Profession of Medicine: A Study of the Sociology of Applied Knowledge* (New York: Harper & Row, 1970).

13. The virtue approach has affinities with the casuistic approach to ethics, a tradition of reasoning which has much in common with legal reasoning. Like the ethics of character, casuistry is also undergoing a revival. In casuistry, the aim is to blend reasoning in both its inductive form, moving from decisive cases toward general norms, with the deductive approach, moving from principles to cases, so that principles and cases mutually influence each other. See Stephen Toulmin and Albert Jonsen, *The Abuse of Casuistry* (Berkeley and Los Angeles: University of California Press, 1988).

14. For an overview of the liberal-communitarian debate, see Markate Daly, *Communitarianism: A New Public Ethics* (Belmont, CA: Wadsworth Publishing Co., 1993). See also David O'Brien, ed., *Communication Thinking: New Essays* (Charlottesville, VA: University of Virginia Press, forthcoming).

15. This is the thesis of the work of Mihaly Csikszentmihaly, *Flow: The Psychology of Optimal Experience* (New York: Harper & Row, 1990).

16. Ibid., p. 65.

17. Ibid., p. 71.

18. Ibid., p. 205.

19. This approach was pioneered by the pragmatic thinkers Charles Sanders Peirce, John Dewey, and George Herbert Mead. See especially John Dewey, *Human Nature and Conduct: An Introduction to Social Psychology* (New York: Random House-The Modern Library, 1930 [1922]) and George Herbert Mead, *Mind, Self, and Society*, ed. George W. Morris (Chicago: University of Chicago Press, 1934). H. Richard Niebuhr developed the implications of this approach as a distinct method for a theological ethics in *The Responsible Self: An Essay in Christian Moral Philosophy* (San Francisco: Harper & Row, 1978 [1963]). Recently, Eugene Rochberg-Halton has argued for the power of this approach in social theory and criticism in *Meaning and Modernity: Social Theory in the Pragmatic Attitude* (Chicago: University of Chicago Press, 1986).

20. Charles Taylor presents a detailed argument for this claim, starting from the value of personal authenticity itself, in *The Ethics of Authenticity* (Cambridge, MA: Harvard University Press, 1993).

21. Forrest C. Pogue, *George C. Marshall: Statesman, 1945–1959.* (New York: Viking, 1987), p. 148.

22. Ibid., pp. 210ff.

23. Daniel Callahan, *Setting Limits: Medical Goals in an Aging Society* (New York: Simon and Schuster, 1987), p. 26.

24. Ibid., p. 19.

25. Ibid., p. 135.

26. Ibid., pp. 97–98.

27. Ibid., p. 96.

28. Ibid., pp. 157–58.

29. Ibid., pp. 197–98.

30. It is noteworthy that Callahan, along with Willard Gaylin, co-founder of the Hastings Center for the Study of Society, Ethics, and Life Sciences, has for twenty years played a sustaining role in promoting ethical reflection of all three types in the health field.

31. See William A. Galston, *Liberal Purposes: Goods, Virtues and Diversity in the Liberal State* (Cambridge, MA: Cambridge University Press, 1991).

32. See William F. May, *The Physician's Covenant* (Philadelphia: Westminster Press, 1983).

33. For example, see Carol Gilligan, *In a Different Voice: Psychological Theory and Women's Development* (Cambridge, MA: Harvard University Press, 1982); and Mary Field Belenky et. al., *Women's Ways of Knowing: The Development of Self, Voice, and Mind* (New York: Basic Books, 1986). See also Jean Bethke Elshtain, *Public Man, Private Woman: Women in Social Work and Political Thought* (Princeton, NJ: Princeton University Press, 1981). For a discussion of the implications of these issues for professional legal judgment and practice, see Rand Jack and Diana Crowley Jack, *Moral Vision and Professional Decisions: The Changing Values of Women and Men Lawyers* (Cambridge, MA: Cambridge University Press, 1989).

34. Quoted by William Greider, *Who Will Tell the People: The Betrayal of American Democracy* (New York: Simon and Schuster, 1992), p. 223.

CHAPTER EIGHT

1. This process of inter-professional competition has been detailed by Andrew Abbott in *The System of Professions: An Essay on the Division of Expert Labor* (Chicago: University of Chicago Press, 1988).

2. This argument has been elaborated in several important studies of the

effects of social cooperation in Western European societies. See Jonathan Boswell, *Community and the Economy: The Theory of Public Cooperation* (London and New York: Routledge, 1990); and Robert D. Putnam, *Making Democracy Work: Civic Traditions in Modern Italy* (Princeton, NJ: Princeton University Press, 1993). Many of the standard views in economics and public policy studies, however, have dismissed the moral dimension and remain tied to the dogma that all social action can be explained as guided by self-interest. For critiques of this position, see Amitai Etzioni, *The Moral Dimension: Toward a New Economics* (New York: Free Press, 1988); also Alan Wolfe, *Whose Keeper? Social Science and Moral Obligation* (Berkeley and Los Angeles: University of California Press, 1989).

3. See, for example, the special issue of the journal of the Kettering Foundation, a publication promoting democratic participation, devoted to professionalism: *The Kettering Review*, Winter, 1994.

4. James Fallows, *More Like Us: Making America Great Again* (Boston: Houghton Mifflin, 1989).

5. Barbara Ehrenreich, *Fear of Falling: The Inner Life of the Middle Class* (New York: Pantheon, 1989).

6. Robert B. Reich, *The Work of Nations: Preparing Ourselves For 21st-Century Capitalism* (New York: Alfred Knopf, 1991).

7. Christopher Lasch, *The True and Only Heaven: Progress and Its Critics* (New York: W. W. Norton, 1991).

8. Joseph A. Raelin, *The Clash of Cultures: Managers and Professionals* (Boston: Harvard Business School Press, 1986).

9. Ibid., p. 251.

10. Among thinkers who have consistently and helpfully confronted the problem of elites in American democracy, the work of historian William Appleman Williams and sociologist E. Digby Baltzell stands out. See William Appleman Williams, *The Contours of American History* (New York: W. W. Norton, 1966); and E. Digby Baltzell, *Puritan Boston and Quaker Philadelphia: Two Protestant Ethics and the Spirit of Class Authority and Leadership* (Boston: Beacon Press, 1979). See also David V. Hicks, *Norms and Nobility: A Treatise on Education* (New York: Praeger, 1981); also Barbara Hargrove, *The Emerging New Class: Implications for Church and Society* (New York: Pilgrim Press, 1986).

11. See Tony Hiss, *The Experience of Place: A Completely New Way of Looking At and Dealing With Our Radically Changing Cities and Countryside* (New York: Alfred A. Knopf, 1990).

12. Ibid., p. xii.

13. See, for example, Jane Jacobs, *Cities and the Wealth of Nations: Principles of Economic Life* (New York: Random House, 1984); also Daniel Kemmis, *Community and the Politics of Place* (Norman, OK, and London: University of Oklahoma Press, 1990).

14. Hiss, *Experience*, p. xii.

15. Ibid., p. 192.

16. Ibid., pp. 204–5.

17. Ibid., p. 207.

18. Ibid., p. 208.

19. Harold Perkin, *The Rise of Professional Society: England Since 1880* (New York: Routledge, 1989), p. 437.

20. Ibid., p. 501.

21. Ibid., p. 515.

22. R. H. Tawney, *The Acquisitive Society* (New York: Harcourt, Brace, and Howe, 1948 [1920]), pp. 92 and 98.

23. Ibid., p. 150.

24. Fred Block, *Postindustrial Possibilities: A Critique of Economic Discourse* (Berkeley and Los Angeles: University of California Press, 1990), p. 63.

25. Alfred North Whitehead, *Science and the Modern World* (New York: Macmillan, 1967 [1925]), p. 196.

26. See Mihaly Csikszentmihaly, *The Evolving Self: A Psychology for the Third Millennium* (New York: HarperCollins, 1993), p. 221.

27. See Marcus Aurelius, *The Meditations*, trans. G. M. A. Grube (Indianapolis, IN: Hackett Publ., 1983), bk. viii, 32, p. 79.

INDEX